# UNBREAKABLE

# UNBREAKABLE

*The Woman Who Defied the Nazis*
*in the World's Most Dangerous Horse Race*

## RICHARD ASKWITH

PEGASUS BOOKS
NEW YORK LONDON

Unbreakable

Pegasus Books, Ltd.
148 West 37th Street, 13th Floor
New York, NY 10018

ISBN: 978-1-64313-210-5

10 9 8 7 6 5 4 3 2 1

# Contents

# 1.

# Old Women's Gorge

The hill falls down so steeply you can almost touch the flaking bark at the tops of the high conifers, slanting up from below. Patches of undergrowth sprout feebly from the balding earth. The dry soil is rough with trampled scraps of tree; the air, sweet with pine, is still.

We are just below the brow. The gusting April wind has vanished. So has the low moan it carried from the next valley, of traffic on its early evening rush south-west from Prague on highway No. 4.

A rusting chain-link fence, barely kept vertical by cracked concrete pillars, separates us from a tiny pebble-dash cottage that clings awkwardly to the slope. The walls are blotched with damp. The black roof tiles are newer. 'This is what it used to be,' says the man with ash-white hair, kicking at some jagged red fragments among the dusty twigs. 'Asbestos.'

Jan Pospíšil stamps out his Lucky Strike in the debris. 'They'll have electricity now,' he adds. 'And running water. They didn't then.' His eyes glisten, perhaps from the smoke.

'She was my favourite aunt,' he explains. 'Well, great-aunt. There were three of them living here, three sisters. I liked Lata best. I was five or six when I first came here.

She must have been about seventy. My mother would leave me here to stay for a few days. There wasn't much room: just two bedrooms. You could fit two single beds in each, and the sides touched.

'Lata was strict about table manners. But she was kind. She used to send me out to play in the woods. Sometimes she'd give me her gun and some ammunition, and tell me to play with that ...' Later, in his teens, they would sneak away into the woods together and Lata would share secret cigarettes with him.

Behind us, up on the hill, a car can be seen, moving noiselessly on the lane that runs along the ridge. Back then, in the 1970s, it was more likely to be a man on a horse; sometimes more than one. 'The secret police liked to keep an eye on things round here.'

There is no sign of the cottage's current occupants, nor of any neighbours. Other dwellings are just visible through the trees, but these are recent additions. You wouldn't expect their occupants to remember Jan's great-aunts. Yet the elderly sisters must have made an impression on someone. The rocky stream at the bottom of the valley is known as Babí rokle, or 'Old Women's Gorge'. Lata would spend much of each day going up and down the hill to fetch water from a well by the stream, even though she could no longer walk without a stick.

'But she never complained,' says Jan. 'None of them did.'

§ - § - §

For a small nation, the Czechs have an extraordinary gift for producing sporting champions of luminous greatness. Still more remarkable is their rulers' gift – especially in the twentieth century – for disowning them. Emil Zátopek, the runner; Věra Čáslavská, the gymnast; Olga Fikotová-Connolly, the discus thrower; Martina Navratilová, the tennis player; the near-invincible national men's ice-hockey team of 1947–9 … All dazzled and conquered their chosen worlds, only to be denounced as traitors or enemies of the people. Some were punished; all were shunned. But none fell so far or for so long as Lata Brandisová, the steeplechase jockey, who displeased not one totalitarian regime but two – having already struggled through years of prejudice on account of her gender.

In her prime, between the world wars, Jan's great-aunt was fêted by statesmen and socialites, acclaimed by chanting crowds. Her achievements in the saddle made headlines not just in Czechoslovakia (as it then was) but across Europe: they were astonishing in sporting terms but more astonishing still in the courage and resilience that made them possible. In an age of prejudice she refused to be constrained by convention. At a time of despair she embodied hope and patriotism. Her aristocratic glamour added to her celebrity, but she was also a figure of deep and serious significance for her nation, her sport and her gender.

She faced her ultimate challenge in middle age, confronting the warrior-athletes of the Third Reich in a sporting contest so extreme in its dangers that some would question its right to be called sport. That day alone should have been enough to earn her immortality. Instead, she was stuffed into history's dustbin.

She remained there, in that little cottage in the woods, for thirty years, forgotten and unmentionable. Her sisters would leave at dawn, walking to catch a train, to work all day in a factory on the edge of Prague. Lata, still unsteady on her feet from sporting battles gone by, would stay at home, cleaning, washing, chopping wood, fetching water, with only a dog for company.

Later, as age and hunger gnawed at their bones, the sisters became increasingly reclusive. But once a week they would walk to church, always sitting in the same pews, always returning in single file, always alone with their thoughts – 'like the three kings,' says a villager who used to watch. Then, nearly forty years ago, even that procession stopped.

Lata's death, in 1981, was barely reported. She is buried abroad. As far as most of her compatriots are concerned, her story might as well have been buried there with her. A few pilgrims say a mass for her each year at the family shrine in the woods above her old home – hundreds of miles from her actual resting place. Apart from that, you'll struggle to find a Czech or Slovak who has heard of her, outside the hardcore racing community. In the West, she is almost entirely forgotten. Yet the life of Lata Brandisová was too remarkable to deserve such oblivion. Her character, courage and achievements made a mark that mattered in European history, and made a permanent difference to the opportunities available to the women who came after her. If ever an athlete deserved to have a permanent record set down of who she was and what she did, she does.

Some would say it is too late. There are too few witnesses, too many missing documents. In a cheerful bar among the bleak high-rises of the Prague suburb of Chodov, the respected journalist and racing historian Martin Cáp spends several hours kindly explaining the difficulties to me. He himself has spent twenty years researching a still-unfinished book about the Czech Derby; his knowledge of his nation's incomplete racing archives is unrivalled, and he is painfully aware of every gap. 'It's a fascinating story,' he tells me, 'but it will be terribly hard. So many records have been lost.'

Martin Šabata, a television pundit famous among Czechs for his encyclopaedic knowledge of the blood-curdling horse race that made Lata a sporting legend, tells me much the same a few days later, in a café in the eastern Bohemian town of Pardubice. 'The story of Lata Brandisová is an extremely interesting one. I would love to be able to share all the details with you. But I can't. They are lost.'

These men know what they are talking about; it would be prudent to listen. But although I have tried many times to talk myself out of writing this book, somehow I haven't been able to stay talked out of it. Each surviving detail of Lata Brandisová's lost life throbs with the same message: her story demands to be told. Her very obscurity adds to the urgency

In any case, the trail is not quite cold.

§ - § - §

A few miles from Old Women's Gorge, her old family house still stands, on the edge of a quiet, low-lying village at whose heart is an ancient fish pond. It is a small, low stately home, overlooking a tree-shaded courtyard, where Lata's privileged parents taught her to ride and raised her (in vain) to be a well-bred bride. Water was pouring through the ceiling when I first visited. The coat of arms above the front door had peeled away long ago, and patches of stucco were missing from the outside walls. On the sagging stables – on one side of the courtyard – 'Danger: keep out' signs stated the obvious.

Indoors the house is warm and welcoming, but there are still traces of its clumsy repurposing as an institution in the Communist era. It is hard to imagine that this was once the home of a family of aristocrats – let alone that one of the twentieth century's most celebrated sportswomen lived here.

Lata and her sisters were driven out in the 1950s, long before Jan was born. The property came back to the family under 'restitution', following Czechoslovakia's Velvet Revolution of 1989. Jan has lived here (most of the time) since 1993. He shares the old property with his wife, Gabriela Křístková, along with two dogs, three cats and six horses. They support themselves with a portfolio of activities that includes forestry and riding tuition. Time or energy that remains is devoted to undoing the damage of the Communist era. 'It had been reconstructed in the socialist way,' explains Jan. 'There were trees growing from the roof.'

One day they hope their home will feel more like the home that Lata lived in, but the restoration is a thankless task. The passing seasons nibble insatiably at house and garden; it's battle enough to prevent further degradation. Behind the house, wild boars have made a wasteland of the sloping fields in which Lata learned to ride; the forest on the hill beyond would quickly become an impenetrable wilderness without constant intervention by its owners. Like a profligate ex-spouse, the estate endlessly renews its demands for maintenance.

The couple stick at it, determined to honour the memory of their most remarkable relative. In one small room, they have even assembled a 'mini museum' in Lata's honour. There isn't much in it yet: a few dozen photographs; a cupboard of clothing and rosettes; a small glass case full of souvenirs. But that may soon change.

In 2006, Jan's Aunt Eva died. She was eighty-four, unmarried – and the longstanding custodian of family memories. Jan found himself the unexpected owner of ten large boxes stuffed with papers, photographs and newspaper cuttings. It was the kind of legacy that can take years to unjumble – if you ever get round to making a start on it. With Aunt Eva's boxes, the process is almost complete. The contents have sometimes proved baffling; most concern family members who do not come into this story. Yet every now and then there is a priceless clue to its heroine – because Eva was Lata's niece.

Much of what follows is based on lines of enquiry that began with these boxes, some of which led in unexpectedly fruitful directions. Other family members, and countless friends, acquaintances and witnesses, have also contributed generously. The resulting picture is not complete: occasionally I have been reduced to joining the dots, speculatively, between known facts. (I have made it clear when I am doing so.) But the picture is drawn from life. There really was a countess whose nation took away her privileges one by one, yet who became its figurehead in its time of need. There was – and still is – a steeplechase so extreme in its demands that some consider merely taking part in it to be a sign of insanity. There was indeed a band of Nazi paramilitaries, seemingly invincible on horseback, who chose that same steeplechase as an arena in which to

7

prove their credentials as a master race. And there really was a woman, shy, modest and awkward in company, who tried to stop them; and who refused – in that as in much else – to take no for an answer.

§ - § - §

A photograph from Aunt Eva's boxes shows Lata in her prime. It is cut from a newspaper, yet her joy fills the faded picture. Head held high, strands of fair hair drifting from her helmet, she is breathless and shining, minutes after her most famous victory. Her eyes seem glazed with thrill and wonder. This is the Lata Brandisová who astounded Europe: bold, defiant, radiant with self-belief.

Beside her stands a pale horse, inches from her head. It, too, appears to be in a kind of trance. The two lean towards one another in unconscious intimacy.

Both seem euphoric. Both seem proud. Both seem to glow, like victorious warriors, with the joy of survival. Much of Lata's greatness can be sensed from this preserved moment. To win her glory she required fighting spirit and physical and moral courage to a degree more usually associated with warfare than with sport; and she required a loyal comrade – no less indomitable – from another species. Both points are central to her story.

Lata Brandisová came of age as one empire was collapsing and died as another was approaching its overdue end. In between came two world wars, depression, occupation, revolution – and world-changing technological upheaval. She and her sporting contemporaries wrestled with forces – sexism, class hatred, nationalism, fascism – whose shadows darken today's world too. Her struggles, to which she brought an unbreakable courage beyond most imaginations, were never just about sport.

Nor were they just about her. In her death-or-glory moments, she rode for her nation, and for her gender; perhaps even for freedom. And she did so – as she never forgot – as one of a partnership, between rider and ridden, in which she was the weaker link. That is perhaps the strangest thing about this strange story: at its heart lies the age-old mystery of collaboration between human being and beast, in which, in the right hands, a dumb, powerful, half-ton brute not only consents to serve the feeble biped on its back but does so sometimes with an enthusiasm that seems indistinguishable from the conscious pursuit of human goals.

What follows is a quest to recover the lost life of one of the bravest, oddest, most unjustly forgotten figures in all the annals of sport. Our first steps will be tentative: there are multiple trails to pick up, personal, sporting and historical. But soon they converge, and the pace quickens. They intersect at a climactic moment in the tragedy of the 20th century, when all too many Europeans failed to rise to the challenge of their times, and Lata found herself riding with the hopes of a doomed nation – and a failing democratic project – on her shoulders.

There are many reasons for rescuing Lata Brandisová's story from oblivion. Only two really matter. She stood up for what was right. And she was that rarest kind of sporting hero: one who achieved what was generally agreed to be impossible.

# 2.

# The little countess

It is not immediately obvious which child is which, but you can easily guess the one destined for greatness. Even as an eight-year-old, Lata has a strange, ungovernable air. Her seven siblings glower or simper with varying degrees of submission or resentment at the photographer's demands. Their tired-eyed mother sits tensely in the middle of the composition. Lata, fair-haired and serious, seems detached. She leans slightly for a better view past her brother and gazes intently into the distance beyond the photographer's shoulder. Her grey eyes are alert, but she is deep in her own thoughts. Others in the tableau may well be more prone to mischief. Lata has a more subversive quality: independence.

This is the heroine of our story: Marie Immaculata Brandisová, fifth child of the Count and Countess Brandis – a noble family with Austrian roots who lived in the twilight years of the Habsburg empire, in the central European region of Bohemia (later part of Czechoslovakia and now in the Czech Republic).

You could guess their approximate status without knowing their title. All eight children in the picture are scrubbed, brushed and formally attired. The girls wear stiff, matching dresses, with lace bib collars; the boy wears a heavy suit. The two eldest sisters keep watch at the back for signs of mutiny. The whole tableau creaks with upper-class respectability.

Yet there is less to the Brandis family's privilege than meets the eye; and what there is of it is fragile. In contrast to most tales of sporting greatness, this is a riches to rags story.

The studio photograph was taken in 1903: a time when the Czech lands of the Austro-Hungarian empire were awash with inherited wealth. In the lushly wooded hills south-west of Prague, noble families lived in chateaux that would not have looked out of place next to Versailles. Even today, you gasp when you see them: the Colloredo-Mansfelds' seat in Dobříš; the Schirndings' in Mníšek pod Brdy; the Schwarzenbergs' in Orlík; the Pálffys' at Březnice; the mighty royal castle at Karlštejn. Yet the Brandis chateau in Řitka – right in the centre of this belt of architectural splendour – was little more than a large farmhouse by comparison: a stucco-fronted quadrangle, straggled with ivy, with stables along one side of the sloping courtyard, a granary on another, staff quarters on a third and just one low, two-storey block available on the north side for the count, the countess and their fast-growing family.

Their financial resources were barely adequate even for that. Count Brandis, observed one snide neighbour, 'is more blessed with children than with earthly possessions'. By normal standards, of course, he was fabulously fortunate. The 500-hectare estate, about seventeen miles from Prague, originally included three villages, two farms, several fish ponds, a brewery, a distillery, a brickworks, a forest packed with game and a dependent, rent-paying population of more than 300 people. It needed careful managing, and the revenues were modest; but it was a lot better than having no estate at all.

The Brandis family came here in 1896. Count Leopold, Lata's father, was a former cavalry officer turned chamberlain at the imperial court, with limited cash but plenty of dash. As a young lieutenant in the Hussars, he swam across the Danube and back on horseback for a bet, in full uniform, earning himself a spell under house arrest and the lasting admiration of his fellow officers. Later, having left the army with the rank of lieutenant colonel, he found part-time employment tutoring princelings in Vienna (including the future Emperor Charles I) in, among other things, horsemanship. He also dabbled in horse breeding.

His wife, Johanna, was sixteen years younger, the daughter of a wealthy Viennese-born politician, Christian von Schäffer. Leopold courted her when she was barely fourteen. The resulting quarrel with her father was so violent that shots were fired, and Leopold was barred from the house for the rest of Christian's life. Family tradition blames this incident for Christian's premature end soon afterwards – although the official cause of the fifty-five-year-old's death, in 1885, was 'exhaustion'. Whatever the truth, the romance survived the mishap. Leopold and Johanna married two years later and set up home with Christian's widow in the Schäffers' neo-Renaissance chateau at Úmonín, in the central Bohemian region of Kutná Hora.

Children followed quickly: six in nine years. Lata, the fifth, was born on 26 June 1895, moments before her twin, Kristýna. The only account I have heard of her earliest years involves her sleeping outside in a double pram with Kristýna, under the supposed supervision of their four older siblings – who were actually practising driving a horse and carriage with the help of an eighteen-year-old coachman. But we can be sure that the family did not lack for comfort: the chateau at Úmonín was not only large and well appointed – with extensive stables – but employed half a village's worth of servants.

Shortly after Lata's first birthday, the family moved out. Christian's widow had bought another estate, in Řitka, sixty miles to the west, and in August 1896 she sold it to Johanna. It is not clear what prompted this transaction, but one possibility is that Leopold needed to be closer to Vienna. Another is that life in Úmonín had become strained. Christian von Schäffer had been a pillar of respectability: a member of the Bohemian parliament, a director of the local sugar refinery and a canny investor in the stock market. He had restored and developed the chateau at Úmonín, but beyond paying for a new vicarage for the neighbouring village of Křesetice he was not extravagant. His widow – who was later accused of tampering with Christian's will to ensure that the estate passed to her rather than their sons – was more of a spender than a saver: one local chronicler was scathing about her alleged extravagance. Eventually, in 1902, mounting financial problems resulted in the estate being taken out of her hands and passed to her youngest son. Her eldest son had emigrated by then: he died drunk in Berlin a decade later. Count Brandis, whose grand friends included at least one royal archduke, may not have relished being linked too visibly with such family turmoil – or seeing his wife's potential inheritance squandered. The twenty-five-year-old Johanna borrowed money to fund the purchase of Řitka, and it was there that the formative years of Lata's life would be lived.

§ - § - §

Over the next six years, Leopold and Johanna added three more children to the six they had brought with them from Úmonín. The final line-up comprised: Marie Therese (b.1888); Gabriele (b.1890); Leopold (b.1892); Mikuláš (b.1893); Lata and Kristýna (b.1895); Alžběta (b.1898); Markéta (b.1899); and Johanna (b.1901). To raise all nine in the manner expected of the nobility was a daunting financial challenge. Leopold was ill-suited to it. He was known as a friendly, good-natured kind of chap, but he may have pined for the more fashionable pleasures of Vienna, to which he made frequent visits.

Responsibility for the day-to-day running of the estate fell on the shoulders of its legal owner, Johanna. The fact that she also had nine children to raise may account for the bags under her eyes in the photograph referred to earlier. None the less, according to village tradition she managed Řitka well. She balanced the books; she managed the workforce (many of whom lived on the premises); she kept land and buildings in good repair; and – in contrast to the allegedly rapacious vendor from whom her mother had purchased it in 1890 – she cared for the wellbeing of workers and tenants. That's something they still talk about in Řitka today. Sick villagers were cared for; staff received financial gifts upon marrying; locals with a taste for reading were encouraged to borrow books.

Leopold found work in Prague: as director at a bank and, from 1901, as a member of Bohemia's regional parliament. Some say that he also found time to squander most of the revenues generated by Johanna's efficiency, spending long periods away in Vienna, where he still had a permanent entry pass for the imperial court. But there were opportunities for squandering closer to home as well. Leopold had an eye for fine horses and fast carriages, and there were some fabulously wealthy neighbours to keep up with. The financial position deteriorated; those three villages would dwindle to one before Lata came of age. The arrival of Leopold's elderly mother, who lived with them until her death in early 1901, is unlikely to have made things easier for Johanna; nor is the arrival, much later, of her own profligate mother, who suffered a stroke in Řitka in 1911.

Still, those children had to be raised, and Johanna – aided by Marie Therese, the eldest, and, from 1900, by a young live-in governess, Marie Rothländer – did her best to bring them up in a manner appropriate to the nobility. In practice, this seems to have involved a rather random mixture of discipline and anarchy. Outdoors, the children ran wild, with the entire estate as their playground, including miles of old forest (a mix of spruce, firs, maple, larch, beech and oak) on the hills behind the house. The woods, full of wildlife (including deer, hares, rabbits, pheasant and vipers), were nominally rented out for hunting, but the Brandis children could ride, swim, climb and hide there; or gorge themselves on wild blueberries; or even, as they grew older, shoot. Unusually for children of the nobility they were not entirely banned from contact with ordinary village children when they were small, although they were not supposed to stray far from the boundaries of the main property. There were numerous dogs to play with – one visitor later wrote of 'dogs barking from every window' – and, always, horses. Their number varied: Leopold tried to breed horses commercially as well as keeping them for the family's personal use. But there was room in the stables for around ten (plus carriages); and while there were stable staff, including a coachman, to tend them, that didn't prevent the children from scrambling onto the smaller horses' backs as they grazed in the paddocks that separated the house from the woods.

Indoors, the rules were stricter. An unchanging time-table of meals and schoolwork was rigidly adhered to, and the count was ferociously insistent on good table manners. Prayers were said daily; Sundays were dominated by churchgoing. Everyday communication took place in a very formal kind of German, with Czech reserved for villagers and servants. (In those days, the family probably used German forms of each other's names. For simplicity's sake, I am using the Czech versions throughout.) Daughters of the nobility were also expected to be fluent in French; to understand and help with household management; and to master such lady-like accomplishments as flower arranging, piano playing and needlework. Their mission was to marry, and from their earliest years they were trained for just that.

In fact, the girls' chances of making good matches were slim. Aristocratic brides were expected to be provided with dowries to keep their husbands in the style to which they were accustomed, and Leopold and Johanna were not in a position to make such provision. Still, a good upbringing could do no harm.

The formal part of this upbringing took place in the neighbouring town of Mníšek pod Brdy, not at the local school but with a private tutor, Augustin Černý. Horses took them there and back, sometimes in a small two-wheeled carriage (called a *kočárek*) but also, as they grew in age and number, in the saddle. Lata and Kristýna had their first riding lessons at eight, on horses that their father had first tired out on long hacks. Soon he was taking them for rides; Lata rode an old Irish mare. Within a year they were confident enough to ride unsupervised, although according to Lata it was still a struggle to mount these 'gigantic' creatures. Lata sometimes rode as far as Dobříš, a dozen miles to the south. By the time they were ten the twins could drive a barouche, a four-wheeled carriage – and if the coachman was driving would 'torture' him with requests to take the reins themselves. Lata liked driving, and was particularly attached to the old horse that she used for this purpose: she would feed him oats and braid his mane and tail with red ribbons 'to make the hair nice and wavy'. But it was riding that really excited her. Sometimes a whole line of the children could be seen trotting out to Mníšek, often led by Count Leopold. The girls rode astride, not side-saddle, and wore floppy puff berets rather than helmets. Villagers commented on the beauty of the horses, and on the children's confidence in the saddle.

§ - § - §

The tutoring must have taught them something. The adult Lata had neat handwriting and could speak and write flawless German and French. But it was obvious from an early age that her real gift was for action rather than words. A natural athlete, she excelled at outdoor fun, from tree-climbing to shooting; and the kudos she gained from being best at such games gave her authority beyond her years. One relative described her as 'the uncrowned king' among the siblings.

Her greatest gift was for riding. Her father, a noted horseman whose father and grandfather had also been notable equestrians, was quick to recognise Lata's almost miraculous rapport with horses, and as she grew more assured he used her to help break in younger horses which weren't yet strong enough to carry adult riders. Her secret was simple: she could see the world through a horse's eyes. Most riders hope to make the horse 'an obedient slave' (as Lata later put it); Lata always aimed to make 'a friend – a friend that will gladly put his great strength at your disposal'. She made a habit of imitating horses 'in movement and in temper'. And whereas even the most confident adults tend to harbour a degree of apprehension when they ride, Lata had a naïve faith that no harm could befall her. 'I simply do not believe that a horse could ever deliberately do something bad to me,' she said. She rode 'with peace and love' – and all else flowed from that.

Our knowledge of her siblings is vaguer, but the seven sisters appear to have been close. Kristýna was good at painting and also shared Lata's love of horses. Markéta inherited her mother's gift for herbal medicine. Alžběta was romantic and kind. Marie Therese was described by one family friend as 'the pretty one' and in one photograph wears a ball-dress; Gabriele, plumper than the others, was especially fond of Marie Therese, and of her father. Johanna played the piano and was best at cooking. Lata, the sporty one, was strong-minded and decisive. Within the family, she was considered a natural leader.

Her siblings were charming, clever and well-brought-up, but I have never heard anyone tell a story about any of them in a 'you'll-never-guess-what' sort of voice. With Lata, you rarely hear any other sort. She was the kind of person people exchanged stories about, even when her only remarkable feats involved riding, cycling or climbing.

Gossip about her parents notwithstanding, Brandis family photographs give the impression of a warm, affectionate household, in which people laughed and were kind to animals and life was lived more in the outdoors than in the drawing room. Many of the pictures feature dogs as well as children. When the younger Lata appears in them, she is often messing about, especially when her father is present. Children of all ages wear chunky, solid shoes, laced high above the ankle and well suited for climbing trees.

Count Leopold was handsome, even in middle age, with a soldier's cropped hair, a wide, pointy moustache and a twinkling smile. Although his values were deeply conservative, he had a sense of fun. Countess Johanna was serious but warm. She believed that a mother's role was to 'be good and kind, but if necessary to tell the truth'. Children, she believed, should 'honour' their father; and if anything happened to her she expected her eldest daughter, Marie Therese, to take on the responsibility of teaching them to do so. Therese may have had other ideas.

Their home would have felt crowded at times. There was no corridor on the top floor – people simply walked from one bedroom to another, regardless of who was there. But the interconnected rooms were richly decorated and elegantly furnished. Paintings hung on the walls, often portraying horses or members of the imperial family; or, in one room, Leopold's parents. In the corridors and main staircases, the walls bristled with hunting trophies: a giant pair of elk antlers overlooked the landing. Leopold loved to stalk game in the forest, and when he was in residence he would walk up to the woods every day with his gun. He had also made himself some kind of shooting range there. His daughters were encouraged to join him.

§ - § - §

Yet for all the outdoor activities, Řitka must often have felt like a solemn place. The count and countess were firm and conventional in their Roman Catholic beliefs, and piety was a fact of daily life in their home. The count's elder sister, Maria Theresia, was a nun: a member of the Daughters of Charity of St Vincent de Paul in Austria. In the local church, in the neighbouring village of Líšnice, the Brandis family had their own pews, on either side of the altar. Unless they were away, they never missed a service.

In the woods above Řitka, meanwhile, the count had a small chapel built, near the brow of the hill. It was dedicated to St Anthony of Padua – patron saint of, among other things, lost property, lost people, horses and the sick. No trace remains today, but the wooded ridge, high above the noise and bustle of daily business, is clearly a place that lends itself to contemplation. A few miles further south, just above Mníšek at a spot called Skalka, a whole cluster of small chapels looks out over the same valley from the same woods, like silent, white-robed saints. If you come across these by chance from the trees behind, the peace of the place takes your breath away. People go up there to say prayers for the dead. As Lata was growing up, Leopold and his family often did the same at their small chapel. Leopold, when he did so, would certainly have remembered his mother, who died in 1901; she may not, however, always have been upper-most in his thoughts. In June 1902, four days before Lata's seventh birthday, her eldest brother, nine-year-old Leopold, died of scarlet fever. He was not the only child in Řitka to meet such a fate that summer; but that, for his parents, may have added to the horror. Most noble families banned their children from contact with ordi-nary village children. Had the Brandises' more relaxed approach exposed young Leopold to the infection that killed him?

For a long time the house was chilled with grief. Johanna was still wearing mourning a year later, while for decades to come the family would light candles in lit-tle Leopold's memory every Christmas Eve. Meanwhile, long after the first agonies of loss had calmed, anyone who walked or rode up the narrow path from the house to the woods had only to pass the chapel to be reminded of their loved ones' mortality. At some point, as the sur-viving children became teenagers, the message was rein-forced by the appearance at the lower end of the path of an informal pet graveyard.

Like their Victorian counterparts in Britain, the late Habsburg upper classes seem to have been haunted by existential melancholy. You can feel it in their poems, their songs and their ever-more-elaborate cemeteries: a sad, aching dread. They sensed that, for all their good fortune and sophistication, and the tranquillity of their rural retreats, Death would come for them in the end.

They were right. But what he had in mind for most of them was still a few years off.

# 3.

# Horseplay

Under a grey sky, steam rises from a grey trench. The trench is vast – two metres deep and five wide – with a hedge, almost as high as a man, along one side. Within its depths, a great horse struggles to right itself, rolling on its rider as it does so. Bodies are strewn on the muddy ground beyond: another horse, and too many men to count.

It looks like war. It is supposed to. In another image of the same event, a horse and a rider, a few feet apart, are tumbling, or possibly somersaulting, from a high bank, as if blasted over it by an explosion. It is hard to imagine either man or beast surviving. The bank is higher than the fully stretched length of the horse.

In a third photograph, two riders – both army officers – are on the edge of what looks like a deep stream. One has reached the sodden turf and lies on his back, not necessarily conscious; the other is still up to his waist in the stream, along with his horse, which seems similarly stuck. In the background, a third officer, unsteadily on horseback, gallops out of the picture. A cluster of spectators in the distance is the only hint that this is in fact a sporting contest.

There are even scraps of film footage, although you need a strong stomach to look at them. Horses galloping flat out are halted abruptly and brutally by unexpected obstacles. Their riders shoot forward like human cannon balls, for five, ten, fifteen metres. A horse jumps badly and brings down half a dozen others. When the flailing tangle of legs and bodies resolves itself, two jockeys remain on the ground; they are neither moving nor, it seems, breathing . . .

§ - § - §

I would like to say that no horses were harmed in the making of this book. Sadly – and obviously – that wouldn't be true. Many were, mostly in Pardubice, the central Bohemian racecourse where these scenes and many like them took place. Sometimes Lata Brandisová was present; more than once she was involved. Yet this is not a tale of brutality or cruelty. It is the story of a woman whose distinguishing feature was her compassion for and empathy with horses – someone who, in the words of one friend, 'would have given her life for her horses – I'm certain of that'. It is also, despite appearances, a story from a time and a place in which horses were valued more deeply than they are today.

To understand that paradox, and hence to understand properly the story of Lata Brandisová, we need to shift our focus for a moment and explore not her life but her world. This is an adventure from a rougher, more reckless age than ours: a time when men were men and women were their chattels, and horses were not the cherished pets they are now. Even aristocrats shrugged off daily discomforts that we would struggle to tolerate. Horses were expected to be as robust as their riders.

Yet horses were also cared for, as prized assets. Lata grew up in an age more horse-focused than any before or since, at a time when the ancient bond between the equine and human species had not yet been broken. Horses, and people who understood horses, and people whose lives revolved around horses, could be found in every corner of society. Peasants and farmers used them for work, the rich for leisure and war, and all who could for day-to-day transport. Only a minority had no contact with them at all. The rural economy was largely made up of local, horse-based micro economies. Řitka, with its stables, stable staff, farm and farm horses and its network of local suppliers, was just one small example. In Pardubice, ninety miles to the east, the phenomenon was replicated on a far grander scale.

The people involved may sometimes have exposed the horses in their care to great danger, but they were not indifferent. Rather, with few exceptions, they would normally do their very best to keep them out of harm's way, just as today we try not to damage the cars we drive.

Decent people felt affection for their horses, too, but that didn't mean that they never took risks with them – especially the fast ones. And ideas of acceptable risk, for both horse and rider, were very different from ours. In Lata's world, the crazy horseman who risked a broken neck for the sake of a moment's glory was admired for his pluck, not censured for his folly. The fact that that neck might sometimes belong to the horse rather than the rider was barely considered as a concern in its own right. Ideally, no necks would be broken at all; and if you did end up losing your co-participant, well, it was like losing a comrade in battle. You dealt with it and moved on.

It is important to understand this, because this is a story in which many necks were broken.

§ - § - §

The seeds of Lata's story were sown long before her birth, in the early nineteenth century, among the upper echelons of Austro-Hungarian aristocracy. Decades of disastrous war had just ended on the killing fields of Waterloo, in 1815. In the aftermath, two empires dominated Europe. The British, the new superpower, claimed credit for vanquishing Napoleon; the Habsburg lands – or at least their ruling classes – rejoiced at being liberated from his yoke. Both welcomed a new age of (relative) peace and prosperity. Both saw military strength and martial values as the key to making it last.

The British honed theirs in endless colonial skirmishes. The armies of Austria-Hungary, lacking this option, developed instead a barracks-based military culture obsessed with displays of bravery. The less battle-hardened the officer classes became, the more they were encouraged to cling to the values of the battlefield. Honour was prized, cowardice was abhorred. Boorish rituals – drinking, gambling, whoring – helped to entrench crude stereotypes of testosterone-fuelled manliness. Duelling, in decline elsewhere in the world, was both widespread and tolerated: better a military caste whose members occasionally slaughtered one another on trivial pretexts than one that, softened by years of peace, quailed in the face of death.

But one particular manly virtue was prized above all others: boldness in the saddle.

It's easy to see why. Cavalry remained a crucial weapon of war – at least for a land-based army such as the Habsburgs' – and its components were valued accordingly. Breeders who supplied the imperial war machine with well-bred mounts could become as rich as modern arms dealers. Owners of fine warhorses flaunted them as projections of their own worth and virility. Yet what value were fine horses without riders who could put them to good use in war? The challenge for an army in peacetime was to ensure a reliable supply of skilled, fearless horsemen.

In seeking to rise to this challenge, the officer classes broadened their cult of bravery to embrace the most reckless behaviour. When Leopold Brandis swam his horse across the Danube, he was breaking any number of military regulations, yet the feat was entirely within the spirit of the unwritten military code – as was his exchange of gunshots with his prospective father-in-law. Never mind the potential harm to his fellow creatures: what mattered was his plucky spirit, especially as displayed in the saddle.

Anyone who doubted this code could be swiftly silenced with reference to the example of the British, famous for their foolhardy daring yet enviably successful in war, commerce, science and geo-politics. As the century progressed, the all-conquering liberators of Europe were increasingly adopted as role models. English styles of architecture, dress and manners became fashionable; but what really transformed Austro-Hungarian society was the ruling classes' fascination with their English counterparts' kamikaze approach to horsemanship.

Two British sports particularly impressed the Anglophiles: horse racing and fox hunting. From the 1820s onwards they began to imitate them, with competitive enthusiasm. Wealthy Hungarians such as Count István Széchenyi and Count Móric Sandor and wealthy Czechs such as Count Oktavian Kinský and Prince Franz Liechtenstein imported English thoroughbreds and hounds and organised hunts and races to show them off. Hungary's first English-style race meeting took place in 1826, Bohemia's in 1839. Bohemia's first English-style hunt was organised by Kinský in 1836, near the then little-known town of Pardubice – where, in 1841, a permanent hunting society was established. The society organised a race meeting the following year that included several 'steeplechase' races.

The richest aristocrats splashed out not just on horses but also on the finest English trainers, grooms and, as racing took hold, jockeys. Dozens of Englishmen who were skilled with horses made the journey to central Europe from the mid-nineteenth century onwards: for badly paid, barely educated stable staff, it was a rare chance to convert their talent into prosperity. The far-away countries in which they ended up must have seemed terrifying in their strangeness, but the potential rewards justified the upheaval – rather as they do today for South Americans and Africans who seek fame and fortune in Europe's football leagues.

The story of the English racing diaspora to the Habsburg lands in the nineteenth century deserves a book of its own. (I recommend the excellent *The Velká Pardubická and the Grand National*, by John Pinfold and Kamila Pecherová, to which this chapter and the next are heavily indebted.) Some localities were transformed by the influx: the town of Alag, for example, became known as 'the Hungarian Newmarket' – while some of the migrants became little short of celebrities. Previously obscure Englishmen who found fame and fortune on the central European racing scene included Richard Fletcher, a hard-drinking jockey from Northenden, near Manchester, whose riding for Prince Thurn und Taxis was rewarded with a substantial hunting lodge at Loučeň; Henry Huxtable, another Mancunian, whose work for the Hungarian Prince Festetics earned him a mansion in Alag; George Williamson, a horse dealer's son from Nottingham whose successes in the saddle and in Alag real estate were matched by a string of romantic conquests in high society (the Baroness de Buren and Daisy, Countess of Warwick, were among his 'wins'); and Walter Earl, a farmer's son from Northamptonshire who made a name for himself first as a jockey in Lednice and then as a trainer for Prince Auersperg – on whose Slatiňany estate Earl's memorial stone can still be seen.

It was much the same with hunting. Bohemia's best-known – and best-paid – early huntsmen were English expatriates who had acquired their skills the hard way in their native land before coming abroad to be properly rewarded for them. Examples include Thomas Sketh (employed by Prince Franz Liechtenstein at Lednice); Rowland Reynolds (recruited by Prince Ferdinand Kinský during a hunting trip to England to be his Master of Horse at Heřmanův Městec); and Samuel Stevens and Charley Peck, from Buckinghamshire and Lincolnshire respectively, who were both employed by the Pardubice hunt.

Attitudes to horsemanship in Bohemia were trans-formed by their work. The Anglophile aristocrats didn't have much appetite for killing foxes – they were more likely to hunt deer, which they often did not kill – but they grasped that fox hunting was the key to the uniquely crazy British way of riding. Thanks to the enclosure pro-grammes of the seventeenth and eighteenth centuries, those who followed hounds on horseback in England could do so successfully only if they could ride at high speed through countryside criss-crossed with field boundaries. This meant frighteningly large amounts of daredevil jumping: jumping hedges, jumping fences, jumping gates, jumping ditches; jumping unexpected combinations of these – all at a gallop, regardless of the going or the weather, in an atmosphere of ferocious snob-bery in which perceived reluctance to take risks could see you ostracised as a 'funker'. As a result a spectacularly gung-ho approach to horsemanship evolved. This kind of riding, which could be tested in steeplechase races as well as hunts, was barely safer than duelling. But it was hard to imagine a better way – short of genuine warfare – of making cavalry officers battleworthy.

§ - § - §

At first the upper classes tested their own mettle in hunts but left the steeplechasing to specialist jockeys. But some aristocrats felt that this was not enough. Where was the fun in paying some Englishmen to take all the risks on their behalf?

The Hungarian Count Móric Sándor was the most notorious example of a nobleman who wanted all the horse-related glory to himself. Known for his reckless riding, Sándor had a string of extreme feats to his name, including riding from Vienna to Pest (now part of Budapest) in thirty-one hours without changing horse; riding across the ice of the Danube as it was cracking beneath his horse's hooves; and jumping clean over three horses, side by side, as they pulled a moving cart in Nagyhéd Street in Pest. He rode in several steeplechases in Pardubice, and won at least one, but ended his riding career – and wrote off a horse – in a head-on collision with an iron railing in 1850.

Sándor's contemporaries sensed that his kind of horsemanship went beyond the bounds of decency. The count was nicknamed 'The Devil Rider', and it was reported that, at his funeral, the horses charged with pulling his hearse shied away and bolted.

Count Oktavian Kinský, whose principal residence was in Chlumec nad Cidlinou in eastern Bohemia, was similarly imprudent, but somehow more human. Known for his acrobatic skills – he could stand on his head in the saddle – he shared Sándor's penchant for riding his horses indoors, especially up the grand staircase of his magnificent baroque-gothic castle, Karlova Koruna. He would also race his coach around the castle's high terrace-balcony, allegedly turning corners so fast that the outer wheels hung in the air. No doubt he would have driven it into a swimming pool, had any of his castles possessed one. In short, he was a hellraiser, whose favoured tool of mayhem was the horse. Yet there was a bond of affection between master and horses that seems incompatible with deliberate cruelty, or even with neglect. When Kinský lay on his deathbed in 1896, his horses were led into his room, one by one, for him to bid them farewell.

Oktavian was by no means the only Kinský to make his mark on the horse-racing world. His family had been breeding horses for centuries, and had officially done so for the imperial cavalry since 1723. Their rewards included fabulous wealth, vast estates and power and prestige on a scale more usually associated with monarchs. (One branch of the family, from Choceň, had been elevated to the rank of princes.) The Kinskýs had access to some of the finest horses and stables in Europe, and most members of the family knew how to use them. For example: Count Rudolf Kinský, an early promoter of races in Pardubice; Count Zdenko Kinský, Oktavian's nephew and adopted heir and an influential owner and jockey in his own right; and the more flamboyant Count Karel Kinský, who caused a sensation in the UK in 1883 by becoming the first foreigner to win the Grand National. His horse, Zoedone (purchased with winnings from a bet on the 1882 Cesarewitch), was fancied to carry him to a second Aintree victory in 1885; instead, it was nobbled by a mystery poisoner. Karel, a diplomat in the Austro-Hungarian embassy in London, honed his remarkable jumping skills by hunting in Northamptonshire, and also found the time and energy to conduct a sizzling love affair with Winston Churchill's mother, Lady Randolph Churchill.

It is worth dwelling on Oktavian Kinský in particular, because without him there would be no story. Born in 1813, 'Taffy', as his intimates called him, was a lanky, long-armed, bushy-moustached man, with dark hair and wild blue eyes. Some considered him brutish in appearance

('It is impossible that we had such apes in our family!' protested a later count, Norbert), and his behaviour often compounded the impression. His temper was explosive, his appetite for thrills insatiable, his sensitivity to the needs of others limited. He loved practical jokes. Cruder examples included convincing a guest that he had just cleaned his teeth with Oktavian's personal 'arse-brush'; filling another's pillow with live frogs; and tricking an untrustworthy horse-dealer into submerging himself in a barrel of muck. At the more sophisticated end of his repertoire, he announced his own death at least once, to see how people reacted. He is said to have particularly enjoyed the moment when an estranged relative, who had returned from Vienna specially in the hope of claiming an inheritance, came bounding up the steps of Kinský's castle – to be greeted at the top by the grinning face of Oktavian himself.

He must have been quite annoying to know, and had he been a poorer man his humour might have found a less indulgent audience. Yet there was also something life-affirming about his devil-may-care exuberance – and he was never more exuberant than where animals were concerned. Reckless with their wellbeing, he none the less cared about them deeply. He once leaped from his horse and wrestled a stag by its horns because it was attacking his dogs. As for horses, he believed that they were there to be ridden; and that riding wasn't proper riding unless it included jumping; and that it was hardly worth going to the trouble of jumping unless the obstacles were challenging. Riding, in other words, meant steeplechasing, formal or informal, the more dangerous the better. Nor was he satisfied with making these the guiding principles of his own horsemanship. He wanted all riders to join his adrenaline cult.

His introduction of the Pardubice hunt has already been mentioned. Three years later, in 1839, he was responsible for the creation of the Hunter Stakes, Prague's first steeplechase; while in 1842 he helped ensure that there were several races over jumps at Pardubice's first race meeting. When that wasn't enough to satisfy his appetite, he started his own annual steeplechase, in 1846, in the sloping Lučice meadows near Chlumec nad Cidlinou.

Soon Europe's richest and grandest, including several crowned heads, were flocking regularly to central Bohemia to enjoy Oktavian's exotic new sports – and the spectacular hospitality of Karlova Koruna. The surrounding countryside, most of which Oktavian owned, was perfectly suited to the hunts he organised on the days in between race meetings. And his insistence that all involved in those hunts wore traditional English 'pink' added an extra layer of impenetrable exclusivity to the already elite proceedings. Outside observers were both baffled and impressed; and, then as now, the fads of the super-rich trickled down to become the aspirations of wider society.

For Oktavian, however, even this was not enough. And so it was that, at the age of sixty-one, he devised a more extreme form of sporting entertainment ...

# 4.

# The dance of death

They call it the Devil's Race. It is not clear if they have a particular devil in mind. If they do, it may well be Oktavian. But he wasn't its only creator. Several aristocratic friends accompanied him on the trip to the British Grand National, in 1865, during which the seed of the infernal idea was sown. By the time it reached fruition, on an autumn day in Pardubice in 1874, he had two partners in devilry: Prince Emil Fürstenberg and Count Max Ugarte. The time lag is partially explained by a digression for a brief, shambolic war with Prussia. But it may have taken nine years to work out just how far back the frontiers of common sense could be pushed in pursuit of the ultimate test of horsemanship.

The answer was: quite far. Even today, the Velká Pardubická – the Grand Pardubice – is considered the world's most dangerous steeplechase, and that is despite decades of modifications to make it safer. 'The world's craziest' might be a better description. The *raison d'être* of the race is to test recklessness. It takes place just once a year, over a squiggling four-and-a-bit mile course, with thirty-one obstacles, some terrifying and some much worse than that. A strong, well-ridden horse can complete it in ten minutes – or, just as likely, fail to complete it at all.

Even viewed on foot, many of the jumps make your blood run cold. In the heat and rush of the actual contest, with the muscle-melting effect of miles of muddy galloping factored in and the added danger from fellow competitors, they verge on the suicidal. That's the whole point. They are there, Oktavian would have said, to sort out the men from the boys. You don't have to be unhinged to attempt them, but it helps.

Perhaps 'unhinged' is too crude a diagnosis. But only just. The race has thrived for a century and a half because there are enough people in horse racing who regard labels such as 'toughest', 'most dangerous' and 'most extreme' as red rags, the only acceptable response to which is to charge towards them. 'People think I'm mad,' said the English jockey Charlie Mann, who rode in it in 1994 and 1995, 'but they don't see it the way I do.' Mann had been declared unfit to ride in the UK after breaking his neck in a fall, but insisted, with succinct eloquence: 'If I want to kill myself in Czechoslovakia, that's my business.' To Velká Pardubická aficionados, such an attitude was commendable but in no way out of the ordinary. The race's most famous champion, Josef Váňa, rode to eight victories from twenty-five starts between 1985 and 2011 – the last at the age of fifty-eight. A series of catastrophic falls along the way left him with a permanent limp, a missing part of a lung, half a dozen fewer ribs than he started out with and too many broken bones to list, but failed to dilute the enthusiasm with which he came back for more. Even clinical death – for fifteen minutes in 1994 – only kept him out of the saddle for two months. Why?

He could no more explain than a normal person could understand. But Oktavian would have understood. The race was designed with such competitors in mind.

The Aintree influence is easy to discern. The Velká Pardubická is just a furlong or so shorter than the Grand National – and the jumps are tough enough for merely finishing to be a commendable achievement. Other aspects of the challenge are unique to Pardubice. The route starts and finishes on the racecourse but was not, in those early days, confined to it. The founders insisted that half of the race be run across ploughed fields, and so the route digressed significantly into the local farmland. The stamina-sapping effects greatly increased the difficulty of the jumps; which was unfortunate, because the man overseeing the design of the jumps was Oktavian.

It took several years for the course and its obstacles to settle down into anything resembling their current form. There were only twenty-four when the race was first run, but most of the notorious jumps were there from the beginning and are still there today: the Big English Fence (a thick hedge with a wooden fence on the far side), the Snake Ditch (a wide, water-filled ditch with a drop of about two feet from take-off to landing), the Irish Bank (six foot high and six foot thick, with a small ditch on either side – to be scrambled over rather than jumped), the French Jump (a double hedge with a small ditch in the middle), the Garden fences (two big railed hedges, just eight metres apart). We shall be hearing more of these – just as we shall be hearing a great deal more about the obstacle originally known as the Big Ditch. In the meantime, think of it as a tough cross-country jumping course, transposed to a distinctly unmanicured racecourse, with a couple of miles of ploughed fields tagged on; the crucial difference being that, instead of jumping the vast obstacles one by one as eventers do, the competitors all start at the same time and place, jumping in one monstrous tangle – and whoever finishes first gets the prize.

It sounds like a recipe for mayhem, and it is.

§ - § - §

On a cold Thursday, 5 November 1874, fourteen runners and riders lined up at the start of the first Velká Pardubická. Two had already fallen, the organisers having insisted on a pre-race test jump to check that all involved were fit and competent. The pair who failed were allowed to start anyway. Thereafter, even token pretences of common sense vanished. After six jumps, only eleven horses remained. Four fell at the Wall, the first and biggest (four foot high) of several stone walls. Hansi Fries, riding Kinský's horse, remounted. Like all those riding on this occasion, Fries was a professional: he wouldn't have wanted his employer to think he had done less than his utmost. But Walter Earl and Peter Appleton – two of eleven Englishmen riding – were too badly injured to continue. Earl's distinguished riding career never really recovered from the fall.

The rest of the field charged on chaotically. For much of the race, they were out of sight of spectators, who were not very numerous anyway. But you barely needed to see the action to get the gist of it: more falls, more remounting; more danger and injury; increasing exhaustion. The hurdle at the Big Ditch was trampled flat; some horses preferred to wade through rather than jump over the deep trench beyond it. The Irish Bank claimed a victim; so did the Bullfinch. Only six horses finished. Two had pulled up from exhaustion. Another, Strizzel, was dead, after breaking its neck at the relatively innocuous penultimate fence.

The grim toll provoked justifiable criticism. 'It is inconceivable that such small weight be placed on the safety of horses and riders,' complained one journalist. But it was not enough to prevent the race – which was won by the Germany-based Englishman George Sayers on the German-owned Fantome – from being judged an overall success. It was repeated the following year, although the youngest of its founders, Count Ugarte, did not live to see it. The twenty-four-year-old died in a fall that winter, while racing in Italy. Some might see this as a kind of justice, others as a reminder that life is indeed short – lending all the more urgency to the pursuit of life-transcending excitement in each bright remaining moment.

The Velká Pardubická became a regular feature of the sporting and social calendar, usually on the second Sunday of October. Professional expatriate riders dominated in the early years: twenty-two of the first thirty winners had British riders. But the crowds that came in increasing numbers to watch were drawn from all over the Habsburg empire, and beyond.

§ - § - §

The race's reputation grew with that of its most spectacular and challenging feature. The Big Ditch, as it was initially known, attracted more controversy with each new victim it claimed. It wasn't unjumpable, but the depth of the ditch, which was often flooded, meant that mistakes could be catastrophic. The slanting hurdle at the approach was at some point in the mid-1880s or early 1890s replaced with a large hedge, improving drainage but otherwise making the obstacle more fearsome still. At around the same time, there were serious discussions about the possibility of removing the jump altogether. Instead, the assembled aristocrats were swayed by the intervention of Prince Egon Thurn und Taxis, who said words to this effect: 'Gentlemen, none of us will be jumping it. Therefore I see no reason why we should omit it or make it easier for anybody else.' Perhaps such solipsistic logic makes more sense if you are a prince. It proved persuasive, at any rate; and the jump was officially named after the prince following his death in 1892.

When Lata was growing up, and for most of her adult life, Taxis consisted of a huge ditch, two metres deep and five across, concealed on the approach by a stiff hedge, 1.4 metres high and 1.2 metres thick. A horse jumping it straight would need to soar a minimum of about eight metres to land safely on the far side; a crooked jump would increase the distance still further. The ditch's sides were steep and, as a result, unforgiving to those that fell short. And then there was the biggest hazard of all: all those other horses.

Remarkably, no jockey has yet died jumping Taxis. Some have had their ashes scattered there, but the nearby gravestones are the legacy of a brief period in the Communist era when the course doubled up as a speedway track. Yet the message of the stones is appropriate: this is a life-threatening obstacle. Countless jockeys have suffered disastrous injuries there in the past 145 years. In addition, twenty-nine horses have died. This imbalance is largely explained by the fact that badly injured horses are usually put down, whereas jockeys are not. It still seems obscene. Yet that is how things used to be done. Times have changed since most of those deaths occurred, and the Velká Pardubická is now more merciful – too much so, say hardcore traditionalists. The rules have been tightened and the course has been repeatedly toned down; Taxis, in particular, is not the jump it was. On a dry day you can see the line in the soil where the far slope of the ditch has been made significantly nearer and shallower.

The challenge is still grotesquely hard. Not only must the horse perform a gargantuan leap to land safely on the far side: it must do so without any idea why. Just 'giving full liberty to the horse' – the supposed secret of Count Sándor's prodigious jumping – is not enough. The vast ditch is invisible until well after take-off. None the less, it can be done and usually is. The secret is generally held to be a combination of equine psychology ('Horses will try things as a herd that no individual horse would do of its own accord,' explains Jan Pospíšil) and blind commitment ('When you come to the jump, you have to throw your heart over it,' says Gabriela Křístková, who teaches riding and jumping in the same Řitka paddocks where Lata learned to ride). The best contenders try to be first to the obstacle, so as not to be impeded by the also-rans; the rest charge along in the leaders' wake, hoping to be drawn over by herd momentum.

It sounds a bit vague to inspire total confidence, but it's the best there is. As a result, few approach Taxis without dread in their stomachs. The English amateur rider Chris Collins, who raced here in 1973 – the first Englishman to do so for nearly sixty years – admitted: 'When I saw the Taxis for the first time, I thought those who said it was jumpable were joking.' But they weren't; and, indeed, Collins jumped it successfully that year, although not the next. The British jockey Marcus Armytage, who survived it in 1990 and 1991 but fell badly in 1992, calls it 'the love child of Becher's Brook and The Chair, on steroids'. Charlie Mann, who got over safely both times he raced there in the mid-1990s, thinks, 'It looks bigger than it jumps', while according to the Czech jockey Pavel Liebich (who won the race three times in a row from 1981 to 1983), 'Many people are haunted by the name.' In Liebich's opinion, 'Horses will often do a jump of that size in training, even at a smaller obstacle.' Then, of course, they are not among a crowd of other horses. But the fact remains: if horses more often than not get over it, it is because they are both able and willing to do so. Jan Kratochvíl, who won the 2017 race on No Time To Lose, said afterwards that getting over Taxis was 'largely a question of letting the horse go'.

But Taxis is only one obstacle among many; and, as we shall see, it is by no means the only one that is potentially lethal. The long stretches of ploughed field turn the whole race into a form of Bohemian roulette, especially when the weather has been wet – as it usually has been. The race has been run 128 times (there have been interruptions for war), and there has never yet been a year in

which every competitor finished. In 1909, none finished
at all.

§ - § - §

It is possible that Lata had visited Pardubice by then.
Perhaps she had even watched the race. We do not know.
What we do know is that she and her family were well
aware of the Velká Pardubická, and of Oktavian's role in
its creation. It was impossible to be interested in horses
and not know: it had transformed the sporting culture,
and perhaps even the economy, of central Bohemia.
But there was also another reason: Oktavian was Lata's
great-uncle.

There was a huge gap in wealth and status between the
mighty Kinský family and the struggling Brandis family.
The Brandis's overcrowded home in Řitka would have
fitted unnoticed into the stables of Karlova Koruna. Yet
the fact remained: Oktavian's sister Barbara had married Heinrich Brandis, in 1849. Leopold was their son,
and all his children were Oktavian's great-nieces and
great-nephews. There may not have been much contact
between the two parts of the family in Oktavian's lifetime,
especially after his scandalous late marriage to a former
servant girl forty-seven years his junior. But their paths
may have crossed in Vienna, where Leopold's parents
lived and Oktavian spent his winters, and there was at
least one visit by the Brandis family to Chlumec, during
which the eight-year-old Leopold was allowed to ride
some of Oktavian's horses. And although Lata never met
Oktavian, who died in 1896, shortly before her first birthday, she knew his sister (Lata's grandmother joined her

son in Řitka for the final years of her life), and she would certainly have known about her rich, eccentric great-uncle's pranks, feats and place in steeplechasing history. If his more recent descendants are anything to go by, she will rarely have heard him mentioned without a note of amused admiration, bordering on awe, in the speaker's voice: 'Uncle Taffy? Oh yes, he was crazy! Did you hear about the time ...'

When thinking about what she did and didn't want to do with her future, Lata would have considered Oktavian's example – as well as the example of the equally dashing (but slightly saner) Karel Kinský, a more distant relation. True, the steeplechases with which both men's names were associated were not events in which a woman could hope to compete, no matter how great her talents. Yet it would have been hard not to question the reasoning behind that prohibition, and perhaps even its permanence. It was acceptable for a well-bred woman to follow an English-style hunt: the Emperor's late wife – the beautiful, discontented Sisi – had made endless visits to Britain in her younger years, dazzling English society with her jumping skills as she followed the Pytchley hunt. And if a woman could prove herself men's equal in the most demanding of hunting fields – as the Empress was reckoned to have done – then why should it not be possible one day for a woman to race in one of the great death-defying steeplechases, just as all those dashing cavalry officers did?

It was a far-fetched question, but it was worth dreaming about.

# 5.

# Broken in

Horses are born wild. Even the most pampered thoroughbred is wilful and impetuous until it is broken in. And even then we may assume that the bit sometimes chafes.

It was much the same for children of the ruling classes of the great European empires of the nineteenth century. You started off running wild – often in vast palaces and idyllic country estates. Then, sooner or later, you too had to be taught submission and initiated, patiently but implacably, into the rules and rituals of your caste. For boys, being broken in usually meant being sent to military academy, where habits of unquestioning obedience and dogmatic adherence to military codes were drilled in until they became second nature. For girls, it meant being laced into metaphorical corsets of submissive, lady-like conformity.

It wasn't exactly cruel; nor was it compulsory. It was simply the price of privilege. Yet the sense of unnatural restraint could be maddening. And, just as a horse harnessed to a carriage will occasionally 'kick over the traces' – so that the straps constraining it become instruments of mayhem – so the carefully schooled children of the nobility would sometimes seek escape in mad, destructive abandon.

The gratuitous perils of the Velká Pardubická can be largely explained in terms of such impulses: the race was designed by and for people who abhorred restraint. Much the same could be said of some of the other extravagant excesses through which aristocratic boys in Prague or Vienna liked to let off steam (think Bullingdon Club with uniforms, swords and guns); and, for that matter, of the surprising enthusiasm with which many young officers embraced their rare opportunities to take part in actual battles. The risks were the whole point. It wasn't that anyone wanted to die. It was just that sometimes they felt the need to remind themselves that they were alive.

But what about the girls?

§ - § - §

Shortly after Lata's eleventh birthday, a racecourse opened at Velká Chuchle, a few miles south-west of Prague and a mere twelve-mile carriage ride from Řitka. Leopold became a regular visitor to the track, and the girls, particularly Lata, liked to go with him. The races they watched were mostly flat races. The standard may not have been particularly high. None the less, for a father and daughter who liked being around horses, and who enjoyed one another's company, these were happy excursions.

Two years later, in 1908, Leopold bought his own thoroughbred, a Hungarian mare, through a fellow officer. Lata was allowed to ride it at Řitka – and got her first experience of what a highly strung horse can be like. At one point the mare lay down, with Lata still in the saddle, and refused to get up. The experience did not cool her enthusiasm: on the contrary, she is said to have expressed a wish to compete as a jockey herself. If she did, Leopold did not approve: to have participated in such a rough, rude, public sport would have been scandalous. It was also impossible: there was no such thing as an officially sanctioned race for women, and thus no such thing as a female jockey.

This begged the question of what Lata was to do instead. 'All my young imagination was filled with horse experiences,' she said later. As a result, according to one observer, 'Lata spent more time with horses than trying to find a husband.' This must have worried her parents, although Lata couldn't see what the problem was. Horses were her 'darlings'; a horse, to her, was 'my dearest and most faithful friend'. What was wrong with that? But convention dictated that young noblewomen must marry within the nobility; or grow up to live lonely lives as spinsters, on the margins of high society; or, worse still, marry outside the nobility and lose their privileged status altogether. Finding the Brandis daughters aristo-cratic life-partners would have been the overwhelming priority of their teenage years, irrespective of what they themselves felt about this.

Both parents moved in the highest social circles. Johanna was a regular on Prague's charitable fund-raising circuit, while Leopold kept up friendly relations with members of the imperial court and family – and was part of the delegation that greeted the Emperor Franz Joseph when he visited Prague in 1906. They were on visiting terms with wealthy neighbours, too: the Kasalickýs, for example, who would soon begin to rebuild the already grand house in the nearby village of Všenory; or, later, the Kasts, who acquired the grand chateau in Mníšek in 1909 and similarly lavished vast sums on making it more splendid still (it would eventually include one of the world's first private cinemas). But being well connected did not alleviate the Brandis family's relative poverty – if anything, the strain of keeping up appearances must have added to it. As a result, the biggest social prize of all – finding titled bridegrooms for their daughters – eluded them.

Their daughters may not have been particularly bothered. Indeed, it is said that none of them showed much enthusiasm for marriage. Why should they? They were happy as they were. Their parents loved them; they enjoyed their village and their vast rural playground; they loved the surrounding countryside; and they had horses and dogs and endless opportunities for outdoor fun. It was, in Lata's words, 'a happy youth, growing with nature and with animals'. Who would want to forgo all that, to become the property of a strange aristocrat, far from home?

Male visitors to Řitka were not unknown, but there is no reason to believe that there were swarms of eager suitors. Lata was shy, and disliked dancing. 'I was fond of horses and dogs,' she explained simply. 'I get on well with them.' The subtext was that people were trickier. As for what men thought of her, many would in due course consider her beautiful: she was handsome, blonde, grey-eyed and glowing with fitness. This may not have been enough to offset her awkwardness and lack of a dowry. Spontaneous romance was in any case strongly discouraged in noble families – and was relatively rare as a result. Arranged betrothals to penniless brides were rarer still.

Eventually, three of Lata's sisters would take the radical step of marrying outside the nobility. But that was much later, when the world had changed. For the time being, all seven Brandis daughters were trapped by convention and, like other impoverished young noblewomen, could only wait demurely for a romantic miracle. Or, more wisely, they could seek other forms of fulfilment.

Lata chose the latter course. Horse riding was her most obvious calling: 'the great passion of my life,' she said later. Another was religion. Her parents did not discourage this; indeed, it is said that Lata received some additional education from a monastic establishment in Prague's Smíchov district. If so, she embraced what she was taught with the trusting sincerity of youth. Several of the girls kept commonplace books in which, typically, friends marked visits by inscribing their names, often adding short quotations of an improving nature (e.g. '*Man proposes, God disposes*') or – in the case of Alžběta's book – a romantic nature (e.g. '*The rose smells, the thorn pricks, the violet says do not forget me*'). Alžběta's book even contains a loose scrap of paper arranging a rendezvous 'in the usual place'. Lata's book is full not of names or tender sentiments but, instead, of prayers, all neatly copied out in German, French and Czech. There is something mesmerising about the precise but flowing handwriting: page after page of pleas to her Maker: '*Oh God, help me in your mercy ... Oh Jesus, meek and mild, let me be like you ... Oh Lord of love, I put all my confidence in you ... Make me an instrument of your peace ... Lead me with you to Calvary ...*' It is hard not to sense a fierce, pent-up energy: a yearning to be something more than she was; or, at the very least, to still the turbulence within.

§ - § - §

It would be fanciful to infer from such thin evidence that the teenage Lata was consumed by frustration at the constraints society placed on her because of her gender. It seems unlikely, however, that she welcomed such limits. A photograph in the family's collection shows the aftermath of what seems to have been a regular form of horseborne entertainment. Lata, aged about twelve, stands with four younger sisters by an old wooden bench. It is autumn – the ground is blanketed with leaves – and the girls seem flushed with excitement. They are all dressed as jockeys. Each carries a whip of some kind, and each has a moustache painted onto her face. Lata stands slightly apart, carrying what might be an improvised winner's 'certificate'. On the back of the picture, the adult Lata has written: 'As children, my four sisters and I. After an officers' race (we were all officers).'

This image illustrates well the balance of privilege and servitude in Lata's life. As a child of the nobility, she had drawn a winning ticket in the lottery of life. As a woman, she had not. She was lucky enough to have the wherewithal to take part in pretend races. The road to real officers' races was closed to her. Mikuláš, her surviving brother, could anticipate a future rich with opportunity and adventure, initially to be facilitated by training to be an officer in the largely barracks-bound imperial army. The best Lata could hope for was a life like her mother's: a comfortable treadmill of domesticity and child-bearing, relieved (as Johanna's was) by the occasional foray into polite society. Under the Austrian legal code of 1811, a woman was obliged to do the housework, had to obey her husband in domestic matters and could not embark on a career without her husband's consent – always assuming that she was lucky enough to find a husband. A spinster's horizons were more limited still.

Is it any wonder that, imagining more thrilling adventures for themselves, Lata and her sisters should have begun by disguising themselves as men?

# 6.

# The winds of change

As Lata approached adulthood, her confidence in the saddle grew. So did her faith in her methods of gentle mastery. There were nine horses in Řitka's stables, including a chestnut mare, purchased as a carriage horse by the estate manager, that would allow no one but Lata to approach it. 'The horse is the noblest animal,' she explained, 'unless man has spoiled it by rudeness and lack of understanding. Therefore [a woman] should win the horse like a noble man through love and not through brute force.'

In other respects, life continued upon its preordained lines: for the count and countess, the rituals of polite society; for their children, a largely uneventful jumble of family, pets, friends; for the village, the centuries-old rhythms of the agricultural year. With hindsight, this calm, comfortable world would seem idyllic in its predictability. At the time, for a restlessly energetic young woman with a thirst for adventure, the sleepiness may have been hard to bear.

Small variations in routine were welcome – yet could easily disappoint. Most summers, for example, Count Brandis would allow the imperial army to use the hills behind Řitka for military exercises. The visiting battalions could camp, manoeuvre, parade and drill. Leopold could renew friendships with his fellow officers. For the full-time soldiers it was a welcome change of scene, while Leopold could rekindle his sense of himself as a dashing dragoon.

In the summer of 1912 there was an additional attraction: the visiting officers included Archduke Franz Ferdinand of Austria-Este, heir presumptive to the Habsburg throne. The forty-eight-year-old archduke owned (among much else) a Gothic hunting lodge at Konopiště, about twenty miles to the east. He would probably have known Count Leopold from Vienna. As inspector-general of the army, he often attended such training exercises. He had a reputation for being a demanding critic, but his overall influence was limited: the military establishment was stuck in its old ways from the Emperor downwards. Europe's other great powers were furiously modernising and preparing for war. Austria-Hungary continued to spend three times as much on beer, wine and tobacco as it did on its armed forces.

The watching Brandis sisters may or may not have shared Řitka's excitement at Franz Ferdinand's presence on the hillside of splendidly uniformed soldiers. They would certainly have noticed that everyone involved was male. The fact would have meant something different to Lata's youngest sister, eleven-year-old Johanna, than it did to her eldest, twenty-three-year-old Marie Therese. But it is hard to believe that Lata, who at just seventeen was by far the most proficient in the family at cavalry-related pursuits, did not at some point ask herself why boys, in this as in everything else, had all the fun.

Mikuláš was by now away at cadet school in Moravia – and could expect, in due course, to join in this kind of exercise. He too would be able to manoeuvre and march and ride and drill, and show off his horsemanship, and swagger or hell-raise as he saw fit. He could even dream of putting his mettle to the ultimate test in battle. The girls could only watch and admire – and envy.

If Lata ever wondered why, she will also have known the answer. Things were as they were because that was how they were. This was the principle that held the Habsburg world together. Absurdities and injustices abounded; change was unthinkable. The Emperor Franz Joseph, Franz Ferdinand's uncle, had been on the throne for sixty-four years, fatherly and well-meaning – and perfectly in tune with his inbred dynasty's tradition of constipated conservatism. His inherited empire encompassed eighteen different nations, from Lake Constance to the Carpathians, and the vast machinery of state that held it together for him was obsessed with preserving past glories. 'That was how things were back then,' explained Joseph Roth in his great novel of Austro-Hungarian decline, *The Radetzky March*. 'People lived on memories.' As an aide-memoire, Franz Joseph's whiskery face glowered from near-identical portraits in public buildings and patriotic homes right across his realms, unvarying as the divinely ordained status quo he symbolised.

For those with a stake in the system – aristocrats, army officers, civil servants, and those with old money – there was something deeply comforting in this sense of permanence. All they had to do was observe the established proprieties and honour their elderly Emperor and – as Roth's fellow novelist Stefan Zweig put it in *The World of Yesterday* – 'in even rhythm, leisurely and quietly, the wave of time bore them from the cradle to the grave'.

But those with a stake in the system had three things in common: they were men; they owned property; and they spoke German. Barely a tenth of the Austro-Hungarian population fell into all three categories. And, as Lata was growing up, voices from the excluded 90 per cent had been making themselves heard with increasing volume. Yes, change was unthinkable: everyone knew that. Yet how could things continue as they were? The discontented were everywhere: democrats whose hopes of a less autocratic regime had been crushed following the failed revolutions of 1848–9; have-nots who resented the grotesquely unequal distribution of wealth and land; nationalists who believed that Bohemia should be governed for the benefit of Czechs rather than their Austrian overlords.

There were even a handful of eccentrics who challenged the idea that women should be second-class citizens. They were seen as a lunatic fringe, with little chance of achieving their aims. Yet pioneering feminists such as Františka Plamínková had made slow but significant progress by allying their cause to the Czech nationalist movement. By the turn of the century, opportunities had begun to open up in higher education and in the professions, while in 1905 a Committee for Women's Suffrage had been founded in Prague. In 1912, a woman was even elected to the Bohemian parliament, although she wasn't allowed to take her seat.

For most people, however, no agitation was enough to disturb the inertia of the age. Dreamers could dream all they wanted about a better future; sensible folk were happy in the time-honoured certainty that tomorrow would resemble today. And so, for two more years, the empire, and Bohemia, and Řitka, and the Brandis family, muddled on as before.

Then – well, you know what happened next. On 28 June 1914, in a cul-de-sac in Sarajevo, a bullet fired by Gavrilo Princip brought Franz Ferdinand's life to an abrupt, unanticipated end. Within a month, the empire was at war, with the rest of Europe scrambling to join in. The long twilight of the Habsburg world was sinking into its final darkness.

§ - § - §

Count Leopold was not invited to the funeral but wrote a letter of condolence to Franz Ferdinand's younger brother, who had been living in Prague. He then arranged, at the age of sixty, to return to his old regiment for active service. Lata's brother Mikuláš, forty years younger, enlisted too – having been given special permission to leave cadet school prematurely. Neither man can have imagined the true scale of the catastrophe that had been set in motion, or the terror and obscenity of the industrialised slaughter in which they would soon be engulfed. Even so, those last days of peace must have been melancholy.

In the great horse-racing centres of Bohemia and Hungary, the remaining English expatriates were forbidden to travel. In England, Karel Kinský said his farewells and came home to fight for his Emperor. Austria-Hungary's long love affair with the English was over. Individual friends exchanged reassurances to the effect that (as Kinský put it in a letter to a Newmarket trainer),

'Whatever happens we two will always remain the same friends as ever'; most feared that such declarations would count for little once the blood began to flow. Kinský asked to be sent to the eastern front, so that he would not have to kill any Englishmen.

In Řitka there was a last gathering on 12 September for Mikuláš and his friends. 'Alas,' wrote one of them in a memory book, 'on this dark Earth, what is made to be united is rarely united ...'

Soon, the Brandis home would be inhabited exclusively by women.

There is reason to believe that Lata's mother, Countess Johanna, did not cope well. The loss of her first-born son still grieved her; the fear of losing her other menfolk must have been hard to bear. She had heart trouble, too. And there was the stress of trying to untangle the web of debts left by her own mother. Some family members believe that the countess was absent from Řitka for an extended period. No proof of this survives; but there is a family consensus that, for one reason or another, the countess had by 1914 relinquished much of her role as commander-in-chief of home, family and estate. When Leopold went off to join his regiment, taking with him two horses and the coachman but otherwise leaving a full stable, he paused at the gates of his property, saluted – and left nineteen-year-old Lata in charge.

# 7.

# The breaking of nations

Lata was not the only young woman in Europe to find herself saddled with unexpected responsibility. The great armies drained their nations of men. Women in their millions filled the gaps. Jobs that had been closed to them were suddenly jobs that it was their patriotic duty to do; and while most soon yearned for peace, there was no denying that, for many, war offered a rare and welcome chance to experience the possibilities of work beyond the home.

The paradox applied to Lata, too. Running the estate was probably better than sitting indoors trying to be ladylike. It cannot have been easy. Even without all the worrying about family and friends on the front, war put a huge strain on agricultural estates such as Řitka. With one farmworker in two called up for military service, acute labour scarcity set in. Horses were taken as well. All but one of the eight remaining in the Brandis stables were soon requisitioned. Lata contested each call-up, but could secure exemption only for her favourite, a three-year-old gelding called Sarek. She remembered the assessments as a 'terrible' experience but consoled herself with the knowledge that the chestnut carriage horse that had once been too wild for anyone but her to approach was now so biddable that the acquisition commission commented favourably on its tameness. She cannot have imagined the horror that awaited her 'darlings' on the front line.

The reduction in the horse population made Lata's life easier in some ways: initially she had been feeding and mucking out all eight horses herself, with the help of one small stable lad. But any work the horses had been doing now had to be done in other ways, or not done at all. Fertiliser was also in short supply, while state regulation of food prices made it harder for farmers to make a viable business from what they did grow. Empire-wide, agricultural output would fall by 40 per cent in the course of the war.

Yet the estate still had to function. In peacetime, the main Řitka property was home to more than forty people, only ten of whom were family members. Dozens of others in the village – and their families – were dependent on the Brandis family for their living. The mostly female residues of these populations had somehow to be both managed and looked after.

These were big issues for a nineteen-year-old to handle, yet Lata appears to have done so with confidence. 'She had a rational personality,' according to her nephew, Petr Jaroševský. 'She was almost general-like.' Each sister had a bedroom; Lata set up hers as an office. It had the advantage of being on the ground floor, at the end of the house, with its own external door, where employees and tradespeople could visit her without tramping through the rest of the house.

Word came back that her desk was usually piled high with correspondence, and that the air was thick with her cigarette smoke. Neither detail will have harmed her image as a serious, grown-up estate manager. None the less, there were some who felt that the estate was easy prey. Lata found it necessary to patrol the grounds at night in search of intruders, and on one occasion she apprehended a notorious poacher at gunpoint. 'My horse caught a scent,' she recalled matter-of-factly years later. 'All of a sudden, I'm looking in his face. Right from the saddle I ordered him to put his hands up and drove him in front of me to the police station in Mníšek.'

She knew how to use her weapon, a Flobert hunting rifle that her father had bought her. She had been shooting since her early teens, at least – a photograph shows her doing so in the woods on a sunny day, in a long dress, a cartridge pouch slung from her shoulder – and had become frighteningly accurate. Her father preserved a coin, dented in the middle by a bullet, which Lata is said to have shot in 1913 as it spun in the air. (Some family members dispute this account, but I have seen the coin: a five-crown piece.) She habitually carried her father's revolver around with her. She would probably have been a useful asset to the imperial army. But that, of course, was not a woman's place either.

§ - § - §

War went badly for Austria-Hungary's male warriors. The dragoons fought well at Kraśnik, routing the Russians, and also at Jaroslavice – said to have been history's last true cavalry battle. But those successes took place in the first weeks of conflict. Everything else had been a disaster. The imperial army had lost to the Serbians, to the

Russians, to the Italians. Linguistic barriers between the Emperor's subjects caused communication difficulties; some nationalities, notably the Czechs, seemed reluctant to fight for their German-speaking Emperor at all. Large-scale defections were being reported as early as April 1915. Territorial losses, for example in Galicia, had a disastrous effect on food supply. And with each passing week it became clearer that the army's most cherished tactic – the fearless cavalry charge – was lethally out of date against machine guns. Half of the regular army had been killed before 1915 even began. Among them were Lata's cousin Norbert Kinský, Oktavian's twenty-one-year-old great-nephew, who was shot through the heart while rescuing a wounded comrade on the Russian front.

The lost soldiers were quickly replaced, just as they were in other combatant armies; but their replacements lacked experience. Mikuláš Brandis, also twenty-one and still fresh from his unfinished course at cadet school, was promoted to ensign in March 1915; by August he was a lieutenant. He, too, began the war in the east: like Norbert, he was in the Uhlan cavalry. But he was later transferred to fight with the 2nd Imperial Rifles on the Italian front – considered by many to be the deadliest arena of all.

Back in Bohemia, the most obvious symptom of war was hunger. Rationing, initially just for bread and flour, was introduced in April 1915. In Řitka, 'auxiliary commissions' were organised to work in fields whose owners were serving at the front. Nor was food the only thing that was scarce. Schoolchildren were encouraged to gather scrap metal for use in arms manufacture. The church in Líšnice would eventually lose all its bells and several organ pipes. Leopold, meanwhile, somehow managed to obtain a horse on the front: an old, blind mare called Luska that he sent back to Řitka. According to Lata, 'Her sense of smell and touch were much more developed than with normal horses. I rode with her down the steepest slopes and never fell.' It was probably just as well that Luska could make herself useful. A horse that contributed nothing might have attracted hungry looks.

By 1916, the village had introduced a ban on eating meat on Mondays, Thursdays and Fridays. Beer was prohibitively expensive; salt and coffee were unobtainable; sugar and kerosene were scarce. Yet morale in the Brandis household does not appear to have suffered. All that unsupervised outdoor activity in early childhood had made the sisters self-reliant, and no doubt they had absorbed some of their father's military values, too. Lata's strengths were self-discipline, decisive management, and apparently limitless supplies of energy, athleticism and toughness. Austerity was a challenge rather than an ordeal. So was living off the land. Shooting game in the woods became a valuable source of food. It is unlikely that Lata saw this as a chore.

Towards the end of the year, Mikuláš, fighting in northern Italy, had two brushes with death in quick succession. His 'miraculous' double escape – as he described it – inspired him to contribute 200 crowns towards improvements to Řitka's small roadside chapel. Elsewhere, the winds of change were gathering strength. Tomáš Masaryk, the exiled Czech nationalist leader, had published a manifesto the previous November proclaiming the independence of the 'lands of the Bohemian Crown' – that is, Bohemia, Moravia, Austrian Silesia and the regions of Hungary inhabited by Slovaks. In February 1916 he had established what became known as the Czechoslovak National Council – a kind of government in exile. Since then he had been drumming up international support for the independent nation he dreamed of, while also developing the Czechoslovak Legion – an army of Czechs and Slovaks drawn from expatriates, deserters and prisoners of war that had been fighting against Austria-Hungary with increasing success on the eastern front. The idea that the Habsburg status quo was the natural and immutable order of things was looking increasingly threadbare. Tomorrow could belong to anybody.

§ - § - §

On 21 November 1916, the Emperor Franz Joseph died, aged eighty-six, after a reign of almost seven decades. His nephew Charles, Count Leopold's former pupil, succeeded him; but the spell was broken. The empire's collapse seemed suddenly far from unthinkable, and even the most charismatic ruler (which Charles was not) might struggle to do more than delay it.

In 1917, the increasingly desperate imperial army began to recruit tens of thousands of young women to a Women's Auxiliary Labour Force, in non-combat roles such as telegraph operation. The initiative was controversial: some saw it as a threat to the traditional order of society. But this was the new reality. Old certainties, good and bad, counted for nothing.

Nor was it just the Habsburg world that was crumbling. In March 1917, news reached Bohemia that the Russians had overthrown their Tsar; fleeing members of the no-longer-ruling classes soon followed. It became easier than ever to believe that a similar cataclysm awaited what remained of the Habsburg status quo – especially after the entry of the US into the war on the Allied side that April. In the east, the Czechoslovak Legion threw in their lot with Russia's provisional government. Supporters of Masaryk's independence movement spoke with growing confidence about how an independent Czechoslovak nation might be governed – and one thing that was widely noted was that land reform was high on their agenda. Aristocrats with more than their fair share of land were about to get their comeuppance.

Perhaps this sense of an impending year zero is what prompted the Brandis family to start selling off parcels of land in the southern part of Řitka. Altogether Countess Brandisová (presumably Lata's mother rather than Lata herself) sold about 150 hectares that year, in about fifty small parcels. The purchasers were villagers, many of whose families still live on those plots today. The proceeds were small, but the village appears to have welcomed the sales – and it was better than having the land confiscated.

But land is not the worst thing to lose in war. On 9 July, Mikuláš, still fighting in the Italian Alps with the 2nd Imperial Rifles, was killed at Zugna Torta in the battle of Rovereto. In the great scheme of things, it was just another death: one among 1.2 million men killed fighting for Austria-Hungary between 1914 and 1918. It wasn't even unusual from the village's point of view: eleven other Řitka families lost sons in the course of the war. Yet what consolation was that?

Lieutenant Brandis was honoured, two months after his death, with the Military Merit Cross, 3rd Class; so his parents and sisters knew he had died bravely. But that too offered scant consolation, and the slow, piecemeal return of his possessions from the front only added to the agony. He had been home a few months earlier, on leave, and had posed in his uniform for a photograph. His upper lip bears a few wisps of down rather than a moustache. He was just a boy. 'Nobody can help me,' wrote Johanna soon afterwards. 'I cannot conceal it from myself that I will not be happy until I am reunited with [him] ...'

The count, whenever news reached him, would probably have reflected that he now had no heir. There would be no more counts to carry the Brandis name. And Lata? Mikuláš was one of her closer siblings. He was only eighteen months older than his twin sisters, and since young Leopold's death in 1902 there had been a natural division of the siblings into three age clusters: first Marie Therese and Gabriele; then a three and a half year gap to Mikuláš, Lata and Kristýna; and then another three-year gap before the young ones, Alžběta, Markéta and Johanna. In one family photograph, the middle three can be seen riding together. Lata's taste and aptitude for pastimes traditionally considered boyish would have made Mikuláš a natural playmate. It is unlikely that many in the family will have felt his loss more keenly than she did. But she left no record of her feelings – only those prayers: *'Oh Lord give them eternal rest, and let perpetual light shine upon them ...'*

§ - § - §

By early 1918, the lines between life and death were blurring. Strikes and mutinies broke out across the Austro-Hungarian lands. The crisis in food production became desperate. The cost of living had increased tenfold since the outbreak of war, and daily per capita consumption of flour had fallen to half its pre-war average. In May, a bank clerk from Prague, Josef Pagán, was found starved to death on a Řitka roadside.

In June, a huge Austro-Hungarian offensive against the Italians on the Piave River was comprehensively repelled. The disaster marked the ignominious end of the campaign that had claimed Mikuláš's life; and, to all intents and purposes, the end of the grand military tradition in which he and his father had served. The Italians celebrated their victory on Lata's twenty-third birthday.

On 3 November, following one last military humiliation at Vittorio Veneto, Austria-Hungary concluded an armistice with the Allies. On 11 November the Emperor Charles renounced all participation in the administration of the state. For his Czech subjects, it barely mattered: they had already renounced him. The Western powers had by then officially recognised Masaryk's Czechoslovak National Committee as the government-in-exile of the Habsburg territories hitherto known as Bohemia, Moravia, Slovakia and Carpathian Ruthenia, and on 28 October the new, independent state of Czechoslovakia had been founded.

The war was over, and so was the world that Lata and her siblings had been groomed to inhabit.

# 8.

# A fresh start

As the last guns fell silent on 11 November, Europe's decimated nations turned their faces to the future. Few did so with more optimism than Czechoslovakia, whose first president, sixty-eight-year-old Tomáš Garrigue Masaryk, was elected by the interim National Assembly three days later.

Masaryk was one of history's more appealing statesmen. The son of a poor Moravian couple – a coachman and cook – he was a philosopher and academic before turning to politics in the 1890s. His nationalism was preceded by what he called 'democratism', and although he was ruthlessly effective as champion of an independent Czechoslovak nation from 1914 onwards, he never lost sight of his core values. The use of force was justified 'only in the most extreme case', he insisted, while hate had no place in politics at all. The new nation he believed in had to be based on democracy, freedom, justice and fairness.

His spirit caught the mood of the post-war age, and Czechoslovakia embraced it. As the nation blossomed into what was arguably Europe's most democratic state, Masaryk was repeatedly re-elected: in 1920, 1927 and 1934. His animated face – small, intense, bookish, bespectacled – replaced the old Emperor's whiskery features as the ubiquitous personification of the nation's aspirations. If not everyone shared his beliefs, most approved of his character. He preferred the company of ordinary people to that of the grand and wealthy. His lifestyle was famously modest, his marriage, to the American Charlotte Garrigue, famously happy. His personal motto was homely but catchy: 'Don't be afraid and don't steal.' His new countrymen quoted it with pride.

Mere decency was not enough to undo the devastation of war, but the sense of a fresh, fair beginning offered hope. If the new nation got it right, a better future awaited.

§ - § - §

In Řitka, the Brandis family were mourning the ruined past. No fine words from Masaryk could bring back Mikuláš – or his still-missed older brother. They were not alone in their sorrow: bereavement and trauma clung to the village. But the family's privileged status denied them the consolations of solidarity. As for the new regime, Count Leopold had devoted his life to the service of the old one. He could hardly be expected to celebrate.

The count and countess retreated into a bruised old age. Johanna's health worsened; her own mother's debts from Úmonín continued to plague her. Leopold had four years of fighting to recover from: in photographs taken soon after the war, he looks frail and haunted – although he was still capable of riding for up to three hours at a time. Meanwhile, for all Lata's efforts, the estate was struggling. The scarcities that had crippled the rural economy in wartime would take years to ease.

Masaryk's determination to right past wrongs must have exacerbated the family's worries. Czechoslovakia was barely six weeks old when Law No. 61/1918 Sb. z. a. n. (10 December 1918) abolished aristocratic titles. Four months later, the Land Control Act of 16 April (1919) provided for the expropriation of estates from large landowners.

It was hard to dispute the fairness of these measures. On the eve of the First World War, more than a third of Bohemian land had been owned by 362 families; half of that was owned by a mere thirty-eight families. Almost without exception, these mega-landowners were aristocrats – whose wealth and status reflected their closeness to the imperial regime in Vienna. To have made no attempt to correct the imbalance would have made a nonsense of the idea that the First Republic (as Masaryk's Czechoslovak nation is usually known) would be governed, in contrast to the past, for the benefit of all its citizens. Yet the common citizen's gain would have to be someone else's loss, and Lata's family must have worried. Johanna, updating her will in 1918, urged her surviving children to 'stick together' and to do whatever they could to ensure that Řitka remained in the family's hands. She was still fighting to defend the property in 1924, when the State Land Office formally conceded that – for the time being at least – Řitka would be exempt from confiscation.

It was reasonable for Leopold and Johanna to argue that they weren't really the problem. Their already reduced land-holdings were minimal by aristocratic standards: well under 400 hectares, compared with 58,000 owned by their neighbours, the Colloredo-Mansfelds, or 176,000 owned by just one branch of the Schwarzenberg family, a little further to the south. But their relations the Kinskýs stood to lose tens of thousands of hectares, and most of their grander friends and acquaintances were also affected. In any case, they were – or had been – nobility, and Lata's family were thus caught up in a general nationalist narrative of hostility to titled landowners. In this narrative, the Habsburg regime had been oppressing the Czechs for three centuries, and the super-rich nobility were the obscene symptom. A nation of Czech-speaking Protestants had, it was said, been conquered, plundered and exploited by an aristocracy of German-speaking Catholics, imposed from abroad. This was an oversimplification (and in some respects false); but there was enough truth in it for it to stick.

For aristocrats, the hostility could feel very personal. As an MP in the Bohemian diet, Leopold had represented the Conservative Landowners' Party, and had sworn his oath of loyalty in German. Both he and his party had been swept from power in 1908, following a widening of the electoral franchise. But the taint of speaking German lingered, for all the family. The nationalist Alfred Maria Mayer complained that 'not a single lady of aristocratic origin [can] be found in all Bohemia who speaks and writes correct Czech'. 'Who are the large landowners?' asked the radical newspaper *Venkov*. 'They are almost entirely Germans, most of them ... hating our nation.' The MP František Modráček called for such nobles to be 'expunged' from the history of the nation. It would have been hard for Lata's family to be completely unaware of, or unalarmed by, the public appetite for 'settling accounts' (as Mayer put it) with the nobility. They had heard about the 'red terror' instituted by the post-war

Communist regime that had been established (briefly) in the former Habsburg land of Hungary. In the new Soviet Union, meanwhile, 'enemies of the people' were being executed at a rate of about 500 a week.

At the very least, the Brandis family would have felt isolated. In the census of 1921, citizens were required to record their mother tongue. In the village of Řitka (population: 362) the only German-speakers were the Brandises and their governess. Everyone else, apart from one Russian exile, spoke Czech.

There is no evidence of specific tensions between the Brandises and the villagers. Relations with those who depended on the family for a living remained cordial. That 1918 will of Johanna's included a sizeable bequest to a long-time servant, Václav Širl, with the proviso that the Brandis family look after it for him 'until Širl settles down and can no longer squander the money'. But Řitka clearly did not regret the passing of the old order. In 1920, villagers established their own branch of Sokol – a mass sport-and-nationalism movement, dating back to the mid-nineteenth century, that specialised in huge gymnastic displays in traditional costumes. The Habsburg regime had been suspicious of Sokol, whose Czech patriotism had given it a subversive edge, but the Brandises appear to have welcomed its emergence in Řitka. Some years later, Lata would give the local Sokol a substantial chunk of land for its activities.

Meanwhile, there was at least one respect in which the remaking of their nation represented a dramatic improvement for Lata, her mother and her sisters. Masaryk's sense of fairness extended to gender politics. Democracy, he believed, was 'first and foremost the equality of woman and man'. He had been campaigning for such equality for years, arguing that, in confining women to the home, 'we lower their horizons, deaden their energy, and waste their talents'. In a well-ordered nation, he declared, 'the woman would cease to be a slave (cook, housekeeper, wet nurse and concubine) and the man would cease to be the lord over the woman'. His eloquence earned him the admiration of feminist campaigners: 'The name of Masaryk has and will have in the Czech women's movement a significance rarely accorded by women to men,' wrote one activist.

There was every reason to believe that, in office, the philosopher-statesman would live up to this reputation. The Czechoslovak declaration of independence – written by Masaryk and published with Allied approval just before the end of the war – had specifically stated that women would be 'placed on a level with men, politically, socially and culturally'. Eight women were included in the National Assembly that governed the new state for the eighteen months between independence and the first nationwide elections. So it was not exactly a surprise when equality between the sexes was enshrined in the Constitution that passed into law on 29 February 1920.

It was, none the less, a landmark in European history. Even Britain, which had enfranchised women over thirty in 1918, had yet to give all adult women the same voting rights as men. (That would happen in 1928.) Františka Plamínková, the most prominent Czech feminist of the age, rejoiced: 'The position of women in the Czechoslovak Republic today with respect to political rights may be regarded as the realisation of the boldest hopes of those who have laboured for the civic rights of women.'

In practice, equality under the Constitution took a long time to translate into equality of opportunity – or even into equality under the legal code (especially family law). Many would argue that it never did so. Yet Article 106 of the Constitution could not have been more explicit: 'Privileges of sex, birth and occupation will no longer be recognised.'

Lata Brandisová was no longer a countess, but nor was she a second-class citizen.

# 9.

# Riding out

Řitka is not a glamorous place; nor was it in the 1920s. Photographs suggest a world barely changed since Napoleon's day. Dirt roads fade dustily into unkempt verges; oxen pull ploughs; crops are harvested with scythes. The village's name can easily be misheard, by mischievous ears, as an obscenity roughly equivalent to 'arsehole'. This risk was arguably exacerbated in 1924, when villagers agreed to update the name's spelling (from Řidka to Řitka). That may have been the most exciting thing that happened in the village all year.

Even in the chateau, life must often have felt unsophisticated. Electricity didn't arrive until 1929. The main courtyard, pecked by chickens, was dominated in winter by a large dung heap, packed around the water pump to prevent it freezing. The smell would have been the first thing a visitor noticed. Life wasn't squalid – there were still five servants in residence – but by aristocratic standards it was basic, and it certainly didn't feel modern or new.

For some Czechoslovak women those first post-war years felt like a new golden age: a world transformed. 'Today the Czech woman is free ... as if by magic,' wrote the journalist Krista Nevšímalová in 1919. One by one, traditional barriers fell. Female civil servants (including teachers) were no longer required to be unmarried and were recognised as having a right to equal pay. Divorce became easier. Women who were elected to parliament were allowed to take up their seats. By 1922, nearly a quarter of women had jobs.

For Lata, the outlook was greyer. Theoretical freedom is not the same as freedom to do what you want. Her life remained predictable, constrained by convention and duty. Indeed, some of the independence she had enjoyed in wartime melted away now that her nation was at peace. She was still responsible for much of the day-to-day running of Řitka; and by all accounts she continued to exercise those responsibilities well. Ultimately, however, she was not in charge. Her parents were there to be obeyed as well as looked after.

The Brandis family's story continued on the count and countess's terms, while Lata did her best to be dutiful. Appearances were kept up, even though there were no longer any archdukes or emperors to impress. There were visits to and from well-heeled neighbours. Churchgoing and formal meals continued to shape the weekly diary. There was also a rationalisation of the estate. From 1921, much of Řitka's agricultural land was let out, to a tenant farmer called Hugo Polák. This may have ensured a steadier income, although the rent varied according to the price of corn. It also reduced the daily demands on Lata's time. Hunting rights in the woodland were also let out, but the Brandis family remained responsible for its management. Lata liaised regularly with the gamekeeper, who lived in a house provided by the family.

Řitka's stables, briefly replenished after the war, were emptied again, presumably to reduce costs. At one point only Luska remained. The old, blind mare was by now so attached to Lata that she sometimes followed her around 'like a dog'. But Lata still dreamed of adventures on horseback. She would take Luska on long rides in the woods, sometimes accompanied by a sister and usually followed by a dog. Sometimes she would return with game for the pot. And no doubt she sometimes paused by the little chapel on the forest edge to gaze down at the unexplored world beyond Řitka – rolling dark green hills, all the way to Prague. 'I have no longing for the city', she claimed once. Yet it would have been hard not to wonder what excitements she was missing out on.

What life there was grew from the landscape. Low-lying, sheltered and fertile, Řitka brimmed with natural abundance. There were fruit trees on the roadside, wild flowers in the meadows, beehives on the hillside; on the Brandis estate, gardens, paddocks, crops and livestock required constant nurture and restraint. Lata and her family continued to play their time-honoured parts in the resulting cycle of local activities: entertaining villagers when the young men cut down the maypole; supervising the annual draining of the village fish ponds; celebrating the completion of the harvest; helping with births, marriages, sicknesses and deaths. If there were more dramatic happenings, they left no trace. It was almost as if the wave of time had resumed the even rhythm of the Habsburg age. Perhaps, if she chose, it would bear Lata from cradle to grave, leisurely and quietly, as if none of the traumas of the past five years had happened.

In 1920, Lata's younger sister Alžběta, aged twenty-two, became engaged to a dashing young military pilot, Josef Pospíšil. He was not from a noble family, which was a blow to Lata's parents, even though in theory such things no longer mattered. But he did have a reputation for reckless courage – he was said to have flown his biplane under a Prague railway bridge – and this redeemed him in Leopold's eyes. They married in Řitka, on Lata's twenty-fifth birthday, then went to live in Prague.

The following September, it was the eldest sister's turn. Thirty-three year-old Marie Therese married an Austrian knight named Leopold Haan, who took her to live in Austria, in a large hilltop chateau called Reiteregg. Gabriele, the closest to Marie Therese in age, made frequent visits. Kristýna, too, seems to have spent time away – possibly in Germany.

It would have been easy for Lata to feel left behind. But she, too, had dreams. Better still, she understood that dreams rarely come true unless you try to make them do so. 'One should not wait for a miracle from God,' she wrote once, 'but one has to give one's own best.' And so, as soon as she could think how, she took steps to pursue her riding ambitions. Horse racing resumed at Velká Chuchle in 1920. More or less immediately, Lata – probably accompanied by her father – resumed her habit of going to watch. Then, apparently on the suggestion of a racehorse-owning neighbour, she began to make additional journeys to the racecourse alone, between race meetings. One of the trainers who was based there, Karel Šmejda, agreed to let her help with the exercising of some of the horses in his yard.

Šmejda was fifteen years older than Lata, but they got on well. A diffident, thick-set man, rarely seen without a flat cap, he was known for his gentle nature and his love of animals. At work, he preferred jockeys who did not resort too readily to the whip. At home, he kept hens, ducks, geese, turkeys, rabbits and goats, and grew apples and carrots as treats for horses. Like Lata, he may have been more comfortable dealing with horses than with people. He certainly saw at once how horses felt about her: she had a way of greeting each horse she met, her head close to its as she patted it softly on the neck, that seemed to instil calm and cooperation. Her assistance was welcome.

Her first attempts at riding thoroughbreds on the gallops left her 'totally shattered': she had never had to manage such power before. By the fourth morning, however, she had adapted, learning to relax in the saddle as she would with any other kind of riding. On the racecourse, she realised, her philosophy of riding was more important than ever. With 'peace and love for the horse' you could do anything.

Her visits to Šmejda's stable became an important and regular part of her life. She reached it by bicycle, a twelve-mile trip. Then, after a few hours in the saddle, she cycled twelve miles back. Sometimes her father came to watch her, presumably travelling on horseback. In good weather the journeys must have been pleasant for both of them. Velká Chuchle lies in a wide floodplain, at the foot of an isolated hill. The River Vltava winds quietly past, about a kilometre away, while small trains occasionally rattle alongside on the nearby railway.

Šmejda lived in a small house by the level crossing but was usually to be found at the stables by the racecourse at the edge of town. Several trainers kept horses here, and the racing community was growing fast: by the end of the decade there would be more than a dozen stables. The buildings have gone, but the horsey air must have smelled much the same then as it does now: of manure, grass, leather, stale sweat, old and new hay. Lata would have felt at home – in some respects. In others, she may have felt far from comfortable. Šmejda himself was kind, but the locker-rooms of Velká Chuchle were rough and rude. Even in our supposedly enlightened times, women who reach the male-dominated higher echelons of horse racing risk barbaric abuse. (Just ask the British trainer Gay Kelleway, who in the 1980s became the first female jockey to win a race at Royal Ascot and, in the course of a long and distinguished riding career, endured every-thing from aggressive 'banter' to attempted rape.) We should assume that the racing yards of the First Republic were little better.

One young man who worked at Velká Chuchle in the 1920s, Eduard Zágler, became an internationally suc-cessful jockey. He was so disgusted by the crude culture of the racetrack – with its drinking, smoking, swearing, fighting and worse – that he refused point-blank to allow his horse-obsessed son (who still lives close to the race-course) to have anything to do with the sport. Perhaps being known as a (former) countess protected Lata from such behaviour. Perhaps it had the opposite effect. Either way, Lata seems to have developed a defensive shell. She smoked: the stronger the brand the better. She made a point of being wiry and (despite the smoking) fit. Like the men around her, she took fierce care to show no sign of weakness or fear. Unlike them, she kept herself to herself.

Some took this to mean that she was aloof. Zágler, who liked her, thought her shy. 'She wasn't haughty, like a countess,' he told his son – although he always addressed her as 'Countess'. Instead, he claimed, she seemed ordinary: almost like a man. 'She wasn't very talkative. But she loved horses.'

Others who met her saw her differently. I have seen her variously described – by those who didn't know her well – as having a 'direct, hearty smile'; as being 'dignified', 'humble' and 'perhaps a little proud'; as being 'suave in an aristocratic way'; as being 'not at all stiff or affected'; and as being 'the most amiable woman you can imagine'. The only consistent theme – from many sources, oral and printed – was her kindness; and the fact that, in the words of former Velká Chuchle apprentice Jiří Kocman, 'she loved horses very much: she would have done anything for them'.

As long as Lata was only exercising horses (we would call it 'riding out', although it was probably done on the racetrack), it didn't matter too much what people thought of her. It is clear that some of the opinions expressed were unkind: 'If a woman makes a mistake,' she complained later, 'she is rebuked more for that mistake than a man would be. Immediately she hears comments such as: "But of course, a female! Why is she getting involved in this?"' But what distressed her more was the limit her gender placed on her progress. The racing world whose rough edges she was discovering was a world she could imagine conquering. Riding out was all very well, but Lata 'wanted to really achieve and accomplish something' – if only someone would give her the chance.

In 1921, she seems to have driven in at least three ladies-only harness races held at Velká Chuchle, winning once and being placed twice. She also seems to have taken part in some kind of women's riding display in the harness-racing stadium that opened in that May on Letná plain – a fashionable park in central Prague. (Sadly, no official records survive: just a photograph.) But racing itself – riding flat out, on turf primed for speed, in a simple, instinctive contest between horse and horse, rider and rider – was an impossibility. The Jockey Club did not sanction races for women. If any such events had taken place, they would have been mere 'demonstration' races.

For Lata, who was highly competitive, the restriction must have been maddening. The more time she spent at Velká Chuchle, the more she understood what 'real' horse racing involved – and the more she understood her own abilities. She just wasn't allowed to put them to the test. Racing is 'the most beautiful of sports,' she reflected. 'My only regret is that we as women are excluded from this.' Yet perhaps, in Masaryk's new land of equality, it was no longer absurd to wonder if the exclusion might be overturned.

# 10.

# Allies

In February 1923, Alžběta's husband, Josef Pospíšil, was killed in a plane crash – perhaps not a surprising end, given his reputation. Alžběta moved back to Řitka soon afterwards with their two small children, Jan and Eva. With Lata's now frail parents also in residence, as well as the old governess, Marie, it may still have been a warm and loving household, but it was crowded, noisy and far from carefree.

Lata liked to get away sometimes: either on solitary rides in the empty forests or, increasingly, on those bicycle excursions to Velká Chuchle. The escapes sharpened her taste for life beyond Řitka. At the racecourse, she grew confident riding faster, less familiar horses. The hard-living jockeys and stable lads, some more welcoming than others, grew used to her presence. She also got to know some of the leading racehorse owners who frequented the course: Eberhard Mauve, for example, the mining magnate and future Jockey Club official; or Hanuš Kasalický, lawyer, businessman and, by the mid-1920s, president of the Jockey Club management committee that organised Velká Chuchle race meetings. Some of these owners, notably Mauve, liked to compete as amateur jockeys as well – which may have given Lata ideas. But Kasalický had a bigger impact on her life.

Surviving records do not portray him in a flattering light. Eighteen years older than Lata, he was rich, ambitious, short-tempered and ruthless: the kind of man who is used to getting his own way. In pictures you notice his thick neck, clipped white moustache and unsettlingly assertive eyes – usually glowering from beneath a Homburg hat. Born Johan Kasalický in 1877, in Prague, he came to Všenory in 1902 and acquired a large home there – just three miles from Řitka – by marrying Marie, daughter of the wealthy philanthropist Jan Nolč. A pre-nuptial agreement specified that Kasalický should receive half of Nolč's considerable property, and by the 1920s he was in a position to devote considerable time and money to the turf. Enough remained at the end of the decade for him to commission a major programme of improvements to his already magnificent chateau. By then (February 1927) he had formally adopted the old Czech name of Hanuš: a move whose most obvious explanation would have been a desire for greater acceptance as a pillar of post-Habsburg society.

The Brandis family may have seemed shabby compared with some of Kasalický's grand friends on the Jockey Club board (for example, General Václav Chmelař, ex-Count Jan Pálffy and ex-Prince Bedřich Lobkowitz). None the less, they were near-neighbours, and he sometimes paid visits. Since 1921 he had also done occasional legal work for them. He was thus familiar with Lata's riding skills, and impressed by them; and he would have been happy for her to ride the thoroughbreds that Karel

Šmejda trained for him – perhaps even including his Derby-contender filly, Reseda.

Over time, he and Lata became not just family friends but, improbably, friends in their own right who spent significant amounts of time together. It is possible that there was more to it than friendship, on one side or the other. Lata was young, single and, for all her reserve, full of the sap of life. Kasalický probably had a certain alpha-male charisma, and he was not the best of husbands. Maybe he believed in Lata in a way that others didn't; maybe he was attracted by the relative simplicity of her outdoor lifestyle; or maybe he had cruder motives for encouraging her. Or perhaps it was simply that circumstances brought them together. Their shared devotion to horses – and their specific interest in getting the best out of whichever of Kasalický's horses Lata was helping Šmejda to train – would have given them plenty to talk about. In due course, Hanuš Kasalický would play a significant role in Lata's story.

§ - § - §

But he was not the only married man to do so. From 1926 onwards, Lata also saw a lot of her wealthy, charismatic cousin, Zdenko Radslav Kinský. Tall, slim, handsome and athletic, Kinský had a light heart and an excess of playful energy. His small, bushy moustache seemed to bristle with good nature. His main passions were horses, tennis and parties, yet somehow there was more to him than that suggests. Friends and family called him 'Ra'. There must have been some who begrudged him his grand castles and his absurd wealth, which multiplied accidentally as he grew older. But it would have been hard to feel truly hostile to someone with such an obviously sunny nature. Fluent and charming in half a dozen languages, he was a compulsive maker of friends. Fun followed him; caution and inactivity horrified him. Those who enjoyed the brilliance of his presence tended to adore him.

Ra was a year younger than Lata. The son of the previously mentioned Zdenko Kinský (Oktavian's nephew and heir), he had been raised in the splendour of Karlova Koruna in Chlumec, surrounded not just by luxury and horses but by memories of Oktavian. Initiated into the family cult of gung-ho horsemanship in early childhood, he became a fine and fearless horseman, who in due course would compete at Pardubice, although not in the Velká Pardubická itself. In the Great War he had fought bravely with the Hussars on the Russian front before being taken prisoner in June 1916. After two years in captivity he escaped by disguising himself as the servant of a visiting Red Cross representative. He arrived back on Austro-Hungarian territory a few months before the end of the war. In 1919 he had joined the new Czechoslovak army as an interpreter, but he now worked – apparently sporadically – as an attaché to the Foreign Office.

His path may well have crossed with Lata's when they were children or teenagers, but in adulthood there appears to have been little serious contact before the mid-1920s. Ra's company was sought by diplomats and socialites from many countries. He partied tirelessly, travelled extensively, frequented Prague's nobility-only Ressource club, and was president of the equally exclusive Napoleon

Society. He can't have had much time left over for poor relations in Řitka.

Ra had been brought up to consider himself a servant of the Habsburg Emperor. The empire's collapse had hurt him. So, to a lesser extent, had the subsequent programme of expropriation of aristocratic property. Tireless lobbying by its intended victims had softened the impact of land reform: the rural economy was too closely interwoven with existing patterns of owner-ship to be easily unpicked. But it was hard to forget the thought behind it. Noble families had been transformed from pillars of the nation to enemies of the state. 'They had lost the country they loved,' says Kamila Pecherová, biographer of Karel Kinský. 'They had fought for it in the war, but now it was gone.'

But Ra – unlike the Brandises – could not by any stretch of the imagination be described as short of worldly possessions. Notwithstanding land reform, his estates, much of which were devoted to forestry, remained vast beyond any normal imagining. His father, Zdenko, continued to inhabit Karlova Koruna in Chlumec. Ra's main home was the grand family hunting lodge in Obora, eight miles to the west. But it was not the only property to which he had access. In 1921, he had married Eleonora ('Lori'), widow of the fifth Prince Karel Schwarzenberg, and the couple had spent much of their time since either at Lori's palace in Prague (the Clam-Gallas) or at Orlík, the Schwarzenbergs' magnificent cream-coloured cliff-top castle overlooking the Vltava between Příbram and Tábor. Strictly speaking, Orlík belonged to Ra's step-son, the sixth Prince Karel Schwarzenberg, who had inherited it at the age of three, but that didn't prevent Ra and Eleonora from enjoying extended periods there. Such palace-hopping was not unusual for the high nobility. It had little in common with the lifestyle of the cash-strapped Brandises, whose only home was shabby and full of pets.

But Orlík was barely thirty miles from Řitka, and in 1926 Ra paid his first visit to the Brandis home. This led to an invitation for Leopold to pay a return visit – and to bring Lata with him. Despite the gulf in wealth and status, Ra and Lata had much in common. Both had strong moral principles; each had lost a brother in the war. They also shared a lighter side. They thrived outdoors and loved to express their athleticism and energy in exuberant games. Most of all, they both loved horses.

Ra owned a string of horses for racing, hunting and breeding. He kept most of them in or around Obora and Chlumec, but there were usually quite a few at Orlík as well; including, sometimes, racehorses that he was having trained for steeplechases in Pardubice. For that first visit, Ra took Lata and her father for an 'extensive, brisk' ride through the countryside, on a route punctuated with significant obstacles – which I take to mean the kind of hedges, fences and gates that a Pardubice hunt might have encountered. Lata understood the basics of jumping but had never tried anything on this scale before. At the first obstacle, her horse refused. When it refused again at the second attempt, Ra suggested that, instead, he should take the horse over the obstacle. 'Are you worried about the horse?' asked Lata. 'No,' said Ra – whereupon Lata insisted on a third attempt and cleared the jump successfully. Thereafter, there were no more problems: Lata had mastered jumping. The ride continued 'happily' and, she recalled, 'I jumped everything that came in our way.'

Lata was invited back. She was offered other rides. One of them, in November 1926, was Ra's favourite horse: Nedbal. A fast, well-bred stallion – his sire, Magyarád, won the Velká Pardubická twice – Nedbal had a notoriously difficult temperament. Ra asked Lata to try her hand with him, and although she soon realised that he was, as she put it, 'a very wilful gentleman', somehow she persuaded him to become her willing partner and friend. Ra watched in awe – and the seed of an idea was planted in his head.

Soon Lata was visiting Orlík regularly. She and Lori became warm friends, and in due course Lata became a much-loved aunt-like figure to Lori's children: Karel and František Schwarzenberg, the teenage sons from her first marriage; and, later, Norbert, Génilde and Radslav Kinský (who were born in 1924, 1925 and 1928 respectively).

The journey on horseback to Orlík took much longer than the bike ride to Velká Chuchle, but Lata was happy – when the opportunity arose – to spend most of a morning getting there and to start the long ride back to Řitka before the afternoon was over. She was not averse to making the journey by moonlight, either, on warm nights. Each trip took her several hours, on paths and dirt roads through undulating woodland. It seems reasonable to assume that these were happy times for Lata; but the distances tell us something about her stamina, and about her enthusiasm for developing her jumping skills.

They also tell us something about another attraction. Ra's horses were not ordinary horses: they were Kinský horses.

§ - § - §

The Kinskýs had been breeding horses for centuries. Most were ultimately descended from Old Spanish and Old Italian breeds; from the nineteenth century onwards, however, the family had also imported thoroughbreds purchased in England. They bred from those mainly at the Kněžičky stud and, from about 1836, at Ostrov (both near Chlumec). The resulting horses were admired all over Europe, for their stamina, for their amenable character and, not least, for their striking good looks. Some – roughly two in five – were distinctively coloured, thanks to a gene known as the 'cream dilution' gene. Racing folk call the shade 'buckskin', but 'golden' gives a better sense of its beauty. (In sunlight, according to the modern Czech breeder Petr Půlpán, the best Kinský horses should and do 'shine like molten gold'.) For those who rode for leisure, it was hard to think of a more stylish accessory. When the Countess Kristina Kinský-Liechtenstein arrived at the Congress of Vienna in 1815 with four such horses, it was the talk of high society.

But Oktavian Kinský – Uncle Taffy – was interested in performance as well as looks. In 1838, with that in mind, he bred one of his mares with an English thoroughbred, and tried to register its progeny in the Vienna Jockey Club's studbook. The attempt was rebuffed: the Club objected to the foal's particularly golden buckskin colouring. Oktavian was furious: he was not in the habit of being rebuffed. Rather than admit defeat, he decided that from now on the Kinský horse would constitute its own distinct breed.

In conventional racing language, Kinský horses are 'warm-bloods': part thoroughbred rather than the pure, untainted item. In practical terms, their pedigrees are monitored, managed and recorded in the Kinský stud-book as meticulously as those of any 'hot-blood' thoroughbreds (although much of the breed was wiped out by world war and Communism). Among connoisseurs of rare equine breeds, they are prized for their distinctive elegance and occasionally presented as exquisite gifts: the late Queen Elizabeth the Queen Mother was given one as a hundredth birthday present. Others love the horses for their sheer niceness. Each one is different, but Kinský horses as a breed seem to have something uniquely lovable about them. They are soft to the touch, pleasing to the eye, mostly gentle by temperament, and as curious as puppies about humans and their intentions. I cannot believe that Lata was indifferent to such pleasures.

But the breed also has another idiosyncrasy: its pedigrees are matrilineal. In the Kinský studbook, the primary bloodline passes down through the female line, not the male; and the conventions for naming the horses reflect this. It is said that Oktavian insisted on this relatively unusual quirk, in the hope that it would annoy the Jockey Club. It probably did. It also stands as a neat symbol of the spirit of the Kinskýs and their role in our story. It would be easy to take against them for their vast, unearned privilege. Yet there is something about the family's most prominent members – their charm, their panache, their quirkiness, their appetite for imprudent adventure – that commands sympathy, if not admiration. They were free spirits, when others of their class were not. And occasionally this led them to align themselves with causes far bigger than their own caste's narrow concerns.

§ - § - §

Over the next few months, Lata continued to visit Ra and Lori when she could: mainly at Orlík but also, at least once, at their hunting lodge at Obora. The latter was a ninety-mile journey by train and bicycle, yet Lata obviously felt that it was worth the effort. Over the next few years, she would become a regular visitor.

The lodge was wonderfully situated, just outside Chlumec, in the middle of almost 1,000 hectares of enclosed forest, with a lake so close to the back of the house that you could almost jump into it from a window. Ra saw Obora as an almost spiritual haven: a place where he could return to the innocence of his childhood. But he invited Lata here in 1927 with two specific purposes in mind: to help him get the very best out of the horses he had in training at Chlumec; and to develop the idea whose seed had been sown when he first saw her ride Nedbal.

Accounts differ as to when and how he first expressed this idea to Lata. Some say that he did so in late 1926; others that it was not until she had tamed another of his difficult horses, a pale mare called Nevěsta. What we do know is that, when he did so (no later than early 1927), and when Lata realised that he was not attempting 'a bad joke', she was stunned. She found the proposal in turn astonishing, unbelievable, frightening, upsetting – and indescribably thrilling. The idea was simple. Ra wanted Lata to ride one of his horses for him in a race – but not just any race. The race he had in mind was the Velká Pardubická.

# 11.

# The great game

In Joseph Roth's *The Radetzky March* there is a haunting passage in which, on the eve of the First World War, army officers stationed on the Habsburg empire's eastern border drink schnapps with their Russian counterparts, who will soon be their enemies: 'And none of the Tsar's officers, and none of the officers of His Apostolic Majesty, knew that over the glass bumpers from which they drank, Death had already crossed his bony invisible hands.' It was much the same for the aristocrats and officers – Czechoslovak, German, French, Austrian, Italian, Polish – who raced and partied together in Pardubice in the years dividing the First World War from the Second.

Pardubice in the late 1920s was a very different place from the small provincial backwater in which Oktavian Kinský and his friends had unveiled their great test of recklessness more than half a century earlier. What had been a modest settlement of barely 15,000 people was now a bustling town with a population of around 40,000. It had new homes, new infrastructure, new industries. The latter included the A. C. Nobel factory, in nearby Semtín, which in the Cold War era would become notorious – under the name Explosia – for its manufacture of Semtex plastic explosive. But much of the town's wealth in Lata's day came from the Velká Pardubická, which had helped make it one of Europe's grander tourist destinations.

The rich and fashionable had begun to visit Pardubice almost from the beginning, drawn partly by Oktavian's hunts and hospitality but mainly and more numerously by the risk to life and limb that was his steeplechase's most distinctive feature. For some, the fascination verged – and still verges – on the ghoulish: as an English observer once put it, 'they might as well be at a public hanging'. But many visitors were drawn to Pardubice by a subtler magnetism. To those who understood what was involved, Velká Pardubická horses had a nobility that other horses lacked, while their jockeys shone with that special kind of glamour that attaches only to those who laugh in the face of death. This had been true since the race's earliest days: all that death-defying boldness was magnetic. It often is. Risk takers – mountaineers, adventurers, sky divers, racing drivers – tend to seem more brilliantly alive than the prudent majority. Even when they are not actively flirting with danger, they are fun to be around. Repeated exposure to what the TT motorcycle racer Guy Martin famously called 'that near-death thing' makes them intolerant of boredom; and there is a special intimacy between those who share that exposure, even if they are fierce rivals. Their energy, intensity and focus – their ability to inhabit the moment – serve them well in action but also lend an extra edge to their subsequent celebrations. The more chances they take with their lives, the more fervent their *joie de vivre* becomes.

For some spectators who came to Pardubice in the race's early decades, the competitors themselves were the attraction: George Williamson – the only jockey to win both the Grand National (in 1899, with Manifesto) and the Velká Pardubická (in 1890 and 1893, with Alphabet and Hadnagy respectively) – appears to have been something of a sex symbol. Others were drawn indirectly, by the broader attractions of a town that soon shone with reflected glamour; or perhaps by the hope that, as hangers-on, they would shine by association.

The town grew with its reputation. Its wide avenues acquired bold new buildings, created by fashionable architects such as Josef Gočár and Antonín Balšánek, which would not have looked out of place in Europe's grandest capitals. Luxury hotels were built to entertain the new breed of thrill-seeking visitor. (Not everyone could stay with Oktavian in Chlumec.) The Hotel Střebský (later the Sochor), which was known for its whisky, billiards and gourmet restaurant, became popular with foreigners, especially the English. (After the First World War, the English stayed away and the French and Germans took their place.) Visitors from the Habsburg – and, later, Czechoslovak – lands were more likely to be found at the Hotel Veselka, next to the cavalry barracks and the military riding school. The Veselka – whose owner was father of the daredevil aviator Jan Kašpar – specialised in banquets, balls and piano concerts; Bedřich Smetana and Antonín Dvořák both performed there. By the late 1920s, the Prague Jockey Club had taken to basing itself at the Veselka during the Velká Pardubická meeting, and on race day, according to one account, the hotel was overwhelmed by 'a constant coming and going of racegoers, trainers, owners, gentleman riders, jockeys, etc'.

Many visitors arrived on special race-day trains – the one from Vienna had been introduced in 1886. A few preferred to drive, perhaps less for the convenience than for the opportunity to show off their new-fangled vehicles. The combined effect was that on the day of the race, according to one German visitor who drove for six hours to get there, the town resembled a 'disturbed ant-hill'. It made more sense, if you could spare the time and money, to stay longer, especially since the Velká Pardubická meeting now ran for three days. There were plenty of other fine hotels: the Imperial, for example, or the Bouček or the Zlatá štika. There was a casino, too (in the Střebský); and since 1909 there had been a magnificent new theatre, its vast stone façade – neo-Renaissance with an art nouveau twist – the physical embodiment of the town's confidence and prosperity. For pleasure seekers in touch with the spirit of the age, the buzz was irresistible. Pardubice was not just a place to go, but *the* place to go.

§ - § - §

The reputation fed off itself. The rich attracted the fashionable. The fashionable attracted the rich. Both were a magnet for the not-quite-so-rich and the not-quite-so-fashionable. The process continued until Pardubice was filled to capacity. Nor was it just a question of wealth and style. Politicians and cultural celebrities joined the party. So did diplomats from many nations: it would have been hard to imagine a better place for international networking. There was probably a spy or two among them. And then there were the soldiers.

In the late 1920s, military men – specifically cavalry officers – influenced the ethos of the race to a degree that was out of all proportion to their numbers. Several factors caused this. The English had mostly gone, driven away by war and changing fashions; so, for the time being, had the titled amateur riders. Some of the latter may have felt that, in the new egalitarian climate, it was better to keep their heads down than to take a public role in an event so rooted in aristocratic excess. The result, in any case, was a vacuum. Army officers of various nationalities filled it, both as competitors and as hangers-on.

In October, when Pardubice became a party town, the officers were a small minority. None the less, their talk set the tone. The Velká Pardubická had become an event at which the military celebrated itself, in many languages. Before and after the race, officers from different armies toasted their shared love of boldness and honour. Civilians agreed what a fine thing it was to be a dashing, fearless cavalry officer. The agreement became all the more enthusiastic when All Right II won the 1926 race. Its rider, Captain Rudolf Popler, was as dashing and fearless a cavalry officer as it was possible to imagine.

Most of these officers (including Popler) belonged to the Czechoslovak army; many were attached to Pardubice's military riding school, which under Colonel Jindřich Ott was in the process of becoming one of Europe's finest. A substantial minority wore the uniforms of other nations. All subscribed to codes of honour that required them to scorn fear and rejoice in danger. The very obvious perils of the Velká Pardubická seemed to reinforce their sense of military identity. Those who could, rode in it. The rest, like spectators at a boxing match, swelled with vicarious machismo. If they weren't tough enough to take part, they could at least talk as if they were.

There was a catch, of course. To anyone who stopped to think about it, it was obvious that, if the war for which these officers' careers and codes prepared them ever did break out, they would not all be fighting on the same side. They were trained to kill one another, and riding in the Velká Pardubická was part of the training. But no one was mad enough to imagine – yet – that the killing would actually happen: not again; not already. Instead, courage, patriotism and fighting spirit were channelled into the ritual of a reckless, ridiculous, suicidally dangerous horse race; and those who survived it took pride, as they celebrated, in being part of an exclusive band of brave brothers, united in sport if not in language.

§ - § - §

As a former cavalry officer himself, Ra was part of this tradition. But he did not accept its narrow exclusivity, and what he proposed with Lata and Nevěsta was a direct challenge to it. As he saw it, the race had other traditions: for example, as a celebration of aristocratic bravado and, in particular, of the free spirit of the Kinskýs. No doubt he explained this to Lata.

She already knew that the great steeplechase was her great-uncle's brainchild. Ra would have made sure that she also knew about the exploits of her more distant relative, Karel Kinský, rider and owner of the 1883 Grand National winner and owner of the 1904 Velká Pardubická winner. And he would certainly have talked about Count Zdenko Kinský, his own father, who took over the castle in Chlumec after Oktavian's death in 1896. Famous for his stamina – he once swam down the

Danube from Vienna to Bratislava without resting – Zdenko was one of the first aristocrats to ride in the Velká Pardubická himself, rather than entrusting all his horses to the professionals. He had a fiery temper: when one of his horses ran badly in Vienna in 1893, he was reported to have knocked its trainer to the ground and attacked its jockey with a whip. But no one doubted his hardness or resolve. He achieved a second place and a third place in the Velká in the early 1880s, but was arguably more famous for coming fourth in 1901, at the age of fifty-nine. His grey beard and flowing white hair made a deep impression on spectators, especially when he remounted after falling at Taxis.

Lata must have sensed that, as a Kinský of sorts herself, she had a special relationship with steeplechasing in general and with the Velká Pardubická in particular; Ra may even have argued that she had the pedigree for it. But Lata may also have sensed, and perhaps even discussed with Ra, a wider significance to what he was proposing. Had Zdenko Kinský won in 1901, he would have been the first Czech ever to win the race. Instead, that honour fell to the professional jockey Oldřich Rosák, who won by five lengths the following year on Jour Fix. There was no national celebration: in that pre-war Habsburg world, the Czechs were just one subject people among many. None the less, it was a landmark. And a sense had been starting to develop, even then, that for Czech nationalists there was a particular pleasure to be had from seeing a Czech victor. It wasn't that they begrudged the foreigners their dominance – it was the Habsburgs they resented, not the English. Yet the Velká Pardubická was supposed to be a test of manhood, a challenge that sorted out the real men from the boys. No patriot would have enjoyed the thought that Czech men weren't up to it.

By the late 1920s, the question of nationality had taken on a new, different importance. Czechoslovakia was an independent country; its founder was famous for his love of horses; its most prestigious sporting event was Pardubice's great steeplechase. What could be more natural than for victory in that steeplechase to be seen as a symbol of national vigour; failure as a sign that something was wrong? Just as the British had begun to care deeply about the nationality of the winner of the men's singles at the All-England Tennis Championships at Wimbledon, so Czechoslovaks began to think of the Velká Pardubická in increasingly patriotic terms: as a contest that needed to be won for the nation.

The question then was whether the responsibility for winning it should be left to the military, or whether it was too important for that. There had certainly been a time, before the war, when the race had been as open as it was difficult: a test at which anyone who was brave or talented enough could have a go. Gentlemen riders such as Willie Moore, from Ireland, and Hector Baltazzi, an Austrian-Levantine banking heir, had shown that it was possible for amateurs not just to complete the Velká Pardubická but to win it; the Kinskýs had shown that aristocrats could be contenders, too; František Bartosch, a military vet from Pardubice with a sideline as a trainer who joined Rosák on the race's roll of honour in 1912, had shown that you didn't even have to be rich. War had interrupted that particular train of collective thought, but there was every reason for reboarding it now – especially if you were a German-speaking aristocrat wishing to show your solidarity with the new nation. By 1926, the Velká Pardubická had been going for more than half a century. The 1927 race, in which Ra wanted Lata to ride, would be its forty-sixth running. Its profile had rarely been higher, and its outcome, in consequence, had rarely mattered more. The cavalry officers could think what they liked. For owners, trainers and riders, the race was coming to be seen as much more than a private test of military riding skills. Rather, it was becoming a kind of Czechoslovak dream: a contest of supreme difficulty in which anyone who rode a horse and was brave enough could try to win glory for themselves and their nation.

This was the dream that Lata was now being urged to share, and then to turn into reality. No wonder she felt anxious. No wonder she felt excited. But it can hardly have escaped her notice that there was a difficulty. She had never ridden in an official race before, even on the flat. As a woman, she wasn't allowed to. How could she possibly compete in the hardest steeplechase of all?

# 12.

# Stepping up

In the spring of 1927, Ra was elected president of the Prague Jockey Club. He took his duties seriously and made sure to attend every race meeting at Velká Chuchle. He often visited Řitka on the way from Orlík. Sometimes he even stayed overnight.

His visits lightened the mood of a house bereaved. That January, Lata's mother had died. She was fifty-four. Ill health, bereavement and worry had cast a shadow over her later years; her absence was an altogether darker matter. Leopold was inconsolable. Eventually, he found an outlet for his pain by having a family tomb built in the woods, in a clearing full of birdsong at the brow of the hill, near his favourite spruce, and near the chapel he had built twenty years earlier. The rough stone cross is still there today, although the fittings have been damaged and the woods have closed in. In practical terms, Lata probably had more to do with its construction than Leopold did, but in due course the old count oversaw the transfer of Johanna's remains from the church cemetery in Líšnice, along with those of his mother and his eldest son. It was obvious that he longed to be reunited with them. He did not have long to wait.

Lata mourned, too. Yet in other respects this was a time of exciting and positive change in her life. That same spring, probably with the encouragement of both Ra and Kasalický, she applied to the Jockey Club for a licence as a 'gentleman rider' or amateur jockey. The application was successful, as was that of another female 'gentleman', Růžena Mašková. The granting of the licences may have reflected Ra's influence, or Kasalický's, but may equally have reflected something stranger: times really were changing.

Up to a point, anyway. Early hopes of a golden age of gender equality in the new Czechoslovakia had faded slightly. The Constitution said one thing; legal and social precedent another. Most women were still constrained by traditional preconceptions about the roles of the sexes, and by traditional habits of male behaviour. Yet there was still a sense that, if individual women seized the moment boldly enough, those preconceptions could be changed. In Czechoslovakia, the indefatigable Františka Plamínková had formed the Women's National Council in 1923, to give scores of disparate feminist groups a united and audible voice. There was a sense of change in the wider world, too, as the rhythms of the jazz age made themselves felt. If you read the newspapers, you could see that talented women were achieving fame on a grand scale, and with it wealth and influence. Coco Chanel in fashion, Greta Garbo in film, Josephine Baker in jazz, Georgia O'Keeffe in art, Dorothy Parker in the world of letters: these were movers and shakers as well as high achievers. They had had to fight for their success, far harder than a man would have done. But at least it was success, and perhaps that gave confidence to other women. In Czechoslovakia, women who tried to assert themselves in the 1920s included writers such as Božena Benešová, Jožka Jabůrková, Milena Jesenská and Marie Majerová, who achieved prominence that spanned literature, journalism and radical politics. In parliament, feminists and social reformers such as Milada Horáková acquired real influence. The actress Anny Ondra became not just a screen celebrity but co-founder of a film studio. The fashion designer Božena Horneková created new kinds of 'mannish' womenswear for leisure and sport. The surrealist artist Toyen – born Marie Čermínová – even publicly disavowed his/her birth gender, without adopting a new one. (This required quite an effort of will, given the Czech language's obsession with gender.) The barriers were still there, but for the truly determined they were not insuperable.

It would be a while before the jazz age reached Řitka, and many of these pioneers were in any case far removed, culturally, from the deep conservatism of Lata's family. But she must have sensed the winds of change blowing through the world of sport. Even if she missed the news that the American Gertrude Ederle had in 1926 become the first woman to swim the English Channel, Lata would certainly have heard about the Czech bank-clerk-turned-racing-driver Eliška Junková, the so-called 'queen of the steering-wheel'. The tiny, ever-smiling Junková had astonished both the sporting and the mainstream media with her exploits in the hitherto male world of motor-racing: first as her husband's mechanic and co-driver and then, from 1924, as a driver – and race winner – in her own right. Driving a cigar-shaped Bugatti Type 30, she became the first woman to win a Grand Prix race, in the 3,000cc class, at the Nürburgring in Germany in 1927 – although her big ambition to win the driver's championship remained unrealised. Her racing career would come to an abrupt and tragic end in July 1928, when her husband was killed in a crash at the Nürburgring. She never had the heart to race again. And yet, as she reflected in later life: 'I proved that a woman can work her way up to the same level as the best of men.'

The wider world was increasingly full of sportswomen who wanted to prove similar points in their own fields. One of the most impressive was a Frenchwoman called Alice Milliat. Born in Nantes in 1884, Milliat had excelled as a competitive rower before turning to teaching and translation, from which she earned a modest living. A childless widow, with no visible connections in high places, she had been campaigning with astonishing vigour since the end of the war for women to be allowed to compete at the Olympics in mainstream events such as track and field, rowing, fencing and equestrianism. Baron Pierre de Coubertin, founder of the modern Olympic movement, was contemptuously opposed to the idea: he believed that women's sport was 'against the laws of nature' and asserted that the primary role of women at the Olympic Games should be 'to crown the victors'. Milliat refused to concede. In 1921 she was elected president of the Fédération sportive féminine internationale (FSFI), which she had helped found, and in 1922 she organised the first Women's Olympic Games, in Paris. Czechoslovakia was one of five competing nations. Seventy-seven women took part, watched by 20,000 spectators; the sprinter Marie Mejzlíková was the star Czechoslovak performer.

Four years later, despite the fact that the International Olympic Committee had promised a few grudging concessions on female participation, Milliat's Games were held again. Renamed the Women's World Games – in deference to the angry protests of the 'real' Olympic movement – they were held in Gothenburg, Sweden. Nine nations competed, with the UK, France, Czechoslovakia and Switzerland, which had competed (alongside the US) in 1922, being joined by Belgium, Latvia, Poland, Sweden and Japan. It was striking – at least, it is striking with hindsight – that the world's most democratic nations were keener on this sort of thing than everyone else. The Czechoslovaks once again came fourth in the medals table. Marie Vidláková won gold in the shot put.

Equestrianism never featured in the Women's World Games, despite being a men-only sport in the Olympics. Yet Lata and Ra would have been aware of the movement Milliat had started (especially when Prague was lined up to host the 1930 Games) and so would Ra's colleagues in the Jockey Club. Women in sport were standing up for themselves, with unprecedented confidence, with the implicit support of Czechoslovakia's president. If some of them chose to seek licences to ride competitively, who were the gentlemen of the Jockey Club to refuse them?

That May, as a further sign that times were changing, an officially sanctioned race for women riders – or 'Amazons', as the press insisted on calling them – was held at Velká Chuchle. Kasalický must have been instrumental in making this happen, perhaps for the sole purpose of pleasing Lata. The horse she rode was one of Kasalický's best hurdlers, Vae Victis, a pleasant, obedient horse which Lata probably knew well from riding out. But the six-year-old lacked the speed to win a seven-furlong flat race. Lata finished third, just behind Růžena Mašková. The other two riders, including the winner, Miss Friedländer, presumably had licences from Austria or Germany. Spectators generally were said to have found the event 'extraordinarily interesting'. And although there were some who disapproved – the racing periodical *Dostihy* denounced the race as a 'circus' – *Národní listy*'s reporter was sufficiently impressed to urge: 'It would be good to remember the ladies at future meetings.'

§ - § - §

That summer, Lata continued to visit the Kinskýs when she could: mainly at Orlík but also, at least once, at their hunting lodge at Obora. 'I worked diligently with my horses,' Ra explained later, and Lata 'was a great help to me.' But he, too, was a help to her, advising her on technique during mornings spent riding and jumping at the special racetrack that Oktavian Kinský had made near Kolesa. Then, in the afternoon, they would take the brood mares and their foals to the big Žehuňský pond, below the lodge. The Bohemian interior can be stiflingly hot, and the horses appreciated the still, cool waters.

It may have been at one of those morning sessions that Ra introduced Lata to Nevěsta. Sired by Chilperic out of Nedejse, the mare was in Ra's view 'somewhat crazy'. She may have been past her prime, too. But she knew how to jump, and in Lata's hands she became biddable. 'She began to respond to me particularly well,' Lata recalled later. 'The way she listened to me was extraordinary.' The implication was obvious: Lata should ride Nevěsta in the Velká Pardubická.

There was no final decision: Ra had three other horses lined up for the race as well: Nedbal, Golubčík and Horymír. But with Nevěsta provisionally identified as Lata's ride, her preparations acquired a frightening urgency. It's one thing having a vague plan to ride in a race – or having a broad yearning to compete on equal terms with steeplechasing army officers. Now those aspirations had a specific, urgent focus: this horse, this year, in Pardubice, on Sunday 9 October. Such hard nuggets of reality have punctured many an airy dream. For the first time, Lata had to decide. Was she a doer? Or just a dreamer?

It did not take her long to make up her mind. If Ra was up for it, so was she – even though she had raced formally only once and had been jumping serious obstacles for probably less than a year. There were still several months in which to get to know Nevěsta and, when she could, practise on the jumps at Kolesa. It was a steep learning curve, but it was not insurmountable.

But there was still one big unknown: how would Ra's plan go down with the men Lata would be trying to beat?

# 13.

# The first hurdle

It went down like a plate of steaming horse manure. The boldness of the men who rode at Pardubice did not extend to daring new social attitudes. If they scoffed happily at physical danger, the prospect of riding alongside a woman filled them with horror.

When news broke that Ra had entered Nevěsta in the Velká Pardubická with Lata riding, the backlash was swift and fierce. The other riders protested, with the loudest objections coming from the army officers.

Their argument was as simple as it was forcefully expressed. The Velká Pardubická was a test of manhood; a test of martial virtues. Even war-hardened soldiers were stretched to their limits by it. It was far too tough for a woman; far too dangerous for a woman. No honourable officer of the Czechoslovak army could go along with such a grotesque stunt. And what if, by some freak chance, Lata did not come last? Anyone she beat would be dishonoured for ever.

We cannot say with certainty which individuals led the campaign to keep Lata out of the Velká Pardubická, but we know that there were eight army officers among the twelve other riders who eventually started the 1927 race. Count Alexander de la Forest, a visiting French cavalry officer, seems unlikely to have had much to do with any protests. The other seven were Second Lieutenant Ferdinand Mikeš, Lieutenant Hynek Býček, and captains Antonín Eisner, Sergěj Bezuglij, Josef Charous, Rudolf Pimpl and Rudolf Popler. Of these, the most influential voices would have belonged to Popler, Pimpl, Charous and Býček, old Pardubice hands who had all raced in the previous year's Velká Pardubická and were used to thinking of themselves as being as tough as they came.

They were not bad men. Several were admired for their character. Popler, for example, an instructor at Pardubice's military riding school, had fought on the Italian front as a teenager. This would be his fourth Velká Pardubická; his eventual total would be nine. He had won the previous year's race, on his own horse, All Right II – despite falling at both Taxis and the Big Water Jump. A magnificent horseman – he competed as an Olympic showjumper in Paris in 1924 and would do so again in Amsterdam in 1928 – he was also wonderfully gifted as a nurturer of horses, with a gentle, empathetic approach that had something in common with Lata's. He had bought All Right II for a knockdown price after she had been declared unfit to ride ever again.

By most standards, Popler was a hero: an inspiringly brilliant rider who was also, in the words of a friend, 'every inch a gentleman'. Self-contained yet charismatic, he was idolised by his peers, both for his talent and for his noble, romantic character. He enjoyed female company – and indeed co-owned All Right II with the eccentric Irma Formánková, a keen equestrian and would-be rally driver. But accepting that there was a place for women in horse racing was quite different from accepting that that place was in the saddle, competing alongside experienced soldiers in Europe's toughest steeplechase. Popler's sense of duty required him to protect women from danger, not to allow them to be exposed to it gratuitously.

Hynek Býček, similarly, was and is widely admired, as a fine rider and as a soldier of integrity and courage. In later life he would be a hero of the anti-Nazi resistance; later still, his dissent against the Communists earned him several years in the notorious Mírov prison. His courage was beyond doubt. But I have never heard it suggested that he was socially progressive.

And then there was Josef Charous, older and heavier than the others but no less fearless. He was tough and skilled enough to have come second and fourth in the previous two Velká Pardubickás, as well as competing in the three-day event in the 1924 Olympics. He, too, was a man of integrity, who had fought bravely in the First World War. (In the Second, he would die in Auschwitz.)

You would be happy to have such men fighting alongside you. You would trust them more than most to do what they considered the right thing; but 'the right thing' did not, in their view, extend to treating women as equals – and especially not when it came to physical discomfort and danger. Ra's proposal was not just scandalous, in their view: it was immoral.

Perhaps we should try to put ourselves in their boots. They were soldiers. They lived mostly in the all-male world of Pardubice's cavalry barracks and military riding school, and their values were military ones. Their worldviews were coloured, in many cases, by memories of war; perhaps also by the anticipation of war. The virtues they aspired to were courage, honour, steadfastness, hardiness, patriotism, loyalty to comrades. They were not anti-women, but they saw them as precious creatures, not as equals. Their own kind were men. Women were always the 'other'.

As for progress: it's one thing embracing change if you're a fashionable intellectual in Prague. If you choose to become a soldier, you usually think in terms of defending your country's social traditions, not blithely turning them on their head. Officers such as Popler or Charous would have laid down their lives if their code demanded it. Perhaps it is understandable that they saw that code as immutable.

The Pardubice officers' shared experiences of riding in the Velká Pardubická added an extra layer of insulation against the inclusive attitudes of Masaryk's young nation. Like any contest that takes participants too close to death for comfort, the race created a grim camaraderie among those who rode in it – from which everyone else was by definition excluded. As their horses fidgeted under them at the start, they were united by the knowledge that there was no guarantee that they would all come back in one piece. It wasn't quite like preparing to 'go over the top' in war, but it wasn't all that different. It was, in other words, the kind of time when you remind yourself that you are a soldier: a fighting man, whose code of honour forbids him to shrink from danger.

The idea of a woman muscling in on this territory was as ridiculous as it was offensive.

§ - § - §

The fact that the organisers of the Velká Pardubická meeting raised no objection to Lata's participation signified little: Ra and Kasalický were both members of the three-man management committee. But that didn't make it all right. The officers protested to the Jockey Club in Prague. Lata must have felt tempted to back out when she learned of this; Count Zdenko Kinský, Ra's father, was among those who encouraged her to stand firm. (Lata's father, by contrast, was among those who disapproved of her plan.)

Lata had one obvious advantage in the dispute: the president of the Jockey Club was her cousin. But Ra had an equally obvious difficulty. To use his position to advance his own agenda would be dangerously undiplomatic. If the sport's governing body was perceived to be biased on this matter, the protest could turn ugly.

With artful diplomacy, he referred the matter up to an even higher authority: the English Jockey Club. He wrote to them explaining the problem and asking, specifically, if there was any reason why a woman should not be allowed to compete in a race such as this. The gentlemen of Portman Square, perhaps feeling that it didn't really matter what happened in a faraway country like Czechoslovakia, were remarkably relaxed about it. They wrote back saying that the question didn't really arise in England, as women were happy to ride in separate races and no woman would dare to enter the Grand National; but that ultimately there was nothing in the rules to prohibit such a thing. They insisted, however, that if a woman did ride against men in the Velká Pardubická, she must be provided with a separate changing room.

That seemed to resolve the explicit argument: if Lata wanted to ride in the race, she could. But it would be some time before the ill feeling subsided. The brotherhood of officers remained a brotherhood, and Lata was not a member.

Meanwhile, there were complaints from other quarters. The hazards, according to Ra, were 'reiterated to us from all sides'. The reiterators had a point. Even if you discounted the respectable body of medical opinion that held that (to quote a paper on 'Women's Participation in Athletics' presented to the International Olympic Committee in 1925): 'Sports which tax the muscular frame and put a strain on it ... are, of course, wholly unsuitable for the feminine organism', it was hard to deny that the Velká Pardubická also posed other, less gender-specific risks. Was it really ethical – in terms of traditional values – to expose a lady to such dangers?

Neither Lata nor Ra was swayed. Having taken the matter this far, they could hardly turn back now. The officers had their code, and the Kinskýs had theirs – in which the main items appear to have been reckless disdain for all forms of compromise and caution. In any case, retreat could have intolerable consequences. If Lata didn't exercise her right to compete now, having been given explicit clearance to do so, she could give up all hope of ever competing on equal terms in future.

As the race approached, Lata's father was eventually won round, which would have been an important boost. (He seems to have been the kind of father who could never be unsupportive of his daughter for long.) Lata, meanwhile, spent as much of the autumn as she could at Obora, practising on Ra's private course at Kolesa. The great thing about practising at Kolesa was that the jumps there replicated those at Pardubice. There was even a life-size version of Taxis. Even though Lata could spend only limited amounts of time away from Řitka, the experience was priceless. Nothing could replicate the crowded, terrifying reality of the Velká Pardubická, but by early October both Lata and Nevěsta had a good sense of the jumping challenges they would encounter. At the same time, however, Lata found that the enormity of the challenge was beginning to get to her: 'Just recalling it to mind upset me. I had stage fright during training.' Despite this, 'although I jumped often, I never fell.' But jumping alone is one thing. Doing so in the midst of a charging crowd is altogether more hazardous.

Discussions continued about the possibility of Lata riding a different horse in the big race. Ra still had three entered – Nevěsta, Golubčík and Horymír – and although he planned to ride one of these himself, he was happy for Lata to choose first. But Lata felt comfortable with Nevěsta and, indeed, had developed a 'special liking' for her. Each time they practised, the trust between horse and rider grew stronger.

For the final week before the race, Ra arranged for him and Lata to take accommodation with their horses in Popkovice, a village-cum-suburb right by the Pardubice racecourse. According to Ra, they 'felt very comfortable' there. Part of the attraction was the seclusion. Word of Lata's participation had spread by now, and interest in her preparations threatened to become oppressive. People were still trying to dissuade Ra from allowing Lata to race, but the wider public were fascinated. The organisers and the city council must have been delighted by the excitement. They were concerned about a slight fall-off in the number of super-rich foreigners coming to the race, and they had already increased the prize money on offer to the winner from 15,000 to 50,000 crowns in the hope of boosting interest from abroad. Wild rumours about the involvement of a crazy countess would at least get the event talked about. For Lata, however, the attention can only have added to the pressure she was under. The less time she spent in the public eye, the happier she was.

Nonetheless, she did exercise Nevěsta on the Pardubice racecourse itself. The atmosphere may have been tense, since some of her rivals were practising there at the same time. But Golubčík – the only other horse of Ra's that would actually run in that year's Velká Pardubická – was also there, and Jakub Častora, a professional jockey whom Lata would have known from Velká Chuchle, was probably there with him. So she may not have felt entirely isolated. Meanwhile, the watching journalists had eyes only for Lata – who, they reported, suffered a fall on the course on the Thursday before the race. It looked like a bad one, claimed *Národní listy*, although Countess Brandisová was not seriously hurt. What the press missed was that Nevěsta was left with a sore foot, which was still slightly inflamed when Lata brought her back to the course three days later.

By then it was Sunday 9 October 1927: time for the most important ride of Lata's life so far.

# 14.

# Fight to the finish

She was afraid. Around her neck she wore a medallion with an image of the Virgin Mary; another, depicting St Anthony, was attached to the inside of her helmet. She hoped these would keep her safe. But what she really feared was humiliation. After all that trouble, all that hostility, all that mockery – and now, with all these people watching – what if she made a fool of herself?

Others had had the same thought. Many had come to see for themselves. Pardubice's hotels had been full since Friday, while on Sunday the trains were overflowing. Unofficial estimates put the number of spectators at 20,000. There was no official figure. The weather was pleasant, after two days of rain, and both ticket offices had run out of admission tickets long before the crowds stopped streaming in. Somehow, space was found for everyone, although many missed the earlier races. There were 650 cars packed into the car park behind the main stand – in an age when private motor travel was a novelty.

In the paddock there had been friendly faces. Ra, for example; and Karel Šmejda, who was listed as trainer for both Nevěsta and Golubčík. (Some said that this was just a formality: Ra liked to train his own horses, helped by his own private staff. But Šmejda was too significant a trainer to be engaged as a mere charade.) A pre-race photograph of Lata shows her smiling, the light gleaming from Nevěsta's glossy flanks beneath her. She is thirty-two, but the smile is girlish, suggesting a self-conscious teenager enjoying her day in the sunshine. A well-dressed couple – possibly Ra and Lori Kinský – smile back from the paddock's edge.

The start was a different matter. Lata was alone among her enemies – who, she later claimed, had made a further protest to the Jockey Club that afternoon. There is no record of what form this took, but I presume that it was made at the Hotel Veselka, where the club made a temporary base during the Pardubice meeting. Josef Charous was certainly seen at the Veselka that day. The public excitement surrounding Lata's participation can only have intensified the cavalry officers' resentment, and all the usual pre-race nerves must have been tightened by unspoken hostility. If it's not hard for us to imagine the officers' grumblings, it wouldn't have been hard for Lata to imagine them either. But she brushed her doubts aside. She had to. As she herself once said: 'If you sit on a horse, you must have your nerves properly together.'

She did have one advantage: as a first-timer she had only the vaguest sense of what lay ahead. The old hands knew. Specifically, they felt the shadow of Taxis – the fourth obstacle – which casts a chill over most Velká Pardubická starts. It's not the obstacle itself (which Lata had at least encountered in replica). It's the way that it rushes up on you within moments of the starter's shout. Get it wrong, or get your approach to it wrong, and your race can be over before you've settled into it. Ferocious concentration is crucial; usually preceded, before the off, by ferocious fretting. Lata, by contrast, was a mere irritant. Few expected her to last the course, although *Národní listy* had suggested that morning that Nevěsta might run well, 'even with a woman in the saddle'. The bookies had Landgraf II – winner in 1923 and 1925 and the previous year's runner-up – as 4:1 favourite, with František Gimpl (a professional) riding. All Right II, Captain Popler's winning mount from last year, was on 6:1, along with Editore, ridden by Lieutenant Mikeš. Nevěsta and Golubčík were the joint outsiders, on 33:1.

There was a pause in the crowd's murmurings. The starter shouted. All thirteen runners broke into a gallop, back towards the stands from the racecourse's north-eastern corner. Lata – wearing the Kinský colours of red and white vertical stripes with a red and white quartered cap – settled Nevěsta near, but not at, the back of the field, keeping out of trouble while more experienced contenders manoeuvred for position. The first two jumps, little more than hurdles, caused no problems, and Lata felt her confidence growing. It felt, she said later, much like 'my daily morning training'.

In the third furlong they turned for the Small Water Jump, before galloping westwards, across the middle of the racecourse area but in full view of the stands. This was most spectators' first proper view of the action, and the sight of Lata apparently still in contention added to the excitement. Everyone crossed the water safely – and then came Taxis.

Ferdinand Mikeš led the charge on Editore (whose owner, Josef Charous, was riding Forum) and cleared it first with a 'magnificent' jump. Then came the rest. Lata set Nevěsta as well as she could, but there was no time to think. They leapt, with horses on all sides. The next thing Lata knew, she was flat on the turf, breathless and semi-stunned.

There was such chaos at the obstacle that it is impossible to say with any confidence what happened – except that it was carnage. Landgraf II and All Right II, who probably jumped ahead of Nevěsta, also fell. If they didn't obstruct Nevěsta, they may well have put her off. Golubčík was also a faller: one photograph suggests that Ra's two horses may have impeded one another. Doyen (ridden by Sergěj Bezuglij) fell so horribly that he never got up.

Lata staggered to her feet. Was her race over already? A slight give in the ground may have taken some of the sting out of her fall. It was not enough for the earth to open and swallow her. But there was hope. Popler, Gimpl and Častora were all remounting. She would do the same.

According to John Oaksey, 'There are fools, bloody fools and those who remount in steeplechases.' Oaksey was twice British champion amateur jump jockey before becoming a journalist, so he knew what he was talking about. Yet even he eventually conceded that the culture of the Velká Pardubická is different. This, he wrote later, is a race in which 'the time to give up is when you are in the ambulance and not before'.

Oaksey exaggerated only slightly. Most jockeys would also have some thought for their horse's wellbeing. But the soldiers, at least, took pride in giving little thought to their own, and in those days they were expected to remount if they could. So would Lata. Her plan, as she later described it, was simple: 'to finish the race as long as my horse and I were able to fight.' Her allies – Ra and

Kasalický – had risked ridicule to get her into the race. She could not let them down. She would not give up yet.

But Nevěsta, although unharmed, had bolted. The leaders had reached the next obstacle before she was brought back. By the time Lata had remounted and Nevěsta was back on the move, there were few other horses in sight.

Sadly, the next few runners they encountered were no longer in the race. The 1927 Velká Pardubická turned out to be one of the cruellest in the event's troubled and troubling history. It's not clear why. The going was not noticeably heavier than usual, even over the two miles of ploughed fields. The number of runners was manageable, and most of the horses were hardened steeplechasers, as were their riders. None the less, things kept going wrong.

At the next obstacle, the Irish Bank, Pinguin (ridden by Karel Holoubek) pulled up. Editore, the early leader, fell at the eighth – a relatively straightforward railed fence between two large trees – and his rider, Lieutenant Mikeš, did not remount. Markomann, ridden by the visiting French officer, Count de la Forest, refused at the same obstacle. All this took place out of sight of the stands, behind the woods at the Popkovice end of the course. When the remaining runners re-emerged from the long turn, there were three widely separated groups. Forum, Esáž and Brutus led. Then came All Right II, Landgraf II, Dunka and Eba. And then, far behind, came Nevěsta and Golubčík.

The middle group had the worst of it. Eba fell so badly at the twelfth – a relatively innocuous ditch just before the course winds past Taxis again – that she had to be put down. Popler's All Right II was running strongly when she suffered a freak accident, putting her foot in a pothole and breaking her pastern. Landgraf II pulled up soon afterwards, exhausted and badly lame. Both horses were later shot, in the absence of any other way of putting them out of their misery.

General horror at these ghastly misfortunes meant that much less attention was paid to Lata and Nevěsta than would otherwise have been the case. People were watching the tragedies and other dramas at the front of the field, and that was the focus of subsequent eyewitness accounts.

Thus history records that, shortly after emerging from the Popkovice turn, Golubčík pulled up; and that, for much of the remainder of the race, Esáž and Brutus led. Esáž (ridden by Captain Pimpl) was supposed to be Brutus's pacemaker, but was so exhausted that Brutus (ridden by Jiří Drahoš) kept slowing down to stay with her. We know that Esáž fell at the twenty-second (a simple fence with a punishingly wide ditch) and was out of contention by the time Pimpl had remounted. And we know that Brutus then took up the running, only to have his own disaster, with the finish in sight. But Lata and Nevěsta? All we know is that of the sixteen obstacles that remained after the Popkovice turn, they negotiated only twelve without mishap.

That's all: four more falls. The details are lost, although Lata later dismissed all four as 'harmless'. We can assume that one of the four was the twenty-first, the Big Water Jump, since one photograph seems to show them up to Nevěsta's chest in it. But the others? The trickiest remaining obstacles would have been the eleventh (the Big English Jump), the nineteenth (the Snake Ditch) and the twenty-third (the 'in and out' double jump), but that doesn't mean that those were necessarily the ones that brought Nevěsta down. All we know is that, by the latter stages, the mare's sore foot was troubling her, which may have caused problems with jumping; and that each time they fell, Lata remounted, shrugged off any pain and embarrassment, and patiently coaxed her dispirited but 'loyal' mount into continuing what they had started.

Brutus fell at the final fence. Drahoš remounted (naturally), but by then it was too late to catch Forum, who had been labouring away patiently throughout without once looking like a winner. (Thanks to his solidly built thirty-three-year-old jockey, Captain Charous, he was carrying twelve kilograms overweight.) Still labouring, Forum loped home with a fifty-metre lead, in the unimpressive time of fourteen minutes. Few cheered more loudly than the actor Rudolf Deyl, who had met Charous at the Veselka earlier and, following his advice, had placed a large bet on Forum at 20:1. Brutus was second, with Dunka (ridden by Captain Eisner) a long way back in third, just ahead of Esáž.

And then – history does record this – the fifth and final finisher came into view: Nevěsta cleared the final fence with Countess Brandisová on her back, and the crowd, many of them standing on benches in front of the main stand, greeted the weary pair with 'thunderous applause' as they dragged themselves to the finishing line. The first woman to ride in the Velká Pardubická had stayed the course.

The achievement was so remarkable that *Národní listy* saw fit to record it on its front page the next day. Readers of *Venkov* newspaper were also reassured on another point: at the finish, the young countess had 'looked completely fresh'.

Of the eight military gentlemen who had collectively objected to Lata's involvement, only three had finished. If the others felt dishonoured, they kept quiet about it. Captain Charous, the winner, had the grace to say afterwards that Lata's performance had been 'really impressive'. He had not seen it, of course, but that didn't make the tribute less welcome. In fact, relative to her hopes, Lata had ridden a disappointing race. None the less, she had proved one point: she was not a quitter.

# 15.

# The outsider

Some bruises were quick to heal. Others lingered. Lata was soon fit and riding again. The men whose territory she had invaded remained resentful. They weren't openly hostile: men who feel threatened by a woman's achievements rarely are. Instead, there were mutterings. Some were said to have developed a habit – on the rare occasions when Lata's path crossed with theirs – of leaving any room she entered. Lata's character was blamed. In the words of one racing historian, 'She was considered very grand and arrogant.'

This was unfair. Like all shy people, Lata could seem aloof. Her heart was not worn on her sleeve but instead was kept deep inside, the only clue to her feelings the look of preoccupation in her grey eyes. Something similar could perhaps have been said about several of the officers who disapproved of her. Yet in Lata's case, because of her gender and her aristocratic background, this may have been interpreted as haughtiness. In fact, everything else we know about her suggests that she was modest about her social position – a point on which Řitka villagers who knew her seem unanimous. For example: to Alena Brabencová (now the postmaster's wife) she was 'very kind, very modest'; to Jana Sléhová (the gamekeeper's daughter) she was 'always nice, never reserved or strict'; Vlasta Klabíková, who was a farmhand on the Řitka estate, remembers her as 'very kind, always helping people'. 'She never acted as though she was above the ordinary person,' says Jaroslava Orolová, whose grandfather managed the estate for a while. 'People who worked for her wouldn't hear a bad word about her.'

What Lata did have, however, was a capacity for matter-of-fact assertiveness, when she felt confident that she was right. Some men would have considered this unfeminine. Women who stood up for themselves were often judged in this way. For example: Avery Brundage, the famously assertive senior Olympic official, once complained rather pathetically that Alice Milliat was too blunt and demanding in her campaigning for women to be allowed to compete in the main Olympic Games. The subtext was (and is) that a woman's place is to be yielding. But yielding was not really Lata's thing.

For a while, even so, she retreated from the limelight. She continued to work with Karel Šmejda's horses. When she could spare the time, she worked with Ra's horses, too. But I can find no record of her having raced officially in 1928 or 1929. It is possible that her Velká Pardubická ambitions were temporarily satisfied. She had proved her points: she was brave enough to start the race and tough enough to finish it. Nor could anyone dispute her right to try again if she chose. But Nevěsta had reached the limits of her capabilities, while Ra already had another jockey in mind for his promising young Pročpak colt, Norbert, whom Vojtěch Szabó would ride to eighth place in the 1928 Velká Pardubická. In the short term, a fresh attempt by Lata may not have been a realistic option.

In any case, she had other things on her mind. In Řitka, the anniversary of her mother's death was marked by the death of Marie Rothländer, the Brandis children's former governess and the late countess's closest friend. Marie was considered part of the family and was buried in the tomb in the woods. Eight months later, Lata and her sisters returned to the site to bury their father. The last Count Brandis died on 12 September 1928, aged seventy-four. His later years had been sad and subdued, but his final months were eased by the company of six daughters – one of whom was known across Europe for having ridden in the Velká Pardubická. As far as we know, his death was peaceful.

All his daughters had adored him. It has been suggested that this was one reason why they were slow to marry: other men didn't measure up. Lata was particularly close to him. Yet Leopold's absence gradually transformed Řitka, and some of the change was positive. For as long as anyone could remember, family life had revolved around the need to (as their mother put it) 'honour' the man of the house. Now the house was manless.

Life became simpler and less formal. The family and remaining staff ate meals together in the kitchen. Those of the sisters who smoked (including Lata) did so more visibly. Řitka had never had all that much in common with the kind of stately living that most of us imagine when confronted with words such as 'chateau' or 'aristocracy'. There were no glittering ballrooms and few spacious, polished salons: that was for the Kinskýs. Instead, Brandis home life was cluttered with old furniture and old dogs, riding tackle, guns and mud. The outdoors was constantly having to be kept at bay. And whereas the count and countess had liked to keep up the appearance of living like the high aristocracy, their daughters were happy to let much of that go. They observed the conventions of respectability but had little interest in grandeur.

And so, as time went on, a new order superseded the old. Villagers spoke less of the Brandis family and more of 'the contessas': an almost interchangeable collection of unmarried ladies whose benign influence helped give the village its distinctive character. The sisters in turn felt an almost maternal sense of obligation to the village. They nursed the sick and attended births, just as their mother had done. If a service was held in the little roadside chapel, one of the contessas – usually Lata – would read the litany.

Each sister had different strengths and different duties. Johanna was in charge of the cooking. Kristýna kept the house clean and tidy (although each sister was expected to take care of her own room). Lata was responsible for the woods, which had to be kept in good order so that hunting rights could be rented out. But her main role was as overseer. She was not the most senior sibling in the house: Gabriele was five years older. But, says Jan Pospíšil, 'She was a natural leader. She always took charge of things.' Thus it was Lata who dealt with bills and wages, liaised with tenants and suppliers and attempted to balance the books. And it was she who kept on top of leases and other legal documents with the help of the family's friendly lawyer, Hanuš Kasalický.

At some point, room was found in the house for a distant, German-born cousin from Austria, Alžběta Jarocká – known, to avoid confusion, as Gikina. Elsewhere on the estate lived a Russian exile, Kasian Rusniak, who worked for the gamekeeper. He had arrived in Řitka during the First World War – he may have been a prisoner of war at the time – and had been provided with accommodation in an outbuilding. Later, a White Russian exile, Sergej Jaroševský, was recruited to assist with the estate management and was provided with living space in the servants' quarters. His arrival was of particular interest to Lata's sister Markéta, who some years later married him.

At around the same time – history does not record precisely when, but it must have been after Leopold's death – Kasalický and Lata developed the habit of going for afternoon rides together, starting at Řitka and disappearing into the woods above. This continued for years, increasing in frequency. The village girls who watched them were convinced that they were lovers.

There were plenty of perfectly respectable reasons for the pair to spend time in each other's company. Perhaps they were visiting the family tomb. Perhaps they were discussing leases. More probably, they were discussing horses. Kasalický had several – Büvös, Misserl, Ossiana – in training with Šmejda. It would have made perfect sense for him to seek feedback from Lata; and, equally, for their conversations to take place on horseback.

Yet children see some things that others miss. Lata was human. She left no trace of any other romantic involvements, with men or women. Yet she must have had feelings, and feelings tend to find a focus. Lata had lost her father and her brothers. She may well have welcomed a strong male figure in her life. Kasalický was around, and he appears to have been interested. And while it is hard to feel much affection for the Hanuš Kasalický who emerges from archival records, he may have been more impressive, and perhaps more attractive, in the flesh. His grandson, Jan Doležal, remembers him as 'proud but sympathetic'. We can at any rate infer from the frequency of his visits that he found the modest, feminine character of life at Řitka a pleasing contrast to the luxury and grandeur of Všenory. Perhaps he felt that, in Lata's company, close to nature and away from more materialist concerns, he became a better person; and perhaps in turn she saw that better person in him. But this is speculation. We know, however, that Kasalický had a proper understanding of horses and horse racing. For Lata, that in itself would have made him seem less alien than many men. We also know that Kasalický's marriage was unhappy: his divorce, years later, would be messy. And we know that there were others, eventually, who shared the village girls' suspicions. Even if Lata's friendship with him began as a polite, neighbourly one, it seems likely that it somehow warmed, over time, to a degree that went beyond the polite and the neighbourly.

I cannot believe that Lata would actually have had a physical affair with a married man. Religion was as central to her life as riding; moral firmness was one of her defining characteristics. That is not to say, however, that she did not sometimes yearn for things to be otherwise.

§ - § - §

If Lata sometimes felt trapped by circumstances, there was always the option of taking herself off to the Kinskýs. Such escapes could be only temporary, occasional and brief. Řitka demanded her presence. In any case, she was suited neither by temperament nor by wealth to her

grand cousins' high-society lifestyle. Yet even a few days
in Ra's carefree world could refresh her soul wonderfully.

Her visits tended to coincide with Ra's quieter
moments: periods when he was spending time with his
children and his horses rather than his fellow socialites.
This didn't mean that they were always quiet. At Obora,
he liked to organise amateur dramatics. Energetic outdoor games were another favourite: he particularly
enjoyed showing off his skills at high jump, which he
performed to quite a good standard without the indul-
gence of a landing mat. Lata was always up for outdoor
fun, which made her a popular guest, not least with the
children. 'She was always funny and kind,' according
to Génilde, the second youngest, who was unfailingly
encouraged by Lata in her own riding. 'She loved horses
very much: that was her life. But she also loved dogs and
children.' Lata usually stayed on the first floor of a small
guest house next to the main building. If the children
called her down to play, says Génilde, 'she didn't bother
going down the stairs. She just jumped down from the
balcony. We loved that!'

Lori enjoyed Lata's visits, too. She was a strong, clever
woman, whose unretiring nature had raised eyebrows
in high society long before she married Ra. Compared
with some of the noblewomen Lori mixed with, Lata
must have seemed like a kindred spirit: independent and
unbiddable.

As for Lata, she must have felt happy among the
Kinskýs, or she wouldn't have made the ninety-mile
journey from Řitka. She would take the train to Chlumec
nad Cidlinou, then cover the final eight-mile stretch to
Obora by bicycle. If someone spotted her approaching on

the straight, flat road that led from the town, Ra would ride out to meet her and exchange his horse for her bicycle. They would then complete the journey together.

Yet there is reason to believe that Lata also felt awkward about the gulf in wealth and status between her family and Ra's. She never seems to have talked about her own family while visiting: some of Ra's children appear to have been unaware that she even had sisters. Perhaps she sensed that some would see her as a 'poor cousin': a slight embarrassment. I don't think the Kinskýs really thought in those terms. But Lata clearly fitted in more easily at Obora, in the simplicity of the outdoors, with children and animals to play with, than in the spectacular salons of Orlík, or in Ra and Lori's palace in Prague.

Despite this, the late summer of 1929 saw Lata spending time with the Kinský family at yet another of their homes: at Žďár nad Sázavou, on the Bohemian–Moravian border. The castle there, which Lori had recently inherited, is not the grandest of the Kinský chateaux. It may be the loveliest: a solid eighteenth-century building on the edge of an old monastery, in a little town whose other charms include a small stone replica of Prague's Charles Bridge. There weren't many horses: this was not a playground like Obora. Rather, it was a retreat. From the windows of the chateau's panelled drawing room you look out over a still, small lake. On the far side is a green hill, from whose low top the star-shaped Pilgrimage Church of St John of Nepomuk – the baroque-gothic masterpiece of Jan Blažej Santini Aichel – points quietly up to the heavens. The sense of peace is sublime; and to gaze on the church, with its soft, inverted image in the intervening waters, is to add a whole new layer of meaning to the idea of calm reflection. Lata, whose hungry spirituality made a deep impression on, among others, Génilde, must have gazed on it often.

With Ra, however, nothing remained calm for long. Lata's stay at Žďár coincided with a visit by Lorenzo and Heinrich Hagenbeck, owners of some zoological gardens in Hamburg. For reasons that aren't entirely clear, the brothers had brought four zebras with them. Lata, Ra and František Schwarzenberg (Ra's sixteen-year-old stepson) were soon busy training the unexpected guests to pull a coach and four. Lata then returned, presumably by the usual combination of train and bicycle, to Řitka. The zebras proved so adept in their new role that they were later sold (complete with carriage) to the Maharaja of Kapurthala.

§ - § - §

A month later, the Wall Street stock market imploded. Global depression followed, slowly but inexorably. Within three years US stocks would be worth barely a tenth of their value at their October 1929 peak. In this harsh new climate, central Europe's fragile young democracies struggled to survive.

Within a year, Adolf Hitler's National Socialists – the Nazis – were the second largest party in Germany. Far-right politicians, already in the ascendant in Italy and Hungary, were soon on the rise in Poland, Spain and Portugal as well. In Czechoslovakia, the most obvious sign that the world was changing was a growing tension between Czechs and Germans, particularly in the border area known as the Sudetenland, where German-speakers were sometimes in a majority.

There had been complaints for years about anti-German discrimination in Czechoslovakia. Some were justified. But the rise of far-right nationalism turned low-level grumbling into bitter and divisive hatred. Communities that had rubbed along tolerably for decades were suddenly on edge. Even children were affected. 'We used to play football with the boys from the German school,' a Czech man who grew up in the easternmost corner of the Sudetenland told me. 'Then Hitler came along, and suddenly we were all fighting. No one knew why. It just happened.'

In Prague, news of the Nazis' electoral advances in September 1930 prompted anti-German demonstrations. A number of German citizens with homes in the Czecho-slovak capital had their windows broken. Pardubice, which was neither German-speaking nor part of the Sudetenland, was not immune. The change in mood was abrupt. In 1929 (a fortnight before the great crash), the Velká Pardubická had been won by Gustav Schwandt on Ben Hur. It was the second year running that a German horse and German jockey had won, and the locals had seemed as happy about this as the visitors. The victories were seen as vindication of the organisers' strategy of using increased prize money – and warm hospitality – to revive foreign interest in the event. By 1930, however, such breezy cosmopolitanism was not so easy.

As the Velká Pardubická approached, signs of the new times became visible. A week before race day, the Czechoslovak racing stable Čechoslavia announced that it had purchased a German horse called Gabarit, whose vendor, Lieutenant Mellenthin, would ride the horse – in Čechoslavia's colours – in the big race. News reached Lieutenant Mellenthin's military superiors in Germany. The day before the race he received a telegram forbidding him to compete in Czechoslovak colours. Mellenthin offered to buy back the horse temporarily – so that he could compete in German colours instead. His superiors were not placated. On the morning of the race he was summoned back to Germany. A good German soldier was expected to remember which side he was on.

Such was the fraught context in which eight riders, all Czechoslovak nationals, lined up for the start of the forty-ninth Velká Pardubická on 12 October 1930. The unpleasantness three years earlier about Lata's involvement may have seemed trivial by comparison. Which was just as well, because Lata was one of the eight.

§ - § - §

It had only been a matter of time before Lata tried again. This year was as good a year as any to do so. She was thirty-five – already getting on a bit for such a reckless stunt. There wouldn't be many more chances. And what a chance it was! The prestige of the Velká Pardubická hadn't been so high for years, while interest in female sporting achievements – at least in Czechoslovakia – had never been higher. The third Women's World Games had been held in Prague just a few weeks earlier, in the stadium at Letná: the event attracted 15,000 spectators over three days. The public's enthusiasm must have stirred the embers of Lata's yearning for sporting glory.

Most important of all, Ra had a horse for her. Norbert, the bay colt Vojtěch Szabó had ridden to eighth place two years earlier, was now a fast, confidently jumping six-year-old. Lata had had the chance to strike up a relationship with him while staying at Obora, and both she and Ra felt that he had Velká Pardubická potential.

No one (publicly, at least) objected to Lata's entry. Her battle this time would be the race itself, not getting to the start. She had already proved that she could stay the course. More recently, she had also shown that she had become a much more confident jumper. Riding a horse of her own, an old bay gelding called Boy, she had won a resounding victory with a flawless round in a showjumping contest at Velká Chuchle.

A week before the Velká Pardubická, by way of a warm-up, she rode Norbert in Pardubice, in a two-mile steeplechase for amateur riders. They came third behind Rudolf Popler, on Gyi Lovam!, and Eberhard Mauve on Gabarit. Norbert was well beaten, yet the result was not unsatisfactory. Gyi Lovam!, an eight-year-old Hungarian gelding with a curiously long neck and an extravagant jumping style, had won seven previous races that season and was already being described as a wonderhorse. Lata would have been happy to have kept him within sight, and to have completed the race without mishap.

The following Saturday, still in Pardubice, Lata was unplaced in a 'Drag-Hunt Steeplechase' for amateurs, riding Boy, who showed no great aptitude for racing. Ra and František Schwarzenberg also took part; as did Rudolf Popler who, as was his habit, won.

Then came Sunday. For the second time in her life, Lata prepared to submit herself to Pardubice's trial by ordeal. She was spared the frenzied public interest that had accompanied her previous attempt: the large crowd, more international than it had been in 1927, was primarily interested in the four-legged sensation of the moment, Gyi Lovam!; as were the commentators who, for the first time, were reporting live on the proceedings to radio listeners all over Czechoslovakia. That didn't make the pre-start wait less lonely or intimidating. Lata was, of course, an outsider: not in the tipsters' sense (Norbert was a mere 12:1) but in the sense that she was not part of the Velká Pardubická gang. Popler and his friends were resigned to her presence and were probably polite to her. But she knew that there was jealousy and resentment (she later said as much), and she can hardly have felt welcome. Unlike her, the officers shared the culture of Pardubice's military riding school. Several had experienced war. Some had Olympic hopes or memories. (The riding school's Captain František Ventura had won gold in the 1928 showjumping.) All this was out of bounds to Lata, because of her gender. Meanwhile, her temperament excluded her from many of the officers' habitual pastimes. Even if she had been welcome, for example, she would not have enjoyed the Hotel Sochor's casino, where many of the officers liked to unwind. Nor was she the type to join in the more riotous celebrations at the Sochor, where one rider was rumoured to have ridden his Velká Pardubická horse all the way to the top of the narrow staircase. Even if no one was deliberately giving her the cold shoulder, it was hard to feel much sense of belonging – at least until the race got underway.

When it did, it went more smoothly for Lata than last time. Gabarit – eventually ridden in Čechoslavia's colours by Josef Kohoutek – came to grief at Taxis, bringing down Issa in the process. Soon Hollandweibchen and Chán were on the ground as well. But Lata and Norbert cleared the big jump comfortably, and found themselves in a leading group with Gestor, Talán and Gyi Lovam!. Behind them, the casualties continued. Hollandweibchen, whose jockey, Alexander Alba, had remounted, fell spectacularly at the Irish Bank, performing a complete somersault as Alba flew earthwards alongside. Amazingly, neither was hurt, and they resumed the race, but Alba threw in the towel a few jumps later. By the halfway stage there were only those four early leaders left in the race. Talán went to the front for a while. Then, with only eleven jumps to go, Lata and Norbert took up the lead. They jumped the treacherous Snake Ditch impeccably, and Lata may have toyed with the thought that, notwithstanding Gyi Lovam!, the race was hers for the winning. If so, the thought was short-lived. Two jumps later came the Big Water Jump – in those days, like the Snake Ditch, an unmarked ditch, in which turf was replaced without warning by deep water. Horses are sometimes spooked by such hard-to-see obstacles; and Norbert, despite having taken the Snake Ditch in his stride, refused point-blank at the Big Water.

Lata refused to give up. Eventually, she and Norbert waded through the water. But it was too late to catch up. Worse, Norbert's composure had gone. At the next jump, the Little Taxis (which is exactly what it sounds like), they fell. Lata remounted (naturally) and set off in pursuit at a less ambitious pace. She knew that Norbert was tired; she suspected that he was not as fit as he could have been. Just staying the course would be achievement enough for that day.

The rest of the race was as uneventful as an arduous, dangerous steeplechase can be. The four survivors continued in the same order over the remaining seven obstacles, with Gyi Lovam! far in front and gaining. Gestor and Talán (ridden by Popler's fellow officers, Lieutenant Hynek Býček and Captain Josef Seyfried) claimed second and third. Norbert, breathing heavily, was last home. Fourth place, and just one proper fall, was an improvement on last time, but there was much for Lata to be disappointed about. There was no thunderous ovation: the public had already lavished its enthusiasm on Gyi Lovam! and on the seemingly invincible Captain Popler.

Man and horse deserved the accolades. The Velká Pardubická had rarely seen such an emphatic winner: the time, twelve minutes, was a record. As for Popler, his social traditionalism did not diminish his inspiring talent and boldness in the saddle. Lata described him later as 'maybe our best rider ever'. The rancour between them was healing.

They had much in common. Both were heroic spirits. Both put love and empathy at the heart of their dealings with horses. And both believed in pushing back the boundaries of the possible. Popler's thirst for adventure verged on the crazed. Scarred by war, passionate in his work, unbending in the demands he made of himself, he was always seeking greater challenges against which to test himself. His toughness was matched by unfailing courtesy; gallantry, where women were concerned. The great love affair of his life had ended badly. Some sensed that his broken heart was a factor in his greatness, causing him to scorn lesser pains. Or perhaps he was just naturally restless. A few weeks after his Pardubice triumph, he wrote to Weatherbys in England to enquire about the possibility of entering Gyi Lovam! for the Grand National. It proved a complicated business, but the English were won over by the Czechoslovak officer's good manners and obvious integrity. The boldness of the dream caught the imagination of his compatriots, too. The army gave him special leave to spend nearly three months preparing in England, and he was able to fund the substantial cost of the trip by public subscription. Sadly, although Gyi Lovam! did indeed start the Grand National in March 1931 and coped well with the jumps, the pace proved too fast. Gyi Lovam! fell at Becher's on the second circuit. Popler remounted, but a second fall at the Canal Turn persuaded him that his horse had had enough.

Even the most indomitable warrior must sometimes admit defeat, and Popler cared enough about Gyi Lovam! to do so. He left with a host of English admirers, but perhaps also with a sense that, for an outsider, a crowded steeplechase can be a lonely place.

# 16.

# Mortality

Reports of Popler's adventure fuelled a growing enthusiasm for horse racing among Czechoslovak patriots. In May 1931, President Tomáš Masaryk himself was persuaded to visit Velká Chuchle, where he watched Jiří Esch ride Oskar to victory in the Czechoslovak Derby. It was a big coup for a little course. They had long ago created a race – the President of the Republic's Trophy – in Masaryk's honour. He, in turn, had made a conscious effort to associate himself with his country-men's equestrian traditions since becoming president, and was often photographed on horseback. But he had never yet been to the race. His presence was a boost both for the course and for the notion that horse racing was in some sense the young republic's defining sport. Lata, who was at the meeting, may well have been intro-duced to him.

Later that month, Masaryk was in Pardubice to open a four-month-long exposition, nationwide but centred on the town, that celebrated physical education and sport. It was the biggest such event in Czechoslovakia's history, with 320 exhibitors and 190 events, including one cel-ebrating the Velká Pardubická. Lata is thought to have been among the 1.25 million visitors who attended.

Both town and race revelled in the attention. The scale of the proceedings showed just how far Pardubice had come. The new Grand Hotel opened on the same day as the exposition, with Masaryk as its first guest. Europe's glittering classes followed, and many liked what they saw. Pardubice had so much to offer. The hotels were palatial: the Grand, the Veselka, the Sochor. The main avenues were wide and stately. The public architecture was magnificent. There were banquets, balls, concerts, gourmet restaurants, a magnificent theatre, a busy casino and some very upmarket shops. And – in contrast to Prague, or Vienna, or Baden-Baden, or the French Riviera – there was the mad annual rite of the Devil's Race to justify the pleasure-seeking. Elsewhere, recession and rancour had begun to gnaw at society's fabric. The fact that the Velká Pardubická was so extreme – the fact that only the bravest would expose themselves to its dangers – somehow made it feel like an appropriate form of escapism. None of life's certainties was guaranteed any more. Why not risk everything for a few brief moments of thrills and glory on the turf – or, if that was beyond you, at least come along and join the death-defying party?

By October 1931, it seemed as though half of Czechoslovakia wanted to come along. It was the fiftieth running of the race, and what had once been a cult pursuit for a privileged few was now widely seen as a national sporting ritual. Everyone who could afford to took steps to taste the magic. A new four-storey grandstand, concrete and roofless, had been built alongside the old wooden one to accommodate extra spectators. It was just as well. On race day the road to the racecourse was choked with cars. Streams of pedestrians overtook them on both sides: many had reached the town on a special fast train from Prague.

Gyi Lovam! was not running. Popler was still resting him after his English exertions. But Popler himself was there, riding another of his own horses, Gibraltar II. Ra had two runners: Norbert, ridden again by Lata; and Pohanka, a dark five-year-old mare (by Nedbal out of Piacensa), ridden by the French cavalry officer Lieutenant François Durand. With nine other runners, including two others with Velká Pardubická experience, the race was both open and competitive. Lata's presence no longer seemed exceptional: at least, no one seems to have deemed it worthy of special comment. Perhaps they would have done, had they known what would follow.

The weather was fine, but the autumn had been wet and the course was waterlogged. The race was not so much a struggle between horse and horse as one between horse and nature. The mayhem began before they had even reached Taxis: at the third obstacle, the Little Water Jump. Tuss, ridden by Antonín Albrecht, was first to arrive but jumped sideways at the last minute, bringing down five other horses. Lata and Norbert, who had started at a slower pace, were among the seven who avoided the pile-up. Taxis was relatively trouble-free: Talán refused, but the rest cleared it safely. Renonce – or at least her jockey – came to grief at the Irish Bank, and although there were multiple remountings (and refallings) by the earlier fallers, by the time the runners came back from behind the woods to head past the stands and towards the big ploughed field section, there were just five of them left: Gabarit, Norbert, Gibraltar II, Pohanka and Széles II. Just over half of the race remained. Lata must have felt, once again, that she was in with a chance. Then they reached the fields.

It was like Passchendaele. It was madness to race on such mud. That didn't stop them trying. Sometimes they sank in so deep that even a trot was a struggle; in places they slowed to a walk. By the time they got back to the racecourse proper, it was a challenge to keep going at any pace. No one attempted to jump the Snake Ditch: they waded through instead. Even this presented problems. Gibraltar II got water in his nostrils, and there were fears that he might drown. At the Big Water Jump, the exhausted Norbert struggled to get out of the water. The only horse to complete the course without mishap was Pohanka – who, as a result, won by an enormous distance. The other four contenders trailed in eventually, bedraggled mud-figures, shivering with fatigue. As one commentator observed: 'Everyone was glad that the race was over.'

Once again, it is hard not to question the humanity, let alone the sanity, of racing in such conditions. We can only remind ourselves that, by the standards of the time, this was considered the right thing to do. Decent riders would not push their horses indefinitely. At Aintree, for example, Popler had conceded that Gyi Lovam! had had enough, even though he himself would have loved to continue. But ideas of what constituted 'enough' in 1930s Pardubice were different from ours. In the riders' defence, they spared themselves no more than they spared their horses.

The results read like a battlefield dispatch: J. Rojík, on Gabarit: fell and remounted; R. Popler, on Gibraltar II: fell and remounted three times; F. Albrecht, on Széles

II: fell and remounted twice; J. Linhart, on Holland-weibchen: fell, rider unseated, then fell again; Count K. Rómmel (from Poland), riding Caraibe: avoided jump three times, then refused; A. Csató, on Campana: fell, avoided jump four times, then refused. Yet again, the runners who didn't finish outnumbered those who did. Lata took her share of punishment but coped better than most. Norbert fell twice, refused once and unseated his rider once. The heavy ground must have softened the impact for both of them. Lata remounted each time. Yet again, she finished. Not only that: she finished third. A post-race photograph shows her talking to two fashionably dressed ladies, each wearing a fur stole. Bedraggled or not, she is smiling so widely her face seems about to burst. The battering she has just taken appears to have slipped her mind.

Her glory was eclipsed by the triumph of Ra's other horse, Pohanka. For some, it was also overshadowed by the grimness of the race as a whole. Yet the grimness underlined Lata's achievement: she had proved that a woman – or at least *this* woman – could be tough enough and skilled enough to complete the course, time after time, when highly trained military men could not. Not only that: she was getting better. Fifth, fourth, third: place by place, year by year, she was getting closer to the great prize.

After this, it was rare to hear anyone question the propriety of her participation. She had grasped early on that to win the respect of the male riders who resented her, she had to pay her dues. 'Like any novice, I had to prove myself.' Now she had done so. Even the most traditionalist cavalry officers had to accept that she was no more out of her depth than they were. Popler positively admired Lata by now. He is said to have been impressed by her resilience and grace, and to have envied her ability to bounce up from falls, seemingly unhurt, 'like a cat'. By one account, his feelings extended to the kind of admiration that a romantic soldier traditionally feels for a beautiful, unattainable woman of 'extraordinary grace': not love, nor lust, but a kind of courtly devotion. That may have been wishful thinking on his biographer's part. It is clear, however, that Popler and Lata were now on friendly terms. It is also clear that honour-conscious officers no longer felt compromised by the company of what the German press were soon calling a 'courageous Amazon'. She was not yet a national hero, but she was becoming the next best thing: a national treasure – a strange quirk of Czechoslovak life that her compatriots, notwithstanding her German-speaking background, were happy to claim as their own.

§ - § - §

Reports of the horrors of the 1931 Velká Pardubická did nothing to diminish public interest in the race. The crowds the following year were bigger still. A record sixteen runners took part, including four from Austria, three from Germany and, in Czechoslovak colours, two former winners, Gyi Lovam! and Ben Hur. A scarcely less impressive line-up of VIPs was observed in the stands, including the French ambassador, the Italian military attaché and several government ministers.

Czechoslovakia had missed out on that summer's Olympics. With the nation in the grip of the Great Depression, sending a team to Los Angeles was deemed an inappropriate extravagance. So the Velká Pardubická was the big setpiece of the 1932 sporting year. Brilliant October sunshine held out the promise of a fast, safe race – although some probably hoped that it wouldn't be *too* safe. Just one attraction was missing: Lata.

She was there; but she was watching from the stands, not riding. She would probably have been happy to take her chances again, had a suitable horse been available. But Norbert presumably had no desire to return to the scene of the previous year's ordeal, while Ra's only other Velká Pardubická prospect, Golubčík, already had a rider, a Frenchman, J. Noiret.

It is possible that Lata felt comfortable among the spectators. She was thirty-seven, after all, and arguably a bit grown up for the follies of extreme steeplechasing. She was respected for what she had already achieved. Journalists sought her opinions. (She tipped Golubčík.) Why risk injury or humiliation with another attempt? She had, in any case, been largely preoccupied that year with trying to develop her own string of horses. After a decade of riding other people's race horses, in practice and in competition, she seems to have registered her own colours in 1931: black, with a white crossed sash, and a black cap. Her three-year-old colt, Dante, had run as a complete no-hoper in the 1931 Derby – possibly as a ruse to allow Kasalický to introduce her to Masaryk. Now she had three horses in training with Karel Šmejda: Dante, Dorian and Savoy. The latter was a two-year-old gelding bought from Šmejda himself. Dorian was a three-year-old colt, sired, like Dante, by the fashionable stallion Ossian. (Kasalický and Mauve also had Ossian colts in training with Šmejda.) It's not clear where Lata got the money from. War and revolution have left so many gaps in the paper trail that we can only speculate. It's possible that one or more of the horses was a gift; it is probable that she was able to keep them cheaply. It is also possible that she borrowed at least some of the money: by the mid-1930s, Řitka was quite heavily mortgaged. If so, she was foolhardy. None of the horses won anything. Yet being an owner did allow her to ride out at Velká Chuchle whenever she liked – and to race, too, if she chose. And it meant that, standing among the owners and grandees as the contenders for the 1932 Velká Pardubická headed for the start, she could feel – or at least pretend – that she was one of them: a mover and shaker of the racing world.

It seems more likely, however, that the sight of the race starting without her was agony. Of course, she was less of an outsider, as an ex-countess among the cream of race-going society, than she would have been as a female jockey among the officers of the military riding school. And no doubt the president of the course management committee, Hanuš Kasalický, appreciated her company in the stand. But who wants to be with the grown-ups watching the action when you could be in the thick of it with the boys? Lata had come close enough to glory to have developed a taste for it. Imagine the headlines, if she could win the Velká Pardubická! Five months earlier, Amelia Earhart had been the first woman to fly across the Atlantic, giving a much-needed morale boost to America's impoverished masses. How wonderful it would be to do something similar herself, for her own compatriots – rather than just standing and watching.

If it was any compensation, the race was a thriller, closely fought and relatively disaster-free. Half a dozen horses were in contention until four jumps from the finish, when the boggy ground around the 'willow jump' – a ditch behind a hedge with two willows in it – claimed first Ataraxia, one of the German horses, and then Ben Hur, the favourite. This cleared the way for a desperate battle between Remus – an Austrian horse with an Italian jockey, Rugiero Spano – and Popler's Gyi Lovam!. Less than a length separated them at the line. Many spectators were certain that Gyi Lovam! had won it, an opinion that was clearly shared by Popler. The judges saw it differently. When Remus was declared the winner, there was a storm of whistles and chants of 'Popler! Popler!'

Popler accepted defeat politely. That was his nature. Within, however, he was seething. That was his tragedy. Several friends urged him not to ride in the next race, the last of the day: he seemed too upset. But he insisted; perhaps he saw it as his duty not to succumb to weakness. Within an hour of the Velká Pardubická he was at the start again for the Kinský Memorial Chase, in a four-horse race, on a mare called Ella.

A few minutes later, Popler was dead. Something went wrong at the second: a pair of low wooden bars that, compared with Taxis, barely counted as an obstacle. Some said he had had a heart attack in the saddle. The official cause of death was a fractured skull.

It is difficult to describe the trauma: not just to his family and friends but to the entire horse-racing community. Decades later, Lata said that she could never think of that moment – 'the death of a young athlete, and of a friend' – without pain. Popler's views on gender may have been old-fashioned, but his quiet nobility and fearless horsemanship had been inspirational. He had been revered and idolised, even loved, by his fellow officers, by his fellow riders, by Pardubice racegoers, even by his nation; and seemingly by his horses, too. Now he was a broken corpse. It was a sobering collision between escapism and reality.

It is easy and sometimes fun to talk about death-defying daring. Death's hard fact knocks such glib conceits from our mouths. Some such thought must have occurred to Lata. She may not have drawn the appropriate lesson from it.

# 17.

# Norma

In January 1933, Adolf Hitler became Chancellor of Germany. In March, he was granted unlimited powers. He used them quickly and ruthlessly. The Gestapo, race laws, book burnings, Dachau concentration camp, a ban on parties other than the Nazis: all were launched in a matter of months.

Not everyone saw this as a bad thing. Millions of Germans still believed, at this stage, that the Führer offered the best hope of making their nation great again. Elsewhere, there were plenty who admired his example: in Austria, for instance, where the far-right Fatherland Party was busy setting up its own dictatorship; or in Britain, where the *Daily Mail* argued that 'no one here will shed any tears for the disappearance of German democracy'.

In Czechoslovakia, opinion was divided. For believers in Masaryk's democratic vision, it was obvious that Hitler was a monster. Others argued that, compared with the horrors of economic collapse and Bolshevism, Nazism – or something like it – was merely necessary firmness. Just across the eastern border, millions were dying in a man-made famine in the Soviet Ukraine. In Czechoslovakia, a million people were jobless. The government seemed baffled. At least the Nazis had a plan.

Sympathy for their approach expressed itself in various ways: through support for fascist parties on the fringes of Czechoslovak politics; through increasing hard-right influence in mainstream parties; and, most explosively, through German separatism. More than 3.1 million Czechoslovak citizens (from a population of 10.6 million) were classified as German. Many were happy to be part of Masaryk's nation. A significant number were not; and, for those of them living in the predominantly German-speaking Sudetenland, where unemployment was particularly severe, Hitler's promise of a reborn Germany suggested a radical alternative.

You didn't have to be a Nazi to buy into this. Most German separatists just had a vague sense that they might be governed more sympathetically from Berlin than from Prague; and campaigned, accordingly, for their territory to be ceded to the Third Reich. Others went further. The Sudeten German Nazi Party had more than 60,000 members when the Czechoslovak government finally banned it in October 1933. Meanwhile, the more Hitler's regime consolidated power in Germany, the harder it became to disentangle German nationalist and separatist movements from Nazi nationalist and separatist movements.

The old ethnic dichotomy – 'German or Czech?' – had been one which many good-natured people had felt able to ignore, or to see both sides of. It would be harder to avoid taking a position on the question that now began to replace it: 'Hitler or Masaryk?'; or, more starkly: 'Nazism or democracy?'

§ - § - §

Some places adapted to the new battle lines more quickly than others. Pardubice carried on much as before. There were some local fascists, encouraged by frequent visits from the far-right leader General Radola Gajda; and there were some anti-fascists. But the town's revived tradition as a destination for lovers of horses, thrills and luxury from all over Europe left little room, at this stage, for nationalist rivalries. The 1933 Velká Pardubická would be the most cosmopolitan for a generation. German, French, Austrian and Czechoslovak horses all had a serious chance. For those preparing to ride them, the new hatreds that others were stirring up on their behalf mattered less than their own prospects and preparation, and the strengths and weaknesses of each runner and rider, and the bond they shared with the other jockeys who dared risk Taxis and the rest.

In the months preceding the race, patriotic officers of the Czechoslovak and French armies continued to ride with patriotic officers of the German and Austrian ones, on the racecourses and in the equestrian arenas of several nations. They socialised with them, too, when the chance arose. Unlike us, they didn't know how the rest of the decade would pan out.

Some of the warmest international socialising took place in the Pardubice Zámeček, a small neo-Renaissance chateau set in extensive grounds behind a curtain of conifers on the south-eastern edge of town. This was the home of Leopold von Fugger, a German sports enthusiast who since late 1930 had been renting the property with his wife, Věra, and their four children.

Known to his friends as Poldi, Fugger was a slightly mysterious figure. A keen equestrian, tennis player and aviator, just turned forty, he was a charming but erratic socialite. He was well-dressed, slim and good-looking – with slicked-back hair and big, snake-like eyes – and he made friends easily, at least among Pardubice's German-speaking classes. He was an active member of the tennis club and was on warm terms with many of the officers at the military riding school, notably Captain Popler, before his tragic end, and Captain František Statečný, Popler's fellow Olympic showjumper. He also enjoyed going flying with Major Alois Snášel of the 4th Air Regiment; which, given Fugger's record as a much-decorated reconnaissance pilot in the First World War, was perhaps not surprising.

He kept six servants and a motor car, and, depending on circumstances, between one and three horses, which he rode over a jumps course that he had set up in the grounds of the Zámeček. Yet he appeared to have limited means. The heir to a banking fortune, he was said to be awaiting the outcome of litigation in Bavaria. He had debts in Pardubice – for example, at the saddler's – and he paid his rent irregularly.

Locals also noted that he and his wife were rarely seen together. In fact, since 1932 Věra and the children had lived mainly in Vienna. (The Fuggers would divorce in 1936.) Poldi enjoyed close friendships with at least two much younger women, while his widowed mother, Princess Nora von Fugger, was also a regular guest. But for much of his time at the chateau he was alone with his servants and horses. This may explain the enthusiasm with which – when funds permitted – he entertained his privileged friends.

The Brandis family, 1903 (left): Mikuláš, Lata, Gabriele, Therese, Countess Johanna, ...stýna, Alžběta; front row: Johanna, Markéta

Aftermath of an 'officers' race', the closest the Brandis daughters expected to get to proper race-riding. Lata is on the right.

...e Brandis home at Řitka. ...main house is on the left; on the right is the granary.

Lata on Nevěsta
in Pardubice in 1927 . . .

. . . and on Norma
at the water jump in 1933

Lata (left) after falling with Norma (out of picture) at Taxis in 1935

Lata and Norma (far left) at the water jump in the 1934 Velká Pardubická

's cousin, Zdenko Radslav Kinský ('Ra'), at his stables in Chlumec nad Cidlinou

lanuš Kasalický: more than
just a neighbour to Lata?

Karel Šmejda: the first trainer to
recognise Lata's talents

Leopold von Fugger at the
Pardubice Zameček

SS-Untersturmführer Hans Schmic

. . . and SS-Scharführer (later SS-Obersturmführer) Oskar Lengnik

'That was not a crowd. That was a nation . . .'
Mourners in Prague for the funeral of Tomáš Masaryk, September 1937

Lata, riding Norma, successfully negotiates
a water obstacle in the 1937 Velká Pardubická

Willibald Schlagbaum, riding Quixie (right), does likewise

'The race is mine!' Lata and Norma
approaching the finish of the 1937 Velká
Pardubická

The first and only woman to win
the Velká Pardubická dismounts
after her victory

Lata and Norma are led through the Pardubice
crowd following their historic victory

Ra (left) and Josef Soukup (wearing his V for Victory sash) escort the
triumphant Lata and Norma from the finish

Lata's victory
was celebrated
with a ball at
Ra's chateau,
Karlova Koruna

Lata jumps Taxis on
Otello in the 1947
Velká Pardubická

Outside the cottage at
Old Women's Gorge:
's sisters, Johanna and
Kristýna; their cousin,
Gikina Satorieová;
and Lata herself

Lata, apparently still living at Řitka, enjoys her favourite kind of company.
Horses, she said, are 'my dearest and most faithful friends'

Lata at her late sister's castle at Reiteregg, Austria,
in 1981. The Haan family looked after her here for
the last few months of her life

The Zámeček was modest compared with some stately homes, but Fugger employed an excellent cook, Josefa Minářová, and the chateau's arched, polygonal dining room, with underfloor heating, was grand enough for any aristocrat. Aristocratic guests who enjoyed Fugger's hospitality included Count Heinrich Schaumburg, Baron Jan Nepomuk Widersperg, Countess Irena Széchenyi – and, on many occasions, Count Zdenko Radslav Kinský and various members of his family; almost certainly including, at least once, Count Kinský's cousin, Countess Lata Brandisová.

The attractions for Ra and Lata were obvious: not just the fine dining and aristocratic gossip but the company of a man with an eye for horses and a gift for riding them, within easy reach of both Obora and Pardubice race-course. Ra, in particular, enjoyed the company of Fugger, who became a frequent visitor both at Obora and at the Kinský stables at Chlumec. In addition to being a serious horseman, who rode in several races at Pardubice and won at least one showjumping contest there, Fugger was a war hero and, best of all, a gifted tennis player, willing to travel as far as Brno to take part in a tournament. In Ra's world, that made you a decent chap, to be welcomed into the social whirl in which he liked to live.

With Lata, as so often, the evidence is thinner. She was neither a tennis player nor a socialite. But she would have respected Fugger's abilities as a horseman, and would not have objected to spending time with him at the Zámeček, at Chlumec or at Obora, especially when there was riding to be done. Their paths crossed on social sporting occasions, too: for example, the drag hunts that Ra usually organised around the time of the Velká

Pardubická. Lata also got on well with Poldi's mother. If Poldi was not a close friend of Lata's, he was certainly a familiar one.

One day, those carefree moments at the Zámeček would acquire a special significance. In 1933, they were light distractions. Lata was preoccupied with weightier concerns: the future of the Řitka estate – which that year had one of its fields expropriated under land reform; her foray into racehorse ownership; the future of her houseful of contessas – one of whom was thinking of marrying and two of whom were rarely at home; and presumably also her own relationship with Hanuš Kasalický – whose increasing closeness must, at the very least, have been creating confusion in her heart.

§ - § - §

Meanwhile, there was a more practical question to distract her, which needed to be resolved soon. Both Lata and Ra were keen for her to have another go in the forthcoming Velká Pardubická. But which of Ra's horses should she ride? For a long time it looked as though she would opt for Neklan, a six-year-old stallion described by one expert as 'the most beautiful and noble Kinský horse in the [Chlumec] stud's history'. Two weeks before the race, the press was reporting that Neklan would be Lata's mount. Then she changed her mind. She would ride Ra's unfancied isabella mare, Norma.

It was a life-changing decision. Neklan, for all his nobility, would never be more than a decent steeplechaser. Norma, in the right hands, was special. Those hands were Lata's.

What did Lata see in her? At first, not very much. There was little about the six-year-old mare that suggested greatness. She was small – about fifteen and a half hands – with a placid temperament and a tendency to 'round out' when not being trained hard. You might expect a champion-in-the-making to be more aggressive. When Lata first rode Norma, she thought her 'weak' and declared, 'I don't have much confidence in this mare.' Yet she had a charming nature; and, whatever else you said about her, she was pretty.

All Kinský horses are pretty. The pure isabellas are prettiest. Their soft buckskin hide shines pale gold in most lights; their blonde manes are rich as yellow butter. With Norma, white 'socks' and a white star on the forehead completed the effect. If you were designing a horse for a Disney princess, it would look like this.

Like most Kinský horses, Norma was affectionate and interested in humans. It is easy to imagine Lata making friends with her. And it was easy to imagine the two of them as a pair. 'Together with the rider, they made a harmonious, attractive unit that was hard to forget,' observed one contemporary. The observation sounds trite, but many people made it. 'That's a beautiful lady,' a visiting jockey once observed to Ra, pointing out Lata. 'Yes,' said Ra, pointing at Norma, 'just like that horse.' Norma's long mane flowed down the side of her neck in blonde waves: galloping, she could look like a Norse warrior-queen. As for Lata, her blonde hair was already prematurely whitened – which made it all the more striking when, as she sometimes did, she galloped hatless on Norma, both pale manes shimmering.

Yet there was a lot more to Norma than her looks. Like Lata, she had remarkable powers of endurance. She worked hard and, according to one former Chlumec stable lad, 'She couldn't bear having a horse in front of her.' Lata soon retracted her 'unjust' first assessment and admitted that Norma was a 'tough, brave and faithful horse' who 'gives everything'. But there was more to her even than that.

Norma's father was a big English thoroughbred: a dark chestnut called Delibab. Her maternal grandfather was a thoroughbred, too: a Hungarian sprinter named Magyarád. But there may also have been Hutsul blood in Norma's pedigree – the Hutsul being a hardy breed of mountain pony found in the Ukrainian Carpathians. Norma's maternal grandmother, Nedejse, was said to be so close to the breed that her golden isabella colouring was marred by a tell-tale crossed dorsal stripe. Perhaps this was mere rumour. What no one disputes is that, compared with the average pampered thoroughbred, Nedejse was startlingly bright.

One Chlumec groom described her as 'the cleverest horse I ever knew'. She had had some circus training and could answer simple mathematical questions by stamping her hoof an appropriate number of times. This equine trick, made famous in Germany in the first decade of the twentieth century by a horse called Clever Hans, is thought to rely on interpreting unconscious cues from a human rather than on actual calculation. It's impressive none the less. Indeed, such sensitivity to human thought processes seems much more useful, in a racehorse, than mental arithmetic. If Norma inherited any of her grandmother's gifts, it might help explain why she was such a wonderfully responsive ride.

Those who believe that steeplechasing excellence is a matter of pedigree may be interested to know that Norma's mother, Nepal, had a half-brother, Nedbal (also a Nedejse foal), who sired Ra's Velká Pardubická winner, Pohanka. But pedigree is an inexact science. Those who saw Norma in her prime were more likely to enthuse about the mare herself. She had 'chiselled, lean legs', according to one expert observer, and she never had injury problems. Those who were lucky enough to ride her talked about her confident jumping, her sure take-off and confident landing. They also praised her 'toughness, modesty and stamina', her 'brilliant character' and her 'eagerness and calm'. Ra's stepson, František Schwarzenberg, described her as 'a love'. If that makes her sound almost human, we could add the opaque verdict of one of her grooms, Josef Soukup, who called her '*Pan kůň*' – an obscure expression that somehow combines the idea of being 'the guv'nor' with that of being 'all horse'. This seems to have meant, among other things, that she knew her own worth and considered herself any human's equal – scorning treats such as sugar lumps, with which some horses are reduced to slavish sycophancy; and that, although she enjoyed human company, she preferred the pleasures of being a horse. She loved to gallop. She loved to jump. Above all – luckily – she loved to be ridden; especially, it turned out, by Lata.

Their relationship would blossom over several years. In October 1933, it was new. Lata's choice of Norma over Neklan must have seemed perverse. Ra trusted Lata's judgement – but he must have suspected that this was a decision made with her heart rather than her head. He was probably right.

§ - § - §

The afternoon was brilliant and warm. The streams and water jumps were brimful. The public turned out in their thousands. Once again, the stands were packed with dignitaries: ministers, generals, guests from abroad. It was as if people were hoping for a breathtaking spectacle to distract them from the troubled times.

There was plenty of trouble to be distracted from. Six weeks earlier, the German Jewish philosopher Theodor Lessing, living in exile in the Czechoslovak spa town of Mariánské Lázně, had been assassinated by Nazi agents – chilling proof that, even if Czechoslovaks tried to ignore what was happening in Germany, the new German regime would not be ignoring them. Then, at the beginning of October, Konrad Henlein launched the Front of the Sudeten German Homeland, soon to be renamed the Sudeten German Party (SdP). Its agenda was nationalist, separatist and, as it gathered strength, increasingly fascist. (Henlein insisted on being greeted with the words: '*Heil, mein Führer*', and many former members of the Sudeten German Nazi Party were happy to do so.) Its financial support was delivered, covertly, from Berlin. Its calls for German rule, backed by Hitler, would have catastrophic consequences, for Czechoslovakia, for Europe and, ultimately, for the Sudeten Germans.

For some racegoers, such shadows may have added an intriguing new level of contrast to the 1933 Velká

Pardubická. The previous year, Austria's Remus had beaten Czechoslovakia's Gyi Lovam! by half a length, controversially and tragically. Few will have noticed that Remus's owner was Jewish: merely that Czechoslovak hopes had been dashed by German-speaking visitors. Maybe this year such visitors could be put in their place by a local champion.

Those who were actually riding probably took a less partisan view. Most watched the pre-race unveiling of a memorial plaque to Captain Popler on the main grandstand, and some may still have been reflecting at the start on the potentially lethal risks of the impending contest. Others will have been focusing on what they needed to do to win; but the glory they sought was primarily for themselves rather than their nation.

There were thirteen runners. One expert described the field as 'the best in history'. Ferber, from Germany, was the strong favourite, with a string of wins behind him; but there were also three former Velká Pardubická winners to consider: Remus, still trained and ridden in Austria by Rugiero Spano; Gyi Lovam!, being ridden in Popler's absence by the experienced Josef Seyfried; and Pohanka, entrusted by Ra to another French officer, Lieutenant du Corail. (Neklan was now being kept back for next year.) Ataraxia, from Germany, and Clematis, from Austria, were also priced in single figures; and there were three fancied French runners, Jeune Chef, Eckmühl and Regalon, which had arrived by train the previous day. Lata and Norma were the outsiders, at 25:1.

What the punters hadn't bargained for was Lata and Norma's resilience. The challenge ahead seemed to hold no terrors for them, whereas others seemed doubtful.

Ferber was slow to start running at all, then refused at the second obstacle. Pelide refused at the first. Gyi Lovam!, who never really recovered the spring in his step after Popler's death, gave up at the third (a water jump). Wehrwolf refused at the fourth (Taxis).

Lata and Norma continued at a steady pace, near the back, and were able to avoid trouble when Ataraxia fell at Taxis. A French journalist observed that 'she rode very beautifully', while Norma took each obstacle in her stride. It hardly seemed worth trying to overtake: the field seemed intent on defeating itself. Eventually, after the Irish Bank, the survivors settled down, in three distinct groups. In the lead were Eckmühl, Regalon, Jeune Chef and Remus. Then came Clematis, Deputation and Norma, about fifteen lengths behind. Pohanka was a distant last. All progressed without drama until the Snake Ditch, nineteenth of twenty-nine obstacles and frequently the cruellest. On this occasion, the horses were met with a perfect storm of disorienting difficulties: deep water; winding, unmarked ditch; uneven ground (the landing is much lower than the take-off); and, getting worse with each faller, a chaotic, terrifying kaleidoscope of splashing water. Not a single runner jumped it successfully.

Norma was not in the habit of falling, but the chaos was too bewildering even for her. The dynamics would have been simple. Norma, moving at pace, dropped like a stone into the water as the turf vanished without warning and was brought to an abrupt halt when her chest came to rest on the far bank. Lata, consequently, was propelled forward like a projectile from a catapult. I have seen footage in which Velká Pardubická jockeys are propelled twenty feet forward in such falls. All who saw it agreed that Lata's fall was severe, yet neither horse nor rider broke anything. Lata dragged herself to her feet. Norma was led patiently from the water. They regathered themselves. Lata remounted, and off they went again.

There was little hope of winning by now. Rugiero Spano had been fast remounting Remus, and the 4:1 favourite was far in the lead. Eckmühl, too, had resumed very quickly. Yet Lata's tactic of simply keeping going continued to bring dividends. Clematis refused at the twenty-second (Little Taxis); Jeune Chef gave up at the Garden fences (the twenty-third). By the time they had shaken off Deputation and Pohanka – who would be the only other finishers – Lata and Norma were a convincing third, calmly jumping obstacle after obstacle with obvious confidence and little sign of exhaustion.

Remus won, in a record time of 11 minutes 24.6 seconds; Eckmühl was second. But Lata and Norma, approaching the finish, were greeted with an 'enthusiastic ovation'. At least someone was doing something for Czechoslovak pride. The next day's papers described Lata, almost matter-of-factly, as 'the fearless Countess Brandisová'. Perhaps they were desperate for something positive to celebrate, given that the main prize had once again gone to Austria. Yet the epithet was hard to quarrel with.

Four times Lata had ridden in the race. Four times, the non-finishers had outnumbered the finishers. Four times, on three different horses, Lata had been among the minority who were able to complete the course – and on the last two occasions she had been placed. This time, moreover, she had done so on a horse that was, it turned out, slightly lame: Norma had been struck hard on the leg by a flying flag dislodged by a falling horse at, probably, the Snake Ditch. Yet horse, rider and the partnership between them had all proved strong enough to stay the course. This was steeplechase-riding of the highest order, and it underlined a self-evident truth: the idea that Lata was somehow an interloper had been comprehensively demolished. It was the other Czechoslovak riders who were starting to seem out of their depth.

Fearless or not, however, victory was still beyond her. And although she had silenced complaints about her gender, another issue would soon arise. Journalists were too polite to ask the question, but Lata knew the answer: she was thirty-eight. By any sensible measure she was approaching the end of her steeplechasing career.

# 18.

# The Germans

Over the next twelve months, Lata and Norma got to know each other. To facilitate this, Ra put Norma into training with Karel Šmejda at Velká Chuchle. Norma made the ninety-mile journey from Chlumec on foot, with Lata on her back. Their route took them over rough country: along the Labe as far as Kolín, then across densely coniferous hills until they reached the Vltava and, just beyond it, Šmejda's stables. Norma was happy to 'jump over everything they encountered'. Prized racehorses usually did their long-distance travelling by train, but the Kinskýs didn't believe in mollycoddling. Sometimes, Ra would travel from Chlumec to Žďár nad Sázavou on horseback, with his young children following on ponies. The sixty-five-mile journey took them two days, with any number of obstacles to be jumped en route. Everyone was assumed to benefit from the experience. Lata took a similar view with Norma. You don't win the Velká Pardubická by sparing yourself.

There were several advantages to keeping the mare within easy reach of Řitka. Ra had other claims on his attention. For one reason or another – perhaps it was a mid-life crisis, or perhaps there were more ideological motives – he had set his heart on winning the 1934 Velká

Pardubická, come what may. In addition to Norma, he was planning to run four other Kinský horses in that year's race: Čigýr, Padova, Neva and Neklan. Delegating Norma's preparation to Lata and Šmejda gave him one less thing to worry about.

Lata rode Norma at Velká Chuchle regularly, and the two became, in Lata's words, 'real friends'. She began to refer to her by the affectionate diminutive 'Normička', and as time passed 'my confidence in this little mare grew and grew.' Before long, Lata was nursing her own slightly wild Velká Pardubická ambition: 'I believed that, together, one day, we two girls could win that great race ...'

Meanwhile, there was much else to keep Lata at Řitka: notably a two-year-old chestnut colt, Hubertus, whom she bought from Kasalický that spring. Under Šmejda's gentle guidance, Hubertus would eventually become the most successful horse to race in Lata's colours. Lata was closely involved in his development, which limited her opportunities for travel. There were other horses to think about too, including those in Řitka's stables, which appear to have been kept either for work or as a form of transport for Lata and her sisters. Lata used to ride every Sunday to church in Líšnice: observers were struck by how beautifully both horse and rider were turned out. Gabriele, Kristýna, Alžběta, Markéta and Johanna were also conscientious churchgoers, but they may have travelled by carriage. It is possible that Lata rode because it was faster. On Sunday afternoons she often went racing at Velká Chuchle, and it would have been a rush to get there, after church, in time for the first race soon after 2 p.m. (The family had no car; Kasalický sometimes gave them lifts in his.)

The carriage that took the sisters to church was presumably a four-wheeled barouche rather than a two-wheeled *kočárek*; but the *kočárek* was also used, and, when it was, it is possible that Norma pulled it. She certainly pulled a carriage at times, although not necessarily in Řitka. This was unusual for a racehorse still in training but not unique: Brutus, second in the 1927 Velká Pardubická and also trained by Šmejda, sometimes pulled a plough. Ra believed that steeplechasers in general, and Norma in particular, thrived on a combination of recovery, variety and hard exercise; and Šmejda presumably shared that view. Pulling a *kočárek* provided the mare with the first two. Then it was down to Lata to provide the hard exercise.

She did so whenever and wherever she could: around Řitka; on visits to Ra's various homes; and, mostly, at Velká Chuchle, where Šmejda was training not just Norma and Hubertus but also Dante, Dorian, Savoy – and a host of other horses with other owners (including Kasalický), for which he presumably still welcomed Lata's help. It seems unlikely that Lata was regularly riding them all, but even if she just rode two or three a morning she must have been doing an awful lot of riding, and her body must sometimes have protested. Yet her mind, while she rode, was at peace. In the saddle, there was no need to worry about the world's other troubles, or about her own.

§ - § - §

As October approached, the press began to talk about Ra's Velká Pardubická ambitions in unexpectedly nationalist terms: as a showdown between the great Czech stable of the Kinskýs and a powerful contingent of German visitors. If it wasn't entirely true, it didn't need much repeating to become true.

Sport and nationalism were hard to separate in both Czechoslovak and German culture. The Sokol gymnastic movement and its German equivalent, the Turner-Bund, promoted them as two manifestations of the same desirable end: healthy minds in healthy bodies, united by a shared sense of national roots and community. The hardcore nationalists of the 1930s drew on this tradition when they promoted '*völkisch*' ideas of 'blood and soil' – as SdP leader Konrad Henlein (a former Turner-Bund instructor) did to great effect while promoting Sudetenland separatism, and as the Third Reich did in Germany. But there was a sinister difference. The new rhetoric of National Socialism was underpinned by old-fashioned hatreds: of Jews, of socialists, of capitalists, even of democrats. The trick was to vary the mix of wholesomeness and poison to suit your audience, if necessary luring people in with *völkisch* talk and saving the hate for later. The long-term aim was to promote Nazi values; in the short term, what mattered was for as many people to get with the programme as possible.

With that in mind, the Nazis had weaponised sport since their earliest days in power – especially glamorous sports involving fast cars or fast horses, and 'martial' sports (*Wehrsportarten*) that honed the skills and spirit required for warfare. Hitler himself proclaimed that 'a young German must be of slender build, as agile as a greyhound, as tough as leather and as hard as Krupp steel' – clearly thinking of applications for those qualities that went far beyond recreation. Sports enthusiasts who felt inspired were drawn a little further into the Nazi web.

At the same time, several of Hitler's most ambitious henchmen poured money and time into nurturing a new breed of steel-hard German horsemen. They did so initially by developing prestigious equestrian events. The Braune Band von Deutschland, a flat race in Munich – created in 1934 by Christian Weber, Hitler's former bodyguard – was one example. The prize money rose rapidly from 19,500 marks to (by 1936) a staggering 100,000 marks. Hermann Goering in due course responded by rebranding Berlin's big race as the Grosser Preis der Reichshauptstadt (the Grand Prix of the Reich Capital), and this too ended up with a 100,000-mark prize. Major German steeplechases, such as East Prussia's Von der Goltz-Querfeldein, also became more lucrative and prestigious, and attracted interest from much of Europe. Needless to say, money, energy and political will were poured into ensuring that the Germans won most of the prizes.

All this was propaganda: a ruse to make the regime seem successful by association. But the Nazis also used equestrian sports as a way of spreading and enforcing Nazi ideology among those who took part in them. These were mostly rural or upper-class Germans who would otherwise have been hard for the propagandists to reach. Soon after Hitler became Chancellor, the Reich Ministry of the Interior had decreed that all German riding associations must join one of the party's two paramilitary wings: either the original 'brownshirt' Sturmabteilung (SA) – which Hitler was in the process of marginalising – or the more ideologically reliable Schutzstaffel (SS), which would largely supersede the SA as Hitler's main band of uniformed henchmen following the 'Night of the Long Knives' in July 1934. Most German riding associations joined the SA, but in horse-breeding regions such as East Prussia, Hanover and Westphalia, which was where many elite steeplechase riders came from, the SS was more popular.

So it was that, for the rest of the decade, most competitive German riders who were not in the army were members of the Equestrian SS. They may not have joined enthusiastically, or with full comprehension of the organisation's cruel purposes; some may have believed that it was merely a wholesome vehicle for moral renewal. Yet they could not remain untouched by the evil at its heart. Their ultimate leader, Heinrich Himmler, was as viciously fanatical as any senior Nazi. He required all SS members, including horsemen, to train as soldiers. In 1934 he introduced guidelines specifying that members should be Nordic types and at least 1.70 metres tall. Before long, there were exhaustive investigations into their racial backgrounds. Members were also expected to join the Nazi Party and, from 1935, to read the SS's weekly newspaper, *Das Schwarze Korps*, whose bêtes noires included Jews, Communists, freemasons and, not least, 'Amazons' – that is, women who followed traditionally masculine pursuits rather than staying at home to cherish families.

It would be wrong to assume that every German horseman who rode for the SS or the SA in the 1930s signed up to such values, but many clearly did so. Meanwhile, a growing number of Czechoslovaks began to think of them, over the next few years, as Hitler's willing henchmen. Those who followed such matters could see the gathering strength of equestrian sports in the Third Reich; and the pride that Hitler's regime took in German horsemen's successes; and the role – emphasised by Nazi propagandists – that SS members in particular played in them. Günter Temme, multiple winner of the German showjumping Derby, was one much lauded example; Oskar Lengnik, the East Prussian steeplechaser, was another. If you didn't like the Nazis, you would not enjoy seeing such men triumph.

As it happened, Lengnik didn't come to Czechoslovakia to ride in the 1934 Velká Pardubická – although he would enter Lata's story soon enough. Nor, as far as we can tell, did any other SS riders. But Heinrich Wiese, the most significant German horseman in Pardubice that year, was the next-worst thing: a member of the SA, the oldest and most thuggish of Hitler's early support groups. SA-Standartenführer Wiese, whose horse, Wahne, was the big race favourite, had been involved in right-wing paramilitary activities since before the SS existed, and long before it became obligatory to join such a group. A year younger than Lata, he came from Eutin, in the Holstein region, and had originally trained to be a farmer and miller. He fought in the First World War and, though barely out of his teens, was awarded the Iron Cross. After the war, he developed an interest in far-right politics and joined first the Orgesch – an anti-Semitic paramilitary group that was suppressed in 1921 – and then, from 1923, the Stahlhelm ('steel helmets'), an ultra-conservative veterans' group with paramilitary leanings which was later subsumed into the SA. In 1929, he joined the Nazi Party, and since 1933 he had represented the

Schleswig-Holstein region as a deputy in the Nazi Reichstag. This was an occasional and purely ceremonial role, since the Reichstag by then convened rarely, its only function being to applaud and ratify Hitler's diktats. It was not a role for non-Nazis.

Many German riders who went along with the National Socialist programme did so because they felt that there was no safe alternative: by 1934 there were at least eleven dissenting equestrians in Dachau, while another, Anton von Hohberg und Buchwald, had been shot on Himmler's orders. So we should not leap too glibly to judge those who did as they were told. But Wiese appears to have signed up with enthusiasm. If his triumphs in the saddle brought glory to the Third Reich, so much the better, as far as he was concerned. As an SA-Standartenführer, Wiese held a rank roughly equivalent to colonel. He seemed proud of it. With his cropped hair and intimidating physique, he held himself like a soldier: chin high, forehead back, brown eyes staring disdainfully down a large, proud nose. Part of his left thumb was missing, perhaps a legacy of his bravery in war. You would think twice before picking a fight with him; or even, if you were a jockey, before jostling with him for position in the world's most dangerous steeplechase.

It is unlikely that many Czechoslovak racegoers were aware of all these details – or of a comparable back-story involving SA-Sturmführer Helmuth von der Gröben, who was riding Wiese's other horse, Elfe. Sporting biographies were thinner then, and travelled slowly. Yet even without this knowledge, there were good reasons to regard the German visitors with

suspicion. These riders represented a nasty, dangerous regime that used horse racing for its own glori-
fication. They would fight on its behalf, should the
need arise; and, if it did, it already seemed likely that
Czechoslovakia would be on the receiving end. It was
a matter of simple patriotism to hope that, at least
on this occasion, the invaders would be sent back
empty-handed.

All three German horses had a good chance.
Harzburgerin, owned by Count Emich Solms and ridden by F. Hoffmann (about whom little information
survives), had started out as a hunter and was a particularly strong jumper. Elfe, ridden by Gröben, was
a big, experienced mare whose main weakness was
having only one eye, which led her to approach each
jump at an angle. And then there was Wahne, Wiese's
horse, double winner of the Von der Goltz-Querfeldein
steeplechase and so accomplished a racer that, despite
being officially a warmblood, she was handicapped as
if she were a thoroughbred. Owned as well as ridden
by Wiese, Wahne was a dark bay mare, originally from
the Schernbeck stud in Saxony, and Pardubice's punters were impressed by reports of her speed, stamina
and jumping ability. Wahne started as 2:1 favourite, just
ahead of Norma, Neva and Harzburgerin on 6:1, with
Čigýr and Elfe on 8:1. Ra had assigned Neva and Čigýr
to two French officers, Lieutenant P. de Cavaillé and
Lieutenant J. de Granel. Padova, at 20:1, was a less serious
contender, and Ra – somewhat undermining the narrative that this was a fight to the death between two competing nationalities – had given the ride to his German
friend Poldi von Fugger. Nationalists would probably

have claimed a win by Padova as a Czechoslovak rather than a German victory; but the question was unlikely to arise. Lata once again rode Norma, and the odds suggested that locals saw her as their best hope for a Czechoslovak win.

# 19.

# Taking sides

They set off fast. Fugger set off fastest. It had been a dry autumn – the water jumps were mostly empty – and the ground was less treacherous than usual. Poldi was still leading at Taxis, which Padova leapt without difficulty. The other eleven runners jumped close behind. Elfe and Rag were the only fallers. (Both remounted but gave up at the next, the Irish Bank.) Padova tired soon afterwards, and the lead changed hands repeatedly. Norma, Neklan, Upman, Harzburgerin and Wahne: each hit the front at some point, but none seemed keen to force the pace. Unusually, this was shaping up to be a proper tactical race rather than a mere test of durability and luck.

From about halfway, quality began to tell. Madeira dropped out; so did Padova, following a refusal and a fall. Neva, Neklan, Clematis and Čigýr slipped further and further behind, leaving only Upman, Harzburgerin, Norma and Wahne in serious contention. Yet again, victory for Lata was a plausible prospect.

They cleared the fourth from last: the willow jump at the Popkovice turn. Wahne accelerated. Upman and Harzburgerin were too tired to respond, but Norma was still strong. Lata drove her into the lead, the excitement clouding her judgement. The main stand was in sight now, with the winning post somewhere in front of it. Wiese resisted the temptation to react too quickly. Instead, he kept Wahne within a length. Lata made Norma surge again and Wiese once again kept his cool. There was still little to separate them, but by the time they reached the last Norma was tiring. Wahne jumped slightly ahead, and was fresh enough to sprint away, winning by three lengths. The other finishers were far behind.

Second. On the face of it, it was Lata's best performance so far. Yet it was also arguably her worst: she had made her bid for victory a long way from home, and the gamble hadn't paid off. Could a cannier jockey have won the race?

The answer was almost certainly no. Wahne was a superb horse in superb form, with greater natural speed than Norma. Yet the question hung in the air, and it was not just Lata who asked it. Could she have done better? What she needed was another chance – but there was no guarantee that Ra would allow her one.

§ - § - §

Lata got on with her life. In the weeks following the Velká Pardubická, she watched Hubertus race for the first time at Velká Chuchle, over six furlongs. He was unplaced. She also found time to go to an agricultural festival in Nový Bydžov, near Chlumec, where she and František Schwarzenberg took part in a dressage display with Ra and his friends Prince Hans Thurn und Taxis, Count Jenda Dobrzenský and Count Franz Schlick. Presumably she enjoyed it. She was no socialite, but nor was she intimidated by the high aristocracy. And she always felt more confident in herself if horses were involved.

Back in Řitka, the estate kept her busy. There was always something requiring her attention. In 1935, for example, a new gamekeeper, Jan Běhal, arrived from Prague, bringing his young family and a well-behaved eagle owl, which helped him to patrol the woods. Lata made sure that the humans, at least, were properly housed – even donating a large piece of wooden frontage from a building on the main chateau property. She had her own woodland excursions, too, riding in the woods with Hanuš Kasalický on countless afternoons, talking about who knows what, with the young girls gazing curiously up at them from the bottom of the hill.

Her sisters filled much of her life. Alžběta had moved out, taking her children to an apartment in Prague. Gabriele, too, seems to have been mostly absent, staying instead with Marie Therese in Austria. But that still left four contessas: Lata, Kristýna, Markéta and Johanna. Like any bunch of siblings kept in close proximity, they had their quirks and their tensions, but they also enjoyed laughing and messing around together, and their home felt like a happy one. If you had visited them, you would have noticed – in addition to the hunting trophies – the jumble of mugs and glasses on the shelves in the hall (most kept for show rather than use); and a gun-rack with a dozen hunting rifles; and the carved wooden chest on the top landing; the piano in the smoking room, where all except Markéta smoked and Johanna played; Johanna's paintings on the dining-room wall (including, at one point, a caricature of Lata); the pretty writing table in what was still Gabriele's room; and the bright kilim rugs and the desk piled with paperwork in Lata's room. One visitor described the house as 'full of things of which one can say: the older they get, the nicer they are' – which is true of many things but probably not of paperwork.

You would also have noticed the sisters' closeness. Four decades of sharing a home had created an intimacy that must have made communication with outsiders seem laborious by comparison. They lived by a strict timetable: breakfast at 7.30 a.m., lunch at 12.30, afternoon tea at 4 p.m., dinner at 6.30 p.m. Within that inflexible framework, undercurrents of restless activity flowed. This was a house that was lived in: a place in which people were always coming and going and the battle against chaos and clutter was never won for long. There were dogs, too. It would have been hard to visit without noticing them. There were usually at least four in residence – mostly hunting dogs of the pointer variety – and often several canine visitors, since Lata was always happy to look after other people's animals. ('Dogs loved her,' says Jan Pospíšil, 'but she wasn't very good at making them behave.') Outside, in addition to the selection of jumps over which Lata practised, the sisters had created a makeshift volley-ball court on the grass. When Alžběta visited, as she usually did on Saturdays, the whole family would play exuberant games – to the delight of Alžběta's children, Jan and Eva.

And then there were the horses. Those in the Řitka stables – Hostivít, for example, or Egon – were hardy old friends. Šmejda's stable in Velká Chuchle housed Hubertus and, until she sold them, Lata's other racehorses. All required her time and care. It is hard to get bored of such chores, if you love horses. Lata's life was in this respect just like most other horsey lives. Long days of hard work on gallops and in stables piled up behind her. Looking back, the highlights were barely discernible.

One landmark, in June, was Lata's fortieth birthday. She must have reflected on its significance. The infinite possibilities of youth, long receding, were never coming back. Unrealised dreams might have missed their chance. And the stiffness and soreness from riding were never going to get any easier. Even so, she showed no signs of wanting to spare herself, especially when it came to Norma. She exercised her whenever and wherever she could: on the racecourse, cross-country, at home – anything to build up her stamina, and Lata's.

Somehow Lata also found time to travel in August to Hamr na Jezeře, not far from Czechoslovakia's northern borders with Germany and Poland, to ride Ra's Čigýr in a steeplechase. (She came fourth, after falling and remounting.) And although she never rode him herself in a race, she put thought and energy into helping turn Hubertus into a winner. When he was ready, she ran him repeatedly at Velká Chuchle, in September, October and November, over distances ranging from a mile to a mile and a half. It was worth it. Hubertus ended the season with two wins and two seconds to his credit, and Lata ended the season having won a grand total of 10,000 crowns in prize money, from two wins and eight places. This wasn't a huge amount – winning the Velká Pardubická paid eight times as much – but it must have covered most of Lata's costs for the year. And it did help bolster her sense that she was more than a mere nobody in the racing world.

This mattered. Despite everything, Lata probably didn't always feel very valued in racing circles. She had achieved more in the Velká Pardubická than any Czech jockey since Popler, yet there were still those who regarded her participation as freakish and unnatural, and some didn't keep it to themselves. In part this reflected a harsher mood in Czechoslovakia as a whole. Parliamentary elections in May 1935 had revealed a bitterly divided nation. There was a further increase in support for far-right factions; the biggest advances were made by Henlein's increasingly strident Sudeten German Party (SdP). Tomáš Masaryk, elected to the presidency for the fourth time the previous year, was looking alarmingly frail, and so was the fair, inclusive society he had tried to create. Henlein and his followers prized social conservatism, not equality.

Supporters of the SdP could be found far beyond the Sudetenland. One was the East Prussian jockey Hans Schmidt, winner of the 1928 Velká Pardubická, who spent much of the 1920s working in the Sudetenland and joined the Sudeten German Nazi Party in 1925. (He now belonged to the Nazi Party proper and, following a spell in the SA, was an officer in the SS.) Closer to home, from Lata's point of view, was Willibald Schlagbaum, a twenty-four-year-old German jockey working at Velká Chuchle. Born in Bavaria, Schlagbaum had been riding professionally since he was fourteen, initially as an apprentice in Vienna. He had been based at Velká Chuchle since 1927, riding mainly for Count Pálffy and for Count Erwein von Nostitz-Rienck, and was now a leading professional rider – in fact, in 1935 he was the year's most successful jump jockey, with eighteen wins over hurdles and twelve in steeplechases. He was described as a 'vociferous' supporter of the SdP. Lata considered him 'unpleasant', which may or may not have been fair. What's clear is that, probably around this time, the two of them fell out. Some say that Schlagbaum questioned Lata's competence and blamed her failings on her gender. The Czech trainer Martina Růžičková-Jelínková, who has made a study of Lata's life and discussed this matter with Lata's niece Eva Pospíšilová (the Aunt Eva who bequeathed her boxes to Jan Pospíšil), believes that the animosity originated with an incident in which Lata cut Schlagbaum up on the racecourse. 'He hated her from the beginning,' she says.

No doubt Schlagbaum saw it differently. But the animosity, from such a prominent jockey, cannot have done much to make Lata feel welcome at Velká Chuchle. 'It is always worse when a woman is racing,' Lata observed bitterly. 'If anything happens to her, people will say: '"Why did she do that?"'

Lata had learned to shrug off disapproval. This may have felt different. Across society, a new triumphalism could be sensed in the traditionalists' tone: a suggestion that, thanks to the Great Depression, the progressive elite had been discredited as out of touch; and that, thanks to the rise of the Third Reich, Masaryk's liberal consensus was doomed. Some former aristocrats welcomed this, but it was bad news for women.

Meanwhile, it was becoming plainer by the month that the Reich-inspired return to *völkisch* values brought with it much other unpleasant baggage. Hitler was openly preparing for war. In September 1935, the Nuremburg Laws stripped Germany's Jews of their citizenship rights. Henlein and the SdP made little effort to conceal their sympathy for this agenda – and were certainly not among those who called for an Olympic boycott when the German Olympic Committee announced that no Jewish athletes would be representing Germany in the following year's Games in Berlin.

For Lata, who listened to the daily news on the radio, it was impossible to be unaware of such developments, and it would have been hard to dissociate them from Schlagbaum's unpleasantness. She had some personal experience of what it felt like to belong to a group whose members were denounced from on high as enemies of the people; and she probably knew that pro-Reich champions of 'blood and soil' values had inveighed explicitly against women who neglected their duties as home-makers in order to pursue more 'manly' activities. Hermann Goering, Hitler's most powerful ally, spoke for many when he wrote, the previous year, that a woman's proper role was to 'take hold of the frying pan, dustpan and broom, and marry a man'.

As Masaryk had previously argued, and as many others have observed, democracy and gender equality are hard to separate as ideas. The same may be true of their opposites. If Lata didn't feel intimidated, she must at least have felt an urge to fight back. And the obvious way to do so was to give the Third Reich's representatives a bloody nose in the Velká Pardubická.

§ - § - §

Schlagbaum couldn't get a ride in the 1935 Velká Pardubická, which had an unusually small field. But there were some prominent representatives of the Third Reich for him to cheer on, even as he dreamed of making his own first attempt at the race the following year. Last year's winner, SA-Standartenführer Heinrich Wiese, was competing. So was SS-Scharführer Oskar Lengnik. There was also Lieutenant Defendente Pogliaga, from fascist Italy, whose armed forces had begun a war of naked colonial aggression against Abyssinia just a week earlier. Pogliaga rode the fancied gelding, Quixie. A third German horse, Landgraf, was ridden for the Eilenriede stable by A. Peters. The eight-horse field was thus evenly split between Czechoslovaks and the representatives of potentially hostile foreign powers.

Perhaps we should not attach too much weight to the ostensible allegiances of the participants, or to those of other leading German steeplechase jockeys, such as Curt Scharfetter and Heinz Lemke, whose walk-on parts in Lata's drama are approaching. Unlike us, they did not know where these political currents were taking them – only that they faced immediate and terrifying consequences if they tried to extricate themselves from the Nazi machine. Dr Horst Willer, a kind and wise expert on Germany's pre-war racing history, put it well when he told me sadly that Wiese, Lengnik, Schmidt and Scharfetter had been 'captured by National Socialism' during the inter-war years. In another time or place, they might have lived differently.

Yet there could be no doubt about the increasingly raw political divide between Reich and non-Reich jockeys – which was emphasised by a very visible geographical and cultural divide. Many of the best German riders of the time came from East Prussia, a remote 'exclave' of territory on the Lithuanian border that since 1919 had been cut off from the rest of Germany by a chunk of Poland –

and whose people, as a result, took a bitter pride in their regional identity. Many of Europe's best warmblood steeplechasers shared this identity, especially those bred at the great Trakehnen stud near Insterburg, or in the archipelago of small breeding farms that surrounded it. A hardy, sure-footed breed that traced their descent from the warhorses that helped the Teutonic Knights to conquer these flat, pine-shadowed lands in the Middle Ages, Trakehner horses were a living symbol of East Prussian uniqueness and toughness. You could recognise them by their broad foreheads and powerful hindquarters; or, more simply, by the distinctive elk's antler branding on their rumps. A single antler on the right rump signified Trakehner descent; the best horses – locally bred, with their Trakehner credentials recorded in the East Prussian studbook – had a pair of antlers on the left rump.

East Prussians took understandable pride in the excellence of their special breed. And when future SS-Untersturmführer Hans Schmidt won the 1928 Velká Pardubická on Vogler (with Udo von Kummer just behind on Beate), or when Gustav Schwandt won the 1929 Velká Pardubická on Ben Hur, these had been celebrated as East Prussian successes on Trakehner horses. Remus, too (winner in 1932 and 1933), although born in Saxony, was of pure Trakehner origin on both sides. Conversely, Pohanka's victory in 1931 was hailed as a Czech victory on a Kinský horse. This rivalry based on nationality and breed had hitherto been fierce but good-natured. But Nazism had obvious potential for twisting it to its own ends; and East Prussia was more susceptible to malign manipulation than most regions. Its people had suffered badly in the First World War and felt betrayed by the subsequent peace settlement. (A further surrender of territory to Lithuania, in 1923, hadn't gone down well either.) The Great Depression had left its farmers on the breadline, while Hitler's demands for 'Lebensraum' – 'living space' in the east – offered the hope of a longed-for reunion with the rest of Germany. Social and racial attitudes were not enlightened: one of the Von der Goltz-Querfeldein obstacles, a murky water jump, was called Jew's Creek. As for politics: a fading entry in Lengnik's SS records offers a clue. He, too, it seems, had once belonged (like Wiese) to the Stahlhelm. He joined in 1928 – when he was fifteen. It is hard to imagine that happening in a society that was not conservative to the point of extremism. These were perfect conditions for spreading the Nazi virus. An East Prussian victory in Pardubice, on a Trakehner horse, could be almost guaranteed to accelerate its spread.

In fact, in the 1935 Velká Pardubická, not all the national or ideological dividing lines were clear. Ra's Čigýr was again ridden by a Frenchman, Lieutenant de Cavaillé, while Typ was ridden by Martin Münzesheimer, a Prague-based jockey who may well have felt more German than Czechoslovak. Most competitors, in any case, would probably still have felt, most of the time, that the shared bond of the Velká Pardubická ordeal counted for more that the artificial hostilities imposed by other people's nationalisms.

Yet the divisions were still there. Those taking part were aware of them, those watching even more so. Many of the riders will have felt a sense of patriotic duty – or at least of national expectation – as they contemplated the challenge ahead. Lengnik, riding Herold, refused to take part in the pre-race parade. He also skipped the test jump. Instead, his ten-year-old grey Trakehner gelding was led directly to the start. This wasn't a calculated snub: Herold was notoriously nervy in pre-race situations. But it was easy to perceive it as a snub, fuelling a perception that the Velká Pardubická, conceived as a preparation for warfare, was becoming closer in spirit to war itself.

Lata was not intimidated. It was her sixth time at the start. She wore the same red and white Kinský colours as usual, with the same Virgin Mary medallion underneath. Norma, by now as familiar as a sibling, was as fit as she had ever been: in 'sinewy form', according to one cavalry officer. She was used to a little tension on the start line; and at least this time she could count on the support of her fellow Czechoslovaks.

The race began at 3.34 p.m. Čigýr, the 16:1 outsider, led them off at a brisk pace. The autumn had been dry again, and the organisers had once more been forced to put rails in front of the Big Water Jump to make it an obstacle worth jumping. Lata began gently, keeping an eye on Wahne, the evens favourite. The dark bay mare had looked stronger than ever when winning her third successive Von der Goltz-Querfeldein steeplechase in September; she had also impressed at the Ostsee steeplechase in Danzig. But Lata was confident that Norma – who with Quixie and Landgraf started at 5:1 – was stronger than she had been the previous year. All she had to do was stick to a sensible pace and stay out of trouble.

Taxis should have been easier than usual: with only eight horses, there was less risk of getting tangled up in a crowd. Norma was well placed at the approach, set herself well – yet somehow misjudged the moment of take off. She landed just short, crumpling against the far bank of the ditch, and Lata was once again flying over her head in a red and white blur.

Lata later claimed that a fallen horse was involved, too, although it is not clear which one or how. Whatever the detail, the sense of disaster must have been crushing. Lata needed help getting back on her feet, yet Norma, who may well have been hurt herself, remained calmly nearby, waiting for Lata to remount. When they set off in pursuit, there was still hope, although only a faint one.

The field thinned out, as it usually did. Typ, the old chestnut gelding, also fell at Taxis; Münzesheimer was slower to remount – and was soon out of the race altogether, after Typ first refused and then unseated his rider at the Irish Bank. Čigýr continued to lead until the eleventh, after which she drifted backwards. Quixie refused twice but in each case was persuaded to think again and remained in some sort of contention. Monarch fell once, then unseated his rider, and was pulled up at the Big Water Jump. Landgraf, who appeared to be acting as Wahne's pacemaker, lost touch around the Snake Ditch, then fell for the last time at the Popkovice jump, four from home.

But Wahne and Herold appeared to be in a class of their own, jumping confidently and steadily extending their lead. For the final three-quarters of a mile – from the moment the horses came into view again after rounding the Popkovice woods for the second time – it looked as though there were two races rather than one: Wahne against Herold, and then Quixie, Čigýr and Norma vying for third place. The leading pair jumped the last together, whereupon Lengnik, making energetic use of his whip, drove Herold – who had started at 8:1 – to a convincing three-lengths victory. Some time later, Pogliaga roused Quixie into a successful final spurt to claim third place.

Norma trailed in fifth; or, bluntly, last. Perhaps she was still feeling the effects of Taxis. Perhaps the realisation that she was too far behind to win sapped her enthusiasm for the final fight. Or perhaps she – or her rider – simply didn't have what it took.

§ - § - §

Racegoers greeted the German triumph 'coldly', according to one account. So did the national press – in contrast to *Das Schwarze Korps*, whose headline later that month rejoiced at the 'SS riders' triumph in Czechoslovakia'. Some commentators complained that Czechoslovak horses were inadequately prepared, compared with those from the Third Reich. This was probably true. There is no record of Ra's reaction, but he cannot have been pleased.

Soon, however, he had something else to ponder. Two days after the race, without explanation, Poldi von Fugger disappeared. The details are confused. He appears to have gone straight to Germany, although by one account he was still in Czechoslovakia in early November. One way or another, he was never seen again in Pardubice.

The police were quick to investigate. They had long suspected that Fugger was spying for the Nazis. His brother-in-law, Count Heinrich Schaumburg, who had visited Fugger in Pardubice in 1931, was thought to have been engaged in military espionage at the time of his death in a flying accident in 1932. Could Poldi's presence in Pardubice have had a similar explanation? The circumstantial evidence seemed strong.

Fugger was a trained aerial photographer, and while in Pardubice he had displayed a keen interest in aviation. It wasn't just his friendship and flights with Major Snášel from the 4th Air Regiment; he also enjoyed sitting by an airport hangar watching aerobatics. There were also those enthusiastic friendships with Czechoslovak army officers to consider, as well as the proximity of Explosia Semtín (as the A. C. Nobel chemical plant was now called).

A search of the Zámeček unearthed an unusual number of maps, of, among other places, Bohemia, Moravia and Slovakia. The police also confiscated forty photographs, some showing Czechoslovak military premises. None of this proved anything, and rumours about a 'secret transmitter' at the Zámeček appear to have been unfounded. But the fact remained that Fugger had left, apparently in a hurry; and that, after resurfacing at Hildesheim in Germany, he never returned. Instead, he joined the Luftwaffe, for whom he became first an instructor in aerial photography and then an officer in the notorious Condor Legion – which from 1936 to 1939 would provide bombing support for General Franco in the Spanish Civil War (causing untold civilian suffering in, among other places, Guernica). Historians consider the espionage case against Fugger unproven; the court of public opinion concluded, less fastidiously, that he had obviously been a spy. There could, at any rate, be little doubt as to which side he would be on in any coming conflict between the Third Reich and Czechoslovakia.

For Ra, Poldi's good friend, the affair was awkward. Members of the German-speaking ex-aristocracy were already viewed with suspicion. The security services feared that they would conspire against the democratic First Republic in the hope of getting their lands back. That was one reason why the police knew so much about Fugger's habits: his friendships with former nobles such as Ra had prompted them to keep an eye on him.

In fact, the security services could hardly have been more wrong about Ra's loyalties. That didn't make Poldi's flight less embarrassing for him. Ra may also have felt betrayed: on the face of it, Poldi had abused his trust. Yet Ra did remain on friendly terms with members of Fugger's family, as did Lata; so perhaps they weren't too bothered. What was harder to dismiss was a more obvious lesson. The era in which Czechoslovak, German, Austrian, Polish and French horse lovers could share their enthusiasm in one big happy, extravagant Pardubice party was coming to an end. Emotionally, Ra still inhabited the multicultural world of the Habsburgs, in which borders mattered less than class, character and connections, and decent sorts who liked to hunt, dance and play tennis could share their charmed lives without thought of national loyalties. Both he and – to a lesser extent – Lata had had a lot of fun in that world. Now the party was over.

# 20.

# 'A woman? Bah ...'

Lata went home to Řitka. Norma returned to Chlumec. Read into that what you will. Lata had her other horses to think about: in the weeks following the Velká Pardubická she raced Hubertus repeatedly. His successes – a first and a second – soothed her Pardubice disappointment without erasing it.

Ra, equally frustrated, had the fallout from Fugger's flight to distract him; and, in December 1935, the death from flu of his elder brother, František, who was fifty-seven and had no children. This meant that Ra, eight months short of his fortieth birthday, became the new owner of Karlova Koruna, the domed, hill-top chateau that overshadows the town of Chlumec nad Cidlinou.

The inheritance was absurdly magnificent. Another architectural masterpiece by Jan Blažej Santini Aichel, it was a paradise for any confident, super-rich aristocrat who felt comfortable in grand surroundings and whose twin priorities were outdoor leisure and lavish entertaining. It was on Karlova Koruna's marbled stairway and terrace that Oktavian Kinský used to run amok with his carriage. The pillared, octagonal dining room, overlooked by one of central Europe's most magnificent domes, was fit for any king or emperor. (The castle is named after its first guest, King Charles VI.) Its stables were breathtaking in their comfort and convenience, with so much spare space for carriages that the children used one section as an indoor tennis court. (Stable lads were occasionally dispatched to the rafters to retrieve stuck balls.) Outdoors, gardens in the English style, with lawns shaded by artfully arranged exotic trees, sloped down past a summer house, an orangery and other lesser buildings to vast stuccoed walls that snaked around the grassy hill-top impregnably.

Much else that Ra held dear was within easy reach: the hunting lodge of Obora, with all its woods and gallops; the stud farm at Ostrov, Norma's birthplace; and the near-replica of the Velká Pardubická course that Oktavian had constructed near Kolesa. Not least, there was Pardubice itself: magnet for the international movers, shakers, horse lovers and pleasure seekers in whose company Ra was happiest.

For Ra's children – then aged between eight and twelve – it was part paradise, part prison. On the one hand, the idyllic setting gave Norbert, Génilde and Radslav endless scope for mostly unsupervised play. On the other, those snaking walls cut them off from everything else in the world. When the circus came to Chlumec, the young Kinskýs were allowed one brief, segregated excursion, but that was all. 'The other children thought there was something wrong with us,' remembers Génilde sadly. This was the price of noble birth, even in a post-aristocratic age. You were supposed to mix only with your own kind – and as a child you couldn't even do that very much, since a social life was considered an exclusively adult need. The children's closest friendships were thus with one another; with their favourite servants (such as Josef Soukup, the young groom); with their horses; and with their favourite aunt, Lata.

But Lata wasn't much in evidence in Karlova Koruna that year. She had other matters claiming her attention, including her sister Markéta's impending marriage to Sergej Jaroševský, the Russian exile who helped manage the Řitka estate. Whatever was going on between her and Kasalický must have occupied her time as well, or at least her thoughts. Even without such distractions, however, there was a new awkwardness between Lata and Ra. No matter how polite he was about it, he clearly felt that her riding had not given Norma her best chance of winning. And Lata, no matter how polite she was, cannot have felt happy about that.

The cousins were still friendly towards one another. But I am not even sure that Lata visited Chlumec for Ra's fortieth birthday (which fell – incongruously, given Ra's excesses – on Bastille Day: 14 July). The extensive celebrations included a carriage ride, during which Norma, galloping alongside, was ridden by František Schwarzenberg – which suggests either that Lata was absent or, at least, that she was no longer considered Norma's primary rider.

Ra's children entertained themselves with horses instead. They had learned to ride by the age of five, and there was rarely a day when they were not on horseback. Part of the appeal was that, in the saddle, they were allowed to take more or less any risks they liked. Génilde, who had been well taught by Lata, was jumping replica Velká Pardubická obstacles by the time she was eleven – although she was never allowed to try the replica Taxis. There was a prevailing view that children had ten guardian angels,' recalled Radslav in later life. 'So no one was afraid they might get hurt.'

In this, at least, Ra and Lata saw eye to eye. A lack of any normal human instinct for caution appears to be a distinguishing feature of most parts of the Kinský family, including the Brandis branch and their modern descendants. Flick through what remain of Ra's family photographs and you'll keep seeing examples: children climbing around the outside of a house at first-floor level; children riding horses without hard hats; Ra jumping horizontally over his own personal high jump, the bar set at about six feet, with only the hard ground to land on. It's the same with Lata's: you see Lata and Kristýna up a tree; Lata, aged about eleven, firing a rifle unsupervised; Lata sending her six-year-old nephew Jan Pospíšil off to play with what looks suspiciously like a gun in his pocket. It seems to have been an almost moral principle. Decent sorts had a go. Only funkers worried about what might go wrong.

It was a principle that would soon find applications that had little to do with horses.

§ - § - §

Beyond the cream-coloured walls of Karlova Koruna, the air was charged with a sense of impending catastrophe. In December 1935, an ailing Tomáš Masaryk had relinquished the Czechoslovak presidency. In March 1936, Hitler had reoccupied the demilitarised Rhineland. In Germany, thousands of the Nazis' political opponents were in concentration camps. In Czechoslovakia, the economy remained disastrously depressed. The SdP was gathering strength; so, at the opposite extreme, was the Communist Party. The collapse of Czechoslovak democracy seemed far from unlikely.

Many former aristocrats welcomed this – as long as what came next was closer to Germany's Third Reich than to Russian Bolshevism. For nearly two decades the nobility had suffered in silence as Masaryk's rudely egalitarian state had stripped them of their titles, their lands and their prestige. They had been denounced as alien parasites whose participation in public affairs was unwelcome. If Bolshevism triumphed, they risked worse. But now, possibly, a viable alternative seemed to be emerging. In Germany, the high nobility was more Nazi than the general population. Nearly a thousand aristocrats had joined the Nazis before they even took power, and noble families would soon supply getting on for a fifth of senior SS officers. Many of their German-speaking counterparts in Czechoslovakia were similarly inclined: throwing in their lot with the Hitler-friendly German separatists offered the tantalising prospect of a return to the good old days – and an escape from the dangers of the present.

Eventually, when forced to choose, roughly two-thirds of Czechoslovakia's former nobility – who were, after all, mostly German-speakers – would identify themselves as pro-German. But some, including both Ra and Lata, took the opposite view: their loyalty was to democratic Czechoslovakia.

This was surprising, given their families' long histories as German-speaking servants of German-speaking emperors. It seemed particularly strange in Ra's case. As a prisoner of war in Russia during the Great War he had refused the opportunity to obtain his freedom by joining the Czech Legion. But that had been because he considered himself bound by his oath of loyalty to the Austro-Hungarian Emperor. Two decades later, the Kinský family motto – 'God, honour, homeland' – had a different meaning. The multinational homeland of the Habsburgs no longer existed. The choice was now between the idealistic Czechoslovakia to which Masaryk had given birth – or the Germany that Hitler was reshaping in his own image.

Many people who felt that democracy had served them badly preferred not to look too closely at the realities of the Nazi alternative. But Lata and Ra both seem to have understood early on that a Nazi-backed restoration of aristocratic privileges would come at an intolerable human price. The grievances of Czechoslovakia's German-speakers were not without substance, but that didn't make the Third Reich's ideology less hateful. And if you understood the depth of the Nazis' contempt for 'sub-human' Slavs – whose lands they wanted to seize for the Third Reich – it was hard to avoid the inference that to be pro-German in Hitler's world was to be viciously anti-Czech.

For both Lata and Ra, that was a line that could not be crossed. In their different, privileged ways, each dealt with Czechs on a daily basis. The polite society they moved in remained mostly German-speaking, but they were in constant contact with Czech-speakers. Their wealth, their status, their horses, their property: all were sustained by Czech land. There could be no question of betraying the Czechs who looked after it for them.

Over the next few years, this new 'German question' became increasingly important in upper-class life, not least in racing circles. There were some prominent figures, such as Eberhard Mauve (whom Lata knew well as a Velká Chuchle owner and fellow amateur jockey) or Ra's relative Prince Ulrich Kinský, who felt that Czechoslovaks should adapt their ways of doing things to accommodate the aspirations of the Third Reich. Soon, there would be talk of managing horse racing in a more 'German' way – which would ultimately mean excluding Jews.

Those who dissented from such views became, by default, more Czech. Lata's visible support for Řitka's Sokol group should perhaps be seen as a symptom of this. Neither she nor Ra was anti-German: otherwise they would not have remained on warm terms with, for example, Poldi von Fugger's family. (Fugger's mother Nora was Ra's first guest at Karlova Koruna.) But by 1936 both could reasonably have been described as pro-Czech, and anti-Third Reich.

I like to think that this was a symptom of their fundamental decency. It probably was. Yet there may have been another strand to their Czech patriotism: the kind of instinctive, bloody-minded defiance of which Oktavian Kinský would have approved – manifesting itself in an irresistible desire to stick two fingers up at Hitler.

§ - § - §

There was an obvious way for Ra to perform such a gesture: by returning to the Velká Pardubická in October 1936 and making sure one of his horses actually won it this time. Perhaps that sounds trivial. Yet sport was inseparable from politics that year. That August, the Olympic Games had taken place in Berlin. Impassioned pleas for a boycott had come to nothing; so had well-advanced plans for an alternative, non-Nazi Games in Barcelona – which were scotched by the outbreak of the Spanish Civil War a week before they were due to begin. Anti-Olympic feeling was stronger in Czechoslovakia than in most places: at one point there was talk of staging the alternative Games in Prague. None the less, despite angry protests in Wenceslas Square, a Czechoslovak national team was sent to Germany – minus its Jewish athletes, who refused to participate.

Fears that the Games would be abused for propaganda purposes proved well founded. Hitler turned the Olympics into an orgy of Nazi triumphalism, glorifying his regime and attempting to promote ideas of 'Aryan' racial superiority. It didn't always work, thanks to Jesse Owens and others; but it succeeded spectacularly in the equestrian events. The Germans won everything: all three team golds and all three individual golds. It was the only such clean sweep in Olympic history. Low ticket prices ensured that tens of thousands of people saw the world's finest horsemen humiliated by Trakehner horses and German army officers, most of them trained at the Hannover riding school. Only four teams out of fourteen completed the eventing competition. The Czechoslovak team came fourth, with 18,952 penalty points to Germany's 676. They had briefly come within sight of bronze before incurring a vast time penalty in the cross-country, trying to catch a runaway horse. Lieutenant Josef Dobeš, veteran of three Velká Pardubickás, was the most successful individual Czechoslovak rider, in twenty-third place.

Some suspected dirty tricks. In the cross-country, there were complaints from several nations about a particularly tricky water obstacle, for which horses had to land in a deep pond. Most competitors came to grief here, yet the Germans all seemed suspiciously well prepared, finding precisely the right landing spot despite being supposedly as unfamiliar with the obstacle as everyone else. Post-event mutterings did nothing to improve German–Czechoslovak relations.

In the aftermath, Czechoslovaks felt bitter and humiliated. It barely mattered if the Germans had cheated or won fairly: either explanation was unpalatable. Ra's determination to strike a blow for Czech pride in the Velká Pardubická was redoubled. Lata may have paid the price. Ra entered two horses: Neklan and Norma. Both, he decided, would be ridden by men: Neklan by Captain Oldřich Kocourek, from the Pardubice military riding school, and Norma by Defendente Pogliaga, the Italian officer who had come third on Quixie the previous year. The implication was clear: Norma needed a man's strong hand. Lata had been given repeated chances, but had failed to take advantage of them.

It is conceivable that Ra was influenced by a general backlash against women's participation in sport. The World Women's Games held in London in 1934 were the last of their kind. (Thereafter, women's participation in the Olympics was marginally expanded, but on the men's terms rather than Alice Milliatt's.) Two stars of those games – the Englishwoman Mary Weston and the Czechoslovak 800 metres world record holder, Zdeňka Koubková – had scandalised traditionalists in the spring of 1936 by announcing that they had undergone gender reassignment surgery and would henceforth be known as Mark Weston and Zdeněk Koubek. Most people wished them well; but for conservatives who disapproved of any kind of female participation in 'male' events it was salacious proof of sport's defeminising dangers.

All this is speculation. Such matters may not have influenced Ra at all. It is clear, however, that those early ideals of a golden age of equality in Czechoslovakia – with women placed 'on a level with men' – had begun to feel sadly outdated.

That August, Zdeněk Koubek gave an interview to *Time* magazine. It is unlikely that Lata read it. If she had, one passage would have resonated painfully. 'A woman?' said Koubek. 'Bah ... She is nothing. A man? Hah ... He is everything. There is not anything in the world that is not open to him.'

# 21.

# Himmler's cavalry

The fifteen riders who contested the 1936 Velká Pardubická could hardly have been more manly. The line-up at the start shimmered with barely controlled aggression. All four Czechoslovak riders were army officers. There were two officers from fascist Italy (one riding Ra's horse). And then there were the Germans: Oskar Lengnik, Heinrich Wiese, Curt Scharfetter, Hans Schmidt, Heinz Lemke, Otto Backenhaus, Helmut Böttcher; and, from Velká Chuchle, Willibald Schlagbaum. Some had experienced real warfare. Some were accustomed to the brutality of paramilitary work, without which the Nazis could never have risen to power. Several (Lengnik, Scharfetter, Schmidt, Lemke and Böttcher) were proud East Prussians, with all the self-conscious ruggedness that that entailed. This was the most intimidating group of riders the Germans had ever sent to Pardubice. Lengnik, Wiese and Schmidt each had a Velká Pardubická victory to his credit – and each had a horse in 1936 that was capable of winning again.

Germany expected nothing less. The brave horsemen of the Wehrmacht had already wiped the floor with the despised Czechoslovaks at the Olympics. Now it was the paramilitaries' turn to inflict similar humiliation in

Pardubice, in Czechoslovakia's most prestigious steeple-chase, ideally with a clean sweep of first, second and third. If they succeeded, it would demonstrate once again that the Germans were, as the Nazis now openly claimed, an unstoppable warrior race.

Perhaps it seems fanciful to consider a steeplechase in such terms. Yet there were plenty in the Third Reich who discussed sports involving horses in precisely such language. At the Berlin Olympics, the equestrian events were organised by a fast-rising SS riding instructor, SS-Sturmbannführer Hermann Fegelein. The son of a Bavarian riding school owner, thirty-year-old Fegelein was a skilled horseman and political schemer. He had hoped to ride in the Olympics himself but hadn't quite made the grade; his scheming was more successful. More opportunist than ideological, he had joined the Nazi Party in 1932 and the Reiter-SS in 1933. He would eventually become part of Hitler's most trusted inner circle. Now, however, his ambitions were tied up with horses and Himmler. Like the SS leader, he argued that German triumphs in the saddle were evidence of what *Das Schwarze Korps* called 'the new spirit of our nation'; like him, he spoke the language of Nazi mysticism, with its imagery of Grail-seeking Teutonic Knights. He offered to turn the Equestrian SS into an elite fighting force – a fearless Aryan cavalry – and his career took off.

The Olympics boosted Fegelein's reputation further, commending him to the Führer himself. Soon he would be in overall charge of the entire Equestrian SS; later still, he would lead many of its members, on horseback, into battle. For now, though, the triumphs he sought for his organisation were sporting ones.

The horsemen of the SS had already won all three of Germany's big equestrian championships that year (just as they had in 1935 and just as they would in 1937). The Velká Pardubická was their chance to show what they could do on the international stage.

Lengnik was their best hope: he was skilled, brave and tough, in precisely that unflinching way that Hitler thought was the mark of a true Aryan warrior. He was also a committed Nazi; or, at least, well on his way to becoming one. By the close of the decade he would be a Party member, a participant in Himmler's grotesque *Lebensborn* programme (for achieving racial purity through selective breeding), and the proud possessor of a *Julleuchter*: a mock-pagan lantern awarded only to the most valued SS officers. Yet somehow, despite all that, it is harder to dislike Lengnik than most of his fellow paramilitaries. I don't think he started out cruel. On the contrary, he was a sensitive man – described by one contemporary as 'pretty as a picture' – whose relationship with his favourite horse, Herold, was so close that Herold pined disastrously when separated from him. That doesn't excuse his eventual surrender to Nazism. But perhaps we should also see him as, at heart, a hardy horse breeder, from Germany's wildest frontier, who was tough and unyielding, like his horses, because he had to be; and whose fighting spirit the Nazis exploited but did not create.

At all events, he and his fellow SS officers, SS-Scharführer Schmidt and SS-Unterscharführer Scharfetter (both, like Lengnik, from Insterburg), were a fearsome set of opponents for the Czech jockeys in Pardubice to contend with. And if the SS riders failed, there was a strong supporting cast to salvage some glory for Hitler. Among them were SA-Standartenführer Heinrich Wiese, veteran brownshirt; Willibald Schlagbaum, anti-Czech admirer of Henlein's SdP; and SA-Scharführer Heinz Lemke, a rugged East Prussian who had joined the Nazi Party in 1933 but was in the process of being thrown out for being too 'unpleasant'. It is likely that most of these would have thought they were riding for Hitler; and if they didn't, there were plenty watching who did. Pardubice racecourse had become the arena, now and for the foreseeable future, for a symbolic struggle between the Czechoslovak republic and the Third Reich. Victory had never mattered more.

§ - § - §

The Germans won – as usual. The best the Czechoslovaks could say for themselves was that they avoided a complete whitewash. Of the eight finishers, there were only four Germans. But there was no escaping the main headline: the race was another triumph for the Third Reich. SS-Untersturmführer Oskar Lengnik rode Herold to a second successive victory, by a big distance this time. Elfe, ridden by SA-Scharführer Heinz Lemke, came third. In between, on Hetre, came a bitterly disappointed Captain František Aubrecht, who immediately filed a complaint against the winner, claiming that Herold had missed out a jump. The protest was dismissed, to howls of public disapproval.

Of the rest, Lieutenant Josef Dobeš came sixth on Milonga; while Captain Kocourek came eighth and last on Neklan. Schlagbaum, on Quixie, finished fifth.

Glückauf, ridden by Helmut Böttcher, came seventh. Harlekýn, a fourteen-year-old gelding that had been part of Czechoslovakia's humiliated eventing team at the Olympics, embarrassed himself again by falling at the relatively easy Small Water Jump. Norma came fourth. She had run and jumped strongly, but any chance she had was ruined when Lieutenant Pogliaga, emerging into the late afternoon gloom from behind the Popkovice bend, temporarily lost his bearings and, in his panic, went badly off course.

We can only guess what Lata felt about this. No doubt she would have preferred a Czechoslovak victory; it seems unlikely, however, that she would have enjoyed seeing Lieutenant Pogliaga faring better on Norma than she had. Some relief at his failure would have been unavoidable, although she would have concealed it.

The Pardubice spectators were less coy about their feelings. Herold was given a frosty welcome on the home straight, whereas Captain Aubrecht and Hetre, approaching the finish, were greeted 'by louder cheers than the winner', according to one account. Yet Lengnik was applauded by many of his fellow jockeys at the weigh-in, while a spectator's obscure heckle (reported in the German press) to the effect of 'Damn these Germans!' should probably be interpreted as implying grudging admiration. The double Velká Pardubická winner promptly won the next race, the Kinský Memorial Race, as well.

There were celebrations, of a sort, in the usual Pardubice venues. At least one involved a singsong, with revellers adapting a traditional song to praise the great Oskar Lengnik, double-winner of the Velká

Pardubická. But few Czechoslovaks would have felt very jolly, and when they reflected soberly on the outcome the next morning it felt even worse. Yet again, the hosts had had their noses rubbed in the dirt by Germans who despised them. Worse: it was hard to see what they could do to avert a similar outcome the following year. The Germans were simply *better*. They had better horses, better riders, better preparation – and a ruthless will to win that felt uncomfortably close to the spirit of military conquest. The Velká Pardubická had once been the brightest fixture in the Czechoslovak sporting calendar: a source of national pride and joy. Now it was starting to feel like a painful annual ritual, to be endured rather than enjoyed and then forgotten as quickly as possible.

§ - § - §

Lata initially saw it differently. Her thoughts and hopes were already on next year. She still believed she could win. But which horse would she ride? She had had her chances with Norma: if Ra hadn't thought her up to it this year, why would he change his mind the next – when Lata would be forty-two? There were question marks over Norma's future, too. She had also been given repeated opportunities. Maybe she just wasn't the winning type. Next year she would be ten. If Ra was going to breed from her, now would be a good time to start.

At some point, possibly not until early 1937, Lata discussed this with Ra, and heard the news she had been dreading: Norma would not be contesting the next Velká Pardubická. Nor, by implication, would Lata.

This was a dark time for her. She would never have said as much, but the conclusion is hard to avoid. Racing – and the Velká Pardubická, and Norma – had become the main focus of her life. Take that away, and what was left? Life in Řitka was pleasant enough, although the estate was struggling. But it must sometimes have been hard not to feel left behind, and with each passing year it must have grown harder. Four of her six sisters had found love and, notwithstanding Alžběta's bereavement, had families of their own to look after or to look forward to. Lata was still tied to the half-vanished family of her birth. Perhaps she was content with this; more probably, she yearned from time to time for something more. Yet what paths were available to her, apart from God?

Even Velká Chuchle, for so long a place that allowed her to escape her worries, had begun to feel like a troubled place, what with Schlagbaum's dislike of Czechs and female jockeys and a gathering sense (shared by the likes of Eberhard Mauve) that the future was German. There were still friendly faces: Karel Šmejda's, for example. But the place wasn't the haven it had once been. Only the church in Líšnice could be relied upon for solace. Week after week Lata prayed there, kneeling upright in the family pew, hands held high and tightly pressed together, face knotted in concentration. It seemed to be less a duty for her than a passion – as if some fire were burning within.

One probably was. The timing is uncertain, but at some point there was a crisis in Lata's relationship with Hanuš Kasalický. The rides stopped, and he more or less disappeared from her life. It is possible that they fell out over ideology, since Kasalický did eventually throw in his lot with the Nazis. But that may have happened later. More plausible at this stage is some kind of emotional crisis. Perhaps they quarrelled. Or perhaps it was the opposite problem: perhaps years of warm friendship had ignited unexpectedly, as friendships sometimes do, into something more urgent, which one or both of them considered impermissible; at which point the relationship broke under the strain, and those easy, innocent years slipped irrecoverably into the past, unattainable as the forbidden version of the future.

It would be wrong to get carried away by such speculation. It would be more wrong to assume from the thinness of the evidence that nothing significant took place. We know that there was gossip about their relationship. We know that its closeness caused problems in Kasalický's marriage. It seems highly likely that Lata, if she was aware of either fact, would have considered it her duty to end the relationship. And even if they had not yet reached the stage of breaking off contact, it seems reasonable to assume that, by 1937, there was enough intensity in what was going on between them to cause turmoil in Lata's heart.

Kasalický played a big part in Lata's life, for many years. One day, he ceased to do so. That alone tells us something. Of course Lata cared: why would she not have done? If she cared more deeply than she felt was proper, she could not have said so; but she would still have cared – perhaps even more so because of the need for silence. No love gnaws the heart so relentlessly as the unfulfilled love that is also a guilty secret: unsharable, impassable; a grief the lover must both bear and hide.

At around this time, the jockey Eduard Zágler saw Lata at Velká Chuchle and asked her a question. 'Countess,' he said (he still called her Countess, despite having known her for nearly a decade), 'please tell me: how do you bring yourself to jump those enormous obstacles in Pardubice? Aren't you afraid of killing yourself?'

'You know,' replied Lata, 'the thing is: I'm not all that attached to life.'

# 22.

# October 1937

On 14 September 1937, Tomáš Masaryk, founding father of the Czechoslovak nation, died at his summer retreat in Lány, twenty miles west of Prague. It is hard to convey the scale of the collective trauma. Think of the impact of Nelson Mandela's death on South Africa or Winston Churchill's on the UK; or imagine, perhaps, how modern Britain would react to the death of Queen Elizabeth II. The living embodiment of a nation's sense of its better self was gone: vanished from the world. No one could have been surprised: Masaryk was eighty-seven and his health had been failing. His inevitable end still came as a profound shock. For the first time in Czechoslovakia's history, there was no Tomáš Masaryk in the background; and if a world without Masaryk was possible, what else might vanish tomorrow?

The outpouring of grief brought the nation to a standstill. Newspapers' front pages were bordered in black; the flood of impassioned tributes to the 'president-liberator' barely left room for other news. When the body arrived in Prague to lie in state, the Czechoslovak people followed. Quiet and unstoppable as the River Vltava, they flowed into the capital. Over three days, an estimated 750,000 people made their slow way up to the Castle to see the open coffin. 'I remember it as if it were yesterday,' says Alena Šípová, an eighty-six-year-old Prague dweller who was among them, with her parents, as a child. 'We queued for hours. Most people were silent, although some were crying. My mother told me he was the father of our nation.' Traffic came to a virtual standstill. No one could remember such crowds. On 20 September, a three-mile queue of mourners was reported, undeterred by heavy rain and occasional thunder and lightning.

The following day, despite radio appeals for the public to stay away, two million Czechoslovaks were in Prague for the funeral: double the city's usual population. A horse-drawn gun carriage bore the coffin slowly through more than four miles of silent, crowd-lined streets. A vast procession of soldiers, Sokol members, Czech Legion veterans and workers' representatives followed: tens of thousands of them, solemn and orderly; and on every inch of pavement, Masaryk's people looked on, motionless, deep in the reflections of bereavement.

Later, thousands more lined the track as an open train, moving at walking pace and soon piled high with flowers, took the coffin back to Lány, where Masaryk was buried alongside his wife in the village cemetery. Perhaps few of the mourners could have fully explained what drew them. But the London *Times* was not far wrong when it described what happened in that strange, dream-like week as 'a great demonstration of Czechoslovak unity at a moment when the public mind feels that this should be demonstrated'. For *Lidové noviny*, the mourners were united by 'a single desire: to be worthy of this rare and exceptional figure'. For *Přítomnost* magazine, it was simpler still: 'That was not a crowd. That was a nation.'

Whether that was true or not, there was no denying the electrifying animation that spread through the country in the weeks that followed. Czechoslovaks forgot for a while the fractious, demoralised people they had become and remembered the idealism in which their nation had been forged. An era was over as well as a life, but perhaps they could still shape their future.

On the blue, white and red Czechoslovak flag that was draped over the president's coffin while it lay in state, two words were printed: 'Pravda vítězí'. The phrase, adopted by Masaryk as a presidential motto shortly after taking office, remains the official motto of the Czech Republic: 'Truth prevails'.

It was a bold claim to make at the darker end of what W. H. Auden called a 'low, dishonest decade'. For years, Nazi and Bolshevik fake news had been muddying the waters of public discourse, blurring the shocks of a new age of atrocity. Now the shocks were getting bigger. That April, Poldi von Fugger's Condor Legion had killed hundreds of civilians in Guernica. (There is no evidence, however, that he actually took part.) In Germany, a new concentration camp, Buchenwald, had been opened in July to cope with the continuing round-up of those the Nazis hated. In the Soviet Union, Stalin's great purge, in which more than half a million 'anti-Soviet elements' were killed in the space of two years, was at its height. In China, the invading armies of imperial Japan were closing in on Nanking, where they would soon massacre 300,000 people. Yet the watching world, unsure what to believe, seemed sunk in apathy. Unthinkable had become the new normal; so had unspeakable. Masaryk's democratic vision had never looked more noble, or more vulnerable – but who would defend it, now he was gone?

Edvard Beneš, Masaryk's successor as president, was decent and competent. What the Czechoslovaks really needed, though, was someone to inspire them. In its moment of danger, their nation needed a champion.

§ - § - §

The fifty-sixth running of the Velká Pardubická was scheduled for 17 October, three and a half weeks after Masaryk's funeral. There may never have been a sporting event so coiled with political tension. Czechoslovakia was already on something close to a war footing. The military had been building up its border defences against possible German invasion since 1936. In Prague – as in other European capitals – ministers debated the pros and cons of policies with half an eye on what Hitler might construe as 'provocative'. In Pardubice, the Czechoslovak air force was sizing up Pardubice racecourse for military use. (It had served that purpose well enough in the First World War.) Production at the Explosia factory was at full capacity. And at the Pardubice Zámeček, where Lata and Ra had laughed and dined and ridden with Poldi von Fugger, the Czechoslovak army was training its cavalry for a conflict that might break out at any moment.

All this had been set in motion with grim fatalism, by people who remembered the horrors of the First World War and would rather do almost anything than slip into another one. But now something had changed. Masaryk's death had reawakened people's sense of a Czechoslovak dream: a dream that was worth defending. Much had gone wrong with the nation since its birth. Czechs as well as Germans had been at fault in the long-running dispute between the two nationalities. Yet now, remarkably, history had reached one of those rare moments at which patriotism and morality coincide. The Czechoslovaks who hoped that truth and freedom would prevail had right on their side as well as tribal passion. Hitler's Germany had might on its side, but little else. That might was overwhelming; irresistible, according to the well-informed. Yet the air in Czechoslovakia was electric with defiance.

It was still electric when, in the second week of October, the horses and horsemen of the Third Reich began to arrive in Pardubice. Herold, Edenhall and Elfe (ridden by Lengnik, Schmidt and Lemke respectively) were first, reaching the town on the Sunday before the race. Wahne (ridden by Wiese) and Wieland (ridden by Backenhaus) arrived on the Thursday. By then, at least five Czechoslovak horses had already been training on the course for more than a week – including two, Upman and Quixie, which would be ridden by Germans (Scharfetter and Schlagbaum respectively).

Wherever you drew the nationalist dividing line, those on the German side of it were a formidable bunch – especially those who explicitly rode for the glory of Hitler's Reich. Logic suggested that they would be as invincible here as they had been everywhere else recently. Even if Herold, the favourite, failed to complete an unprecedented hat-trick, the credentials of Edenhall and Wahne were barely less strong. The trio (the first two part-owned by SS-Untersturmführer Lengnik, the third owned by SA-Standartenführer Wiese) had just a few weeks earlier taken first, second and third respectively in East Prussia's big race: the Von der Goltz-Querfeldein steeplechase at Trakehnen. For the Velká Pardubická, the longest priced of the group was Wahne, at 6:1. All three were ridden by men who had already won the race, and there was little sensible reason to doubt that one of their number would triumph again this time. The last victory by a Czechoslovak horse had been Pohanka's in 1931; the last by a Czechoslovak jockey had been Popler's on Gyi Lovam! in 1930. With those two exceptions, the run of Germanic victories (five German, two Austrian) went back to 1928. In some Czechoslovak minds, it had begun to seem like a law of nature, like the modern law of nature that dictates that German footballers always win penalty shoot-outs. The Velká Pardubická, it seemed, was a race in which Czechoslovak jockeys and horses rode themselves to exhaustion over four miles of life-threatening fences – only for a German pairing to draw away with irritating ease at the end to claim the big prize.

For the 1937 race, there were six Czechoslovak men who carried their nation's hopes. Most were soldiers. The famously hardy Major František Aubrecht was the most experienced – perhaps a little *too* experienced by now – and his mount, Dagger, was the most fancied of the host nation's horses. Four fellow officers reinforced the military's strength: Captain Zadzora on Romulus, Captain Klement on Lethé, and Lieutenants Růžička and Dobeš on Radomil and Milonga respectively. None could be faulted for pluck or riding ability, but their horses were rank outsiders. Josef Kohoutek, a young professional jockey, had a slightly better chance on Čipera, but only just: he was a 20:1 shot.

Yet that wasn't quite it. There was also a Czechoslovak woman in the field, riding a Czechoslovak horse. The big news had been late coming, but by now it was out: at the age of forty-two, Countess Lata Brandisová was going to make yet another attempt – her seventh – to win the Velká Pardubická.

As far the betting market was concerned, she didn't have much of a chance either. That did not prevent a thrilling, preposterous hope from spreading through the less knowledgeable public. Their noble-born national treasure had already pushed back the boundaries of the possible. What if she still had one more extraordinary moment up her sleeve?

That was Lata's hope, and she was trusting her old partner, Norma, to help her. This had been a late decision, too; or, at least, it had not been finalised until the last minute. Lata had spent much of the year 'begging' Ra to change his mind about Norma, urging him at every available opportunity to delay her retirement and give her one last chance in Pardubice. Ra was deterred by the likely strength of the opposition: there was nothing to be gained from exposing the mare to a humiliating defeat before breeding from her. By July, however, he had relented enough to allow Lata to ride Norma in a two-mile steeplechase in Poděbrady. Her victory suggested that the little isabella mare had lost neither her toughness nor her jumping ability; the narrowness of that victory, against moderate opposition, meant that the question remained open.

Thereafter, Lata and Norma had resumed their long cross-country journeys through the Bohemian hills, rebuilding understanding and stamina. I'm not sure how much travelling Lata can have had time for that summer. August was dominated by a new arrival in Řitka: Markéta's baby, Petr. His five resident aunts took a close interest in the Jaroševský family's latest member. Lata also had the running of the property to oversee, with Markéta presumably taking a less active role than usual. And then there were her own horses to think about, at home and in Karel Šmejda's stable. Hubertus alone raced nine times from July to October, mostly at Velká Chuchle, and it is unlikely that Lata never watched. The five-year-old's single victory came in early September, over a mile and a half, but he also managed two seconds and a third, bringing Lata a season's total of 5,600 crowns in prize money.

Despite all this, Lata found time to work Norma so hard that, as in previous years, the mare's appetite for food gradually declined – giving her that 'sinewy' appearance that signified that she was in peak shape for racing. Lata also seems to have made the long journey to Chlumec at least once, to debate with Ra the case for entering Norma for the Velká Pardubická. Norma presumably went, too. 'I had the feeling that she was on particularly good form,' explained Lata later. Even so, just a few weeks before the 1 September entry deadline, Lata and Ra seriously discussed the idea that instead she might ride another of his horses, Čibuk. Lata was tempted, and the pairing may even have been provisionally agreed. If so, it was not for long. Deep down, Lata believed in Norma. And Ra, deep down, believed in Lata.

The eventual decision made, Lata was able to spend an extended period in the Chlumec area in the last days before the race, practising with her chosen partner. She and Norma were reported to have gone well over the replica Velká Pardubická jumps on the private track at Kolesa. Ra's daughter Génilde, only eleven, accompanied them on an eighteen-hand isabella mare called Neva. She still wasn't allowed to jump the replica Taxis, though.

§ - § - §

In Pardubice, the last hotel room was taken four days before the race; most of the others had gone long before. Much of the accommodation was said to have been snapped up by members of Europe's diplomatic corps. Senior dignitaries of German sports administration were also visiting, along with members of the English, Italian, French, Austrian and Hungarian aristocracy; and, no doubt, a few spies. Rumours that Duke and Duchess of Windsor would also be in attendance turned out to be groundless but added to the atmosphere of feverish expectation.

Not everyone in town could honestly claim to have admired Tomáš Masaryk. Pardubice had its fair share of fascists, notably followers of the anti-Semitic General Gajda; and there were a few, not least among the visiting aristocracy, whose sympathies lay with the Third Reich. But most of these were keeping their heads down. Masaryk had been known for his love of horses – many obituaries had dwelt on his special relationship with his old bay gelding, Hektor. Pardubice, as a town whose *raison d'être* was horses, seems to have felt that this created a special bond with the late president. So, in some eyes, did his efforts on behalf of gender equality. The Women's Club of Pardubice staged a special event at the Veselka in his memory, no doubt realising that it would be a long time before women had such a friend in power again. A public subscription quickly raised funds for a commemorative statue, to be placed in the Square of the Czech Legionaries. Meanwhile, an air of bereavement hung over the town. Dancing at the Veselka, traditionally a popular recreation for cavalry officers, had all but stopped.

Pre-race festivities may have taken place, none the less, especially among the visitors. Some of the German dignitaries were taken on an escorted visit to the state stud farm at Kladruby the day before the race. In the evening, some claimed to have seen German riders drinking – and Schmidt and Scharfetter were known to enjoy a post-race party back in Trakehnen. But the mood in general – and in public – was subdued.

Twenty-five miles away in Chlumec, Ra dispelled the tension by entertaining lavishly at Karlova Koruna. Guests included the Count and Countess of Paris (Orléanist pretenders to the defunct French throne); Lady Rachel Howard, sister of the Duke of Norfolk; Lady Hamilton, who came by private plane; and members of the Schwarzenberg, Fürstenberg, Auersperg, Czernin and Dobrzenský families. Entertainments included an orchestra from Prague, an improvised cinema, and a drag hunt, in which Ra took part along with his children and guests. Some guests were also able to attend the last days of Norma's training at Kolesa; and, later, to watch Génilde demonstrating her jumping skills on Neva.

It seems highly unlikely that Lata took much part in these festivities. If past years are anything to go by, she would have spent the final night, at least, much closer to Pardubice, with Norma nearby. She may well have calmed her nerves with a sleeping pill, as Velká Pardubická jockeys sometimes did; she certainly knew how to get hold of them. Then, ready or not, it was the day: Sunday 17 October 1937.

§ - § - §

The day was dry but neither sunny nor warm. A chill breeze gusted beneath a grey sky. But it was pleasant enough for racing, and the relative cold, at around ten degrees Celsius, did nothing to deter racegoers. On the contrary: by mid-morning, it looked as though the crowds might overwhelm Pardubice. Special trains were converging on the main station from all over Czechoslovakia. Every road into town was at a near or total standstill. The racecourse car park somehow found room for 3,000 vehicles before it shut shortly after mid-day; latecomers made do as best they could.

Total attendance at the racecourse was later estimated at over 40,000, but it would have been hard to count precisely. The stream of latecomers was still in full flood when the sporting action began at 1.10 p.m, and had barely stopped before the big race itself, nearly two hours later. The stands were so densely packed that some people improvised their own, with chairs, stepladders, even stilts. Others preferred to crowd into the various grassy spaces in the middle of the course, hoping to be able to see the most dramatic jumps close up. If you knew what you were doing, you could usually run from one good vantage point to another while the race was in progress, although that might be difficult today. Around the bookmakers' tents, the throng was so dense that many people were unable to place bets. The resulting squabbles led one journalist to report that 'the pushing, pressing crowds ... give the impression that they confuse the Velká Pardubická with a fight in a cloakroom of a Prague movie theatre'.

In the stands, the grander ladies wore fur: leopard, ocelot and beaver were the fashionable choices. One report even mentioned a lady wearing a 'foal coat', although this seems too preposterous to be plausible. The men wore heavy greatcoats and Homburgs – or, in many cases, military uniform. You can see why this may have felt appropriate.

The Czechoslovaks won the first three races – no great achievement, since all the horses were Czechoslovak. The third finished at around 2.30 p.m. Space had by then been found on the course for more or less everyone who wanted to watch the main event. But there was no place for Ra's daughter Génilde. For all her precocity in the saddle, she was not allowed to watch Lata race. Norbert was: either because he was older or (as Génilde suspected) because he was a boy. So she and her younger brother Radslav remained on the Chlumec estate, where they listened to the race in the gamekeeper's cottage, on a crackling radio. Luckily, a new radio booth had just been built on the roof of the main Pardubice stand, giving the commentators an excellent view. There was also a film crew, although, frustratingly, little of their footage survives.

In the chateau at Řitka, Lata's sisters and servants gathered around a larger radio, which was usually kept in Alžběta's room. Others in the village congregated as they could. It would have been hard for anyone in Řitka to have been unaware of what Lata was attempting – and vanishingly unlikely that any villager who was aware of it would not have been willing her to win. It was not just a local thing: it was a Czech thing. All over the country, but especially in the Czech lands, people were rooting for her, huddled around radios and thinking patriotic thoughts. Fairly or unfairly, the impending race was now widely seen as a battle between good and evil. On one side were the Third Reich's all-conquering Aryan warrior-horsemen, come to crush the Czechs on the racecourse in preparation for doing much the same on the battlefield. On the other were a few brave Czechs, outgunned but defiant, ready to give their all to defend the ideals of Tomáš Masaryk's nation; and bearing their flag was the unlikeliest of national champions: a silver-haired countess riding a golden mare. No one who understood such things can seriously have imagined that Lata and Norma would win. But if your soul had been stirred by the events of recent weeks, it was hard not to fantasise about the possibility.

In Prague and elsewhere, Czechoslovak politicians waited anxiously. Some, including Jan Masaryk, future foreign minister and son of the late president-liberator, were hoping against hope for a sporting miracle. Others feared that a German defeat might push Hitler over the edge into war. František Machník, minister of defence, was among several prominent politicians who had come to Pardubice to watch for themselves.

In the on-course stables, Norma was visibly affected by the tension. By the time the big-race runners were led out into the paddock, she was trembling. But she did as she was asked, according to Lata, because 'she's a loyal, nice horse'; and, of course, because she trusted Lata. Herold, as before, skipped the paddock parade, as did Iarbas. In each case, the horse's nerviness was blamed. It still didn't look particularly good.

The clock ticked round towards 3 p.m. The riders mounted; the walk to the course began, through a sea of people. For the first time, the tension seemed to ease. 'Once you're on horseback,' explained Lata, 'you know that the battle is coming – and that's beautiful. There is no more time or space for nervousness.'

On the other side of the stands, thirteen of the fifteen runners paraded in front of the biggest crowd Pardubice had ever seen, then cantered over to the middle of the course and, one by one, skipped over the test jump. And then they were off to the far north-eastern corner of the course, to line up with Herold and Iarbas for the start.

Something approaching a hush seemed to settle over the great crowd. The hour had come.

# 23.

# The Battle of Pardubice

Again, she was afraid. Her whole life had prepared her for this moment, yet now it was here, it was hard not to doubt. She had never felt older. The opposition had never been stronger. The tension between riders had never felt greater. The jumps had never looked bigger. (Some really *were* bigger: several ditches had been widened since Norma first raced here.) More than ever, this felt like the Devil's Race.

The bookmakers rated Lata's chances at 12:1 – not a great deal better than they had been for her first attempt, a decade earlier. But she knew that the public had higher hopes: otherwise, the odds would have been longer. Perhaps for the first time, she felt the pressure of national expectation. Could she really reverse a decade of hurt – and repel the strongest raiding party the Germans had ever sent? She wanted to believe it – 'You have to, when you want to achieve something' – but it wasn't easy. Yet she also knew that, if she didn't beat the Germans today, no one else was likely to.

She wore her medallion, as she always did, trusting in the Virgin Mary to keep her safe; St Anthony, inside her helmet, provided back-up. A horse-drawn ambulance coach, with four horses in train, waited ominously nearby. All around her were soldiers. Counting Lieutenant Henri Massiet, who rode the excitable French horse Iarbas, the line-up of fifteen jockeys included seven army officers and, by my count, five enthusiastic officers of Nazi paramilitary groups: SS-Untersturmführer Lengnik, SA-Oberführer Wiese, SA-Scharführer Lemke, SS-Scharführer Schmidt and SS-Unterscharführer Scharfetter. The civilians included Schlagbaum, who would sign up with the German army at the earliest possible opportunity. Twice that season he had beaten Lata's Hubertus riding a horse called Tank. It seems unlikely that the symbolism was wasted on Lata.

She was used to veiled hostility. Today there was no veil. Many of the men she was up against were real fighting men: trained for warfare and, in some cases, hardened by it. What lay ahead was a fierce and dangerous confrontation. An editorial in the official race-day programme spoke rousingly of 'the Battle of Pardubice', citing stirring examples from military history before boasting: 'Against the foreign invasion we are deploying the best we have.' That very day, in the northern town of Teplice, there were clashes between demonstrators and police at an SdP rally – prompting Konrad Heinlein to call for 'the Sudeten German issue to be decided with the help of the German Empire'. How could any jockey's mind not have been crossed by the thought that they and their rivals would soon be trying to kill one another?

§ - § - §

Shortly after the appointed time, the starter, Antonín Kruliš, gave his long-awaited shout: '*Gehen! Jděte!*' Never had the command to 'go' sounded so much like an order to advance into battle. Fifteen riders urged their horses forward. Within seconds they were charging – and in each mind for a moment there would have been that strange peace that comes when all other worries are forgotten, while the fresh anxieties created by the race have yet to come into focus.

The first three jumps went smoothly, despite the fast pace. Radomil was the early leader, followed by Upman. The others were already manoeuvring to be well positioned for Taxis. But race plans, like battle plans, rarely last long once the action has started. By the time you have jumped the third, the Small Water Jump, it is too late to do very much about changing your position. You need to play the hand you have been dealt and focus on maintaining a straight approach at a pace that suits your horse, giving it the best possible chance of jumping the big one well.

Schmidt, who had recently celebrated the 100th win of his career, had managed to get Edenhall to the front in time to lead the charge at the great obstacle alongside Radomil. Lengnik and Herold were out to the right, slightly behind. They may have been forced further out than they would have liked as they came out of the bend for the Small Water. Lata and Norma were near the centre but also hanging back.

The leading pair jumped Taxis beautifully. So did Norma, avoiding two nearby fallers, Iarbas and Wieland. Herold seemed to take off well, yet something went wrong. The grey Trakehner fell heavily on landing, and

Lengnik was flung from the saddle so violently that he broke his collar bone. Lata would have been too focused on her own safe landing to notice this. But she may have gradually sensed, over the next few obstacles, that Herold was not in sight.

What she couldn't have known, although perhaps she should have guessed, was that all three fallen riders had remounted and continued. Like several others, Iarbas and Wieland struggled at the next – the Irish Bank, which has to be climbed rather than jumped – and thereafter looked increasingly forlorn. Far behind them came Herold, slowly recovering lost ground. Lengnik's agony hardly bears thinking about, but he was not the type to surrender, and certainly not in this battle; and Herold was too devoted to his rider to let him down.

For Lata, the Irish Bank was pleasantly familiar: a puzzle to which she knew the solution. The key here (according to the jockey Václav Chaloupka) is to 'instil the horse with courage'. Norma barely needed help in that respect, and she negotiated bank and ditch without difficulty.

Heading out towards the Popkovice corner, Lata must have felt a cautious optimism. The pace was still very fast, and everyone seemed to be vying for the lead, but things couldn't have gone much better so far. There were, however, still several miles to go.

The route of the course behind the woods had been altered slightly to accommodate the recent expansion of the airport. None the less, the Popkovice fence and the French Jump passed without incident. Coming out from behind the woods, Norma was a comfortable fifth. Schlagbaum led on Quixie, with Edenhall (Schmidt), Elfe (Lemke) and Dagger (Aubrecht) just behind.

The eleventh obstacle, the Big English Jump, defeated both Iarbas and Čipera with its wicked combination of post, ditch, hedge and raised landing – all to be dealt with while coming out of a bend. Their failure made little difference to the leading group but did clear the way a little for the fast-recovering Herold. For a few deceptive minutes, the race continued without drama. Jockeys had a chance to look around them as the dozen survivors wound steadily back through the middle of the course. They jumped the twelfth and thirteenth – Lata was always superstitiously relieved to get the thirteenth behind her – and continued up to the top (by the road) for what by then was called Popler's Jump. Then they turned back down towards the stands. As they jumped the fifteenth (a drop-ditch) and the sixteenth (the stone wall) the field strung out in roughly the following order: Quixie, Edenhall, Upman, Norma, Romulus, Dagger, Wahne, Milonga, Elfe, Herold, Lethé and (for a while) Wieland.

Then they were behind the stands, heading out into the ploughed fields. Some armchair jockeys liked to claim that the plough was easier than it had been in the Velká Pardubická's earliest years, when the race was held several weeks later in the year. 'Without the November mud,' said one opinion piece that day, 'the track is a billiard table.' This was nonsense. The fields were not just ploughed but deeply ploughed, under the personal supervision of the course manager, Jiří Drahoš. In one photograph I have seen, you wonder that the ploughman could get his tractor through it, so deep are the furrows. The going for the course proper was reported to be heavy; and although the fields did not present the kind of near-impassable bog that had reduced the 1931 race to a crawl, the long arc through the mud still made severe demands on stamina. Upman appeared to be handling it best, and moved steadily up the field; but this may have been deceptive. As Lata warned a younger jockey many years later: 'You pay for speed in this place.' Instead, she took Norma on a slightly wider, less direct route than the others, where the going was less heavy, and allowed her to make her own pace. She knew that they could make up any lost time later.

Approaching the stands again, but still behind them, they reached the nineteenth obstacle in mostly unchanged order. This was the Snake Ditch: the worst of several deceptively simple-looking water ditches, 4.5 metres wide, with a treacherous drop from take-off to landing – but no visible obstacle. When the ditch is full, as it was on this occasion, you can see the water trembling at the horses' approach, and it is hard to persuade a horse still recovering from the plough to jump it with any enthusiasm. So it proved now: Wahne, Wieland, Dagger, Upman and Elfe all fell, although only Backenhaus on Wieland failed to remount. Quixie, Norma and Herold jumped it successfully. Shortly afterwards, Upman threw his rider. Edenhall led briefly but was defeated by the Big Water Jump (the twenty-first), bringing Schmidt's race to an end. The watching crowds barely noticed: the real action was by now taking place some way ahead.

On the far side of the track, in full view of the stand, the remaining serious contenders raced from right to left, back towards the Popkovice corner for the second time. Quixie led, followed by Norma, followed by ... actually, it hardly matters. The battle of Pardubice had by now been reduced – assuming no further jumping mishaps – to a two-horse race, with Schlagbaum and Lata in the saddles.

Quixie and Norma were the only horses that had not fallen. Despite this, Schlagbaum, in the maroon-hooped yellow colours of Stáj Quixie, had somehow lost his hard hat. Sensing the chance of victory in the biggest race of his life, he was riding like a man in the fury of battle, sometimes leaning extravagantly to maintain his balance over the bigger jumps. Lata's style was more economical, her body closer to the horse. The red and white stripes of the Kinský colours made her instantly recognisable – as, of course, did the pale golden hide of Norma.

Both pairings continued to jump superbly. Little Taxis (the twenty-second) often presents problems to tired horses, looking more innocuous than it is. (Pavel Liebich thinks 'it would be easier if it was twenty centimetres higher.') But Quixie and Norma soared over it – in that order. They also dealt deftly with the 'in and out' Garden fences, cleared the next two simple ditches, and disappeared behind the Popkovice woods for the last time. As they did so, Lata looked behind her and saw no pursuing Germans. A wild thought filled her heart: 'The race is mine!'

But there was still a fight to be won; and, according to Lata, that fight was now being fuelled by the animosity between the two jockeys. 'He knew I was holding Norma back all the time and was afraid of the finish. Several times he tried to push us aside at an obstacle or a wall.' The hidden stretch behind the woods would have been a good place to do so: there were no giant TV screens, as there are today, on which spectators in the stands could see the flying scraps of turf and the steam of the thundering horses. What happened in the shadows of the Popkovice conifers stayed in those shadows. But if dirty tricks were attempted they did not succeed. Both horses cleared the Popkovice fence and the French Jump, and still Quixie led.

Two jumps to go. The horses could be seen from the stands now. The excitement could have been heard miles away. Lata felt confident: she could feel Quixie's tiredness. And now the moment was near. Just before the second-last, she urged Norma forward. Seeming to sense the finish, the mare charged forward – but Schlagbaum cut across to block her before she could pass. Lata was forced to rein her back, allowing Quixie to jump first. For a few terrible seconds it felt as though all her momentum had gone.

But Lata still believed in Norma. More importantly, Norma believed in her. That was Lata's great secret, and it had never mattered more. She roused Norma, dug in again, urged her towards the jump. There was a quick tap-dance of hooves – and the mare was flying again.

The lost ground was soon made up. Schlagbaum seemed to have cut over a little too far and was no longer riding the optimum line. Quixie, meanwhile, was visibly tiring. As they approached the last, Lata – or perhaps Norma – saw her chance. They flew forward on the inside, soaring over the obstacle and landing in the lead. Lata knew they could win now. She knew they *would* win. Norma knew they would win. As they kicked on for the line, 40,000 spectators knew it too.

One length, two lengths, three lengths ... Quixie could not respond. Norma reached the line with a seven-lengths lead, going away, ears pricked up with what looked remarkably like joy. The noise and emotion were almost too volcanic for the mind to take in. For Lata, afterwards, that was almost the only memory. 'That was my best reward,' she explained, 'the audience's boundless excitement ... In that moment, you feel that you'd be able to win all over again.'

§ - § - §

What followed was a blur. Herold, amazingly, finished a distant third; followed, eventually, by seven other defeated runners. Herold was loudly applauded: whatever uniform Lengnik wore, he and his horse had proved that they were warriors. Lengnik and Lata were able to exchange congratulatory words; some said that it wasn't clear who was congratulating whom. Wiese, too, found time to shake Lata by the hand, saying simply: 'At last, it is done.' Soon afterwards, Lengnik collapsed. The East Prussian would spend several days in a Pardubice hospital before he could return to Germany.

Ra quickly found his way to Norma's side. So did Josef Soukup, the groom, who had earlier prepared a big white V-for-victory sash (actually V-for-*vítězství*), which he was now wearing proudly across his chest, neatly matching the enormous smile on his face. But nothing matched the radiance of Lata's own smile as the four of them – Lata, Ra, Soukup and Norma – made their slow, proud way towards the winner's enclosure. The silk cap had been ripped from her hard hat by then: it is not clear who by.

Someone offered her an overcoat, but she could have kept warm from joy alone. There was so much to celebrate: an 80,000-crown prize for Ra; the third-fastest Velká Pardubická time on record (ten minutes, forty-seven seconds); the pleasure of having stood up to and vanquished a seemingly invincible enemy; and the bewildering realisation that a long-cherished dream had come true.

Yet the greatest happiness, according to Lata, was the fact that the delight was shared. 'I will never forget the moment when thousands and thousands of hands waved and everyone shouted "Norma!",' she said later. 'And when everyone rejoiced, applauding and cheering for our victory, it seemed to me that never before were people so truly and amicably united ...'

For a shy woman who had spent half a lifetime sitting awkwardly on the edge of life's dances, the intensity of the acclaim was disorienting: 'It moved me to tears,' she confessed. At some point she dismounted. In a photograph showing her doing so, she looks as though she is about to swoon from happiness. She was still wearing her capless hard helmet, like a soldier's. Karel Šmejda joined them. Behind him, what felt like an ocean of friendly faces lapped against their little group. Even Norma seemed thrilled, ears still pricked forward, nose held high, keeping her head close to Lata's as she surveyed the excitement.

'I walked with my beloved Norma to the winner's enclosure, and forty thousand people were mad with joy. I could see Norma leading the way, while I enjoyed the delight and the applause of the spectators.' Lata wanted to share the victory with Norma: 'Three-quarters of that glory belonged to the horse.' Since Norma didn't like treats, it was difficult to reward her. 'But I believe she did understand the praise and flattery with which she was showered; and she understood how genuinely I shared the victory with her.'

Then she added, with just the faintest hint of a poignant subtext: 'Never have I known such happiness – the feeling that, far and wide, there was no one who did not like me.'

# 24.

# Rejoice!

Norma's victory was celebrated as few Czech victories, sporting or otherwise, had ever been celebrated. Joyful crowds refused to leave the racetrack for hours. Racegoers who a decade earlier had scoffed at the thought that a woman could even enter their favourite race now shouted the praises of the woman they called 'our Miss', basking in the glory she had won on their behalf.

Then there were parties: in Pardubice, in Prague, in Řitka. In Chlumec, Ra's friends joined his house guests at Karlova Koruna for a ball that night in Lata's honour, with dancing until dawn. A photograph shows Lata sitting on a gilded chair, bare-armed in a black ballgown. A string of pearls is partially hidden by a fur stole, and totally outshone by her gleaming, white-toothed smile. It is the only picture I have seen in which Lata really looks like a countess.

Returning eventually to Řitka, Lata was greeted as conquering hero. There were flowers, tears, hugs: Lata described it as a 'stormy welcome, from people as well as from dogs'. Congratulations poured in from friends and strangers; Jan Masaryk was among those who sent telegrams. A party was held for the whole village. Afterwards, Lata went up to Markéta's room, where three-month-old

Petr was sleeping. She leaned over her nephew's cot and said quietly: 'I won it for you.'

There was no prize money: that went to Ra. There was no trophy. All Lata got to mark her triumph was a small commemorative whip, presented by the Jockey Club to every competitor; and, from Ra, a silk scarf – her only unique physical memento of her day of glory.

But there were headlines by the hundred – Czech, Slovak, German, French, English – and countless thousands of words beneath them. The stream of journalists demanding interviews was unrelenting, until November snow in Řitka discouraged further intrusion. The articles varied from detailed race reports to profiles and interviews. The headlines were mostly variations on a single astonishing idea: 'Woman wins Velká Pardubická'.

Early reports in the Czechoslovak press also emphasised the patriotic aspects of Lata's success. It was a 'victory for our breed', a 'German debacle'; a triumph by 'a Czechoslovak national, on a horse from a Czechoslovak breed'; a defeat of 'the dreaded foreigners' by 'a steeplechaser from our own country'. 'News of this sensational triumph will go all around the world,' proclaimed *Národní listy*.

Then the story was ceded to the features pages, where a succession of articles – many by female journalists – analysed Lata's lifestyle and appearance. Readers were variously reassured that Lata was a 'slim, elegant lady' with 'eyes full of brightness'; that she had 'not lost her feminine grace'; and that she was 'not, as I had anticipated, a man-woman'. She was praised for her firm handshake and 'graceful elegance', but also, more warmly, for having a 'slim girlish figure' and for being 'suave ... but not at all prim'. *Pražanka* magazine celebrated 'a victory for all of womankind' – which might have felt more convincing without the headline: 'Does sport spoil women? Does it ruin their femininity?' A report in *Svoboda-Brno* focused largely on the question of whether Lata should have dyed her greying hair.

§ - § - §

Two weeks later, Konstantin von Neurath, the German foreign minister, was summoned to a meeting with Hitler and some of his senior generals. From now on, declared the Führer, the aim of the Third Reich's foreign policy would be to take over Czechoslovakia and Austria, if necessary by invasion. The objective was to free up food supplies and living space for Germans, to boost military security and 'to preserve and enlarge the racial community'. Up to two million Czechs and Slovaks would be expelled to facilitate this.

There is no evidence that the Germans' failure at Pardubice influenced this accelerated viciousness; but it is not impossible. Hitler did have some awareness of horse racing. Five months later, he would create a lucrative new race, the Union Klub Prize of Honour, with an endowment to provide a 40,000-mark prize for a century. He may well have heard about Lata's triumph. If he did, it isn't hard to guess how he felt about it. Anti-Czech rhetoric in the Reichstag in the week following the race was described by one foreign observer as 'the most violent used by Germany against another country since 1918'.

The Third Reich got its revenge, anyway. In March 1938, Germany annexed Austria, in a non-violent

'Anschluss'. In April, at the SdP's annual congress in Karlovy Vary, Konrad Henlein declared his party's loyalty to Nazi ideals and demanded political autonomy for the Sudetenland. At a meeting in Berlin a few weeks earlier, Hitler had told Henlein how he intended to deal with Czechoslovakia: 'We must always demand so much of them that we can never be satisfied.' Over the next eighteen months, that strategy proved horribly effective.

For Lata, these were strange times. Her wildest dream had come true. She was admired, respected, loved. In Řitka, there was pride and hope. At Velká Chuchle, Hubertus was thriving. As a jockey, she had nothing left to prove. There were many reasons to be happy, yet the wider world was going to hell in a handcart – while who knows what romantic yearnings were draining the colour from life's other pleasures? Erstwhile friends were concluding that it would be more advantageous to swim with the rising tide of Nazi-inspired pan-Germanism, and Kasalický – who was convicted after the war as a collaborator – was at the very least inclining in that direction. This cannot have endeared him to Lata. Perhaps, even now, he and she were still seeing one another. If so, the relationship's days were numbered.

As usual, Lata sought diversion and sanity through horses. At Řitka she kept Hostivít – a two-year-old buckskin Kinský horse – and Egon. These were her main form of transport but also trusted friends. I don't think Řitka had any stable staff left, so Lata was responsible for their daily care. Hostivít and Egon knew her better than most humans did. Riding gear – jodhpurs, long boots, tweedy jacket – seems to have been her default mode of dress.

In racing terms, the year was uneventful but busy. Hubertus raced ten times between April and November, mainly at Velká Chuchle. He came second three times, but that was all. The prize money barely covered his costs. If Lata was indeed on more awkward terms with Kasalický (from whom she had originally bought Hubertus), that would have been an additional reason for taking less delight in her equine pride and joy than she had done in happier times.

She found a less ambiguous pleasure in a springtime adventure on horseback involving Ra and Poldi von Fugger's sister, Sylvie Münster-Fuggerová. Sylvie had decided that she needed to take herself and her horse from Berlin to Vienna; a journey that was most easily accomplished if she rode directly south, cross-country, including a stretch of about 200 miles across Czechoslovakia, for which Ra (given the strength of anti-German feeling in the Czech lands) had agreed to escort her. Lata accompanied them for much of the journey. Few things soothe the soul more effectively than a long, slow, exploratory journey through the countryside. Lata, on horseback, in friendly company, her senses saturated with the sights, sounds and scents of spring, would have struggled to feel much anxiety while it was in progress. According to Ra, she and Sylvie were 'always joking together'. The weather was fine; each bend or hill-brow promised to reveal a bright new slice of the ancient land she loved; the troubles of Berlin and Prague were far away.

The journey ended. The troubles did not. All that summer, Hitler stoked up the Sudetenland 'crisis' with escalating demands. Europe's great and good fretted about where it was leading. Britain dispatched Lord

Runciman to Czechoslovakia, to explore the scope for mediation. Runciman, hoping to ascertain how the country's movers and shakers really felt, had several meetings with Ra and other pro-Czech aristocrats, who tried to persuade him against compromise with Hitler. It is conceivable that at one point, possibly at Žďár nad Sázavou, Lata was present. It did little good. Runciman spent far more time with pro-Reich, pro-fascist aristocrats, and found them far more persuasive. Ra's distant relative, Prince Ulrich Kinský, lobbied with particular vigour in support of Henlein and Hitler, arguing (according to one account) that 'Czechoslovakia is a Bolshevik monster and must be destroyed'.

The pro-Reich faction, which among the aristocracy was far larger, won. Runciman reported that the rise of Nazi Germany had given the inhabitants of the Sudetenland 'a new hope' and that their desire to join the Reich was 'a natural development in the circumstances'. In September, the British, French and Italian leaders – Neville Chamberlain, Édouard Daladier and Benito Mussolini – discussed the matter repeatedly with Hitler, then conveyed to Czechoslovakia's leaders their conclusion: that concessions must be made. Edvard Beneš's government agreed to give the Sudetenland some political autonomy – at which point Henlein upped his demands. What he wanted now was immediate annexation of the Sudetenland by the German Reich. Beneš responded by banning Henlein's increasingly violent paramilitary support group, the Ordnersgruppe. The next day, 17 September, Hitler created the Sudeten German Freikorps: in effect, a German-based paramilitary group whose *raison d'être* was to commit acts of violence on Czechoslovak soil – as it began to do within hours of its creation. Czechs and Slovaks looked on in baffled despair. The Third Reich had all but started a war, and Czechoslovakia's allies showed little sign of coming to the nation's defence. Maybe the Third Reich really was unstoppable.

Then something odd happened. That same day, on 17 September, just after the anniversary of Tomáš Masaryk's death, a small group of Czech nobles, with Ra and his stepson František Schwarzenberg prominent among them, presented President Beneš with a declaration of loyalty. It is hard to convey how surprising this was. The declaration had little practical significance. There were only eight signatories, and the aristocracy was not the political force it had been two decades earlier. Yet there was something quite inspiring – at a time when most influential people were quietly adjusting their values to suit the prevailing Nazi wind – about a gesture that was so plainly not in the interests of those who made it.

The Czech historian Zdeněk Hazdra, who has written several studies of the behaviour of the nobility during the Nazi era, is adamant about two things. First: the nobles had nothing to gain from it. 'In the years right after the First World War, nobles might have had something to gain from emphasising their Czech identity. But not now. A gesture like this could only damage them.' Secondly: each signatory would have been understood as signing the declaration on behalf of his whole family, unless they actively dissented. This wasn't very progressive, but it was significant, because it meant that, when Ra signed, his signature implied the support of the famous Lata Brandisová. 'I am sure she was implicated,' says Hazdra.

'Certainly the Nazis knew that she was loyal to the Czech nation.' They would not forget.

That declaration was swiftly submerged by events. To cut a long story short: at the end of September, at the notorious Munich conference, Chamberlain, Daladier and Mussolini decided, without consulting Czechoslovakia's leaders, that Hitler's demands for immediate annexation of the Sudetenland must be acceded to. Beneš had no choice but to capitulate. The news was greeted with fury in Prague, where there were violent demonstrations, and with jubilation in the Sudetenland – although probably not by the 10,000 or so people who, over the next six months, would be arrested there as 'enemies of the Reich'; or among the tens of thousands of Jews, Czechs and democrats who, over the same period, would flee to what remained of Czechoslovakia. (At least one such family ended up renting a property at Všenory, near Řitka, where they got into a financial dispute with their landlord, Hanuš Kasalický.)

Chamberlain returned to London with a piece of paper, proclaiming 'peace in our time'. German troops poured into the Sudetenland. Henlein, as Gauleiter and Reichskommissar, became the Nazis' supreme representative in the territory. Hitler got on with his plans for war. Czechoslovakia contemplated its own collapse. Overnight, the country had lost much of its industrial base and all of its border defences – which the army (mobilised and ready to fight) was ordered to abandon. President Beneš resigned and went into exile. Masaryk's First Republic died when he did so. An emasculated, Reich-friendly Second Republic took its place, with Emil Hácha as president. Only two political parties were allowed. Censorship was introduced. Most governing was done by decree. Fascists and anti-democrats filled most government offices. More than 20,000 Jews were driven out of public life. The political elite, at least, had recognised that the future was German.

In Pardubice, where there had been repeated demonstrations against such a future, no one had the heart to go through with the steeplechase that had brought so much joy the previous year. The fifty-seventh Velká Pardubická was quietly dropped, notwithstanding a high-class field of entries that included representatives of French, Belgian and American stables. It would be eight years before the race was held again.

A few weeks later, Lata sold Hubertus. We can speculate as to why she did so, just as we can speculate about her choice of purchaser, the Jewish industrialist Otto Ippen. Maybe she was disillusioned with horse racing. Maybe she wished to distance herself from the pro-Reich elite and its policies. Maybe she needed the money. All we know is that, abruptly, her name ceases to feature in the admittedly scanty records of the Jockey Club and the racing press. Racing continued at Velká Chuchle. Šmejda continued to train there. Lata continued to ride out for him. But perhaps, with so much encroaching darkness, the thrills of racing had temporarily lost their lustre.

§ - § - §

Chamberlain's peace wasn't worth the paper it was written on. In March 1939, the armies of the Third Reich marched into Czechoslovakia. Hitler celebrated in Prague Castle the next day. Slovakia, with Hitler's approval, became an independent, pro-fascist state. What remained of the Czechoslovak Republic became the Protectorate of Bohemia and Moravia, with Konstantin von Neurath as Reichsprotektor. Masaryk's former citizens were now Hitler's subjects: in effect, second-class citizens of a Greater Germany.

Still Czechoslovakia's Western allies did nothing. This may have encouraged the new regime to proceed with relative restraint. Thousands of dissenters were arrested over the next six months, but thousands of others weren't. Jews were excluded from public life but not, as yet, rounded up. For those not on the receiving end of such policies, it was still just about possible to make a meaningful choice between implicitly accepting them or showing disapproval. Some tried to protest subtly, through culture: patriotic Czech films, plays and musicals proved particularly popular in Prague that summer. Some participated with extra enthusiasm in Sokol activities. A fearless few attempted to establish an underground resistance network. Most people simply kept their heads down.

The nobility, on the other hand, were mostly enthusiastic about their nation's new German rulers. Some, such as Count Max Egon Fürstenberg, immediately began to lobby for the return of their former property; a few, such as Karl Khuen-Lützow (who described Hitler as a 'guardian angel'), suggested that they might be allowed to use their abolished titles again. Karel Belcredi and Hugo Strachwitz helped set up a Czech Union for Cooperation with the Germans. Many others did little, but none the less felt what Prince Alfons Clary-Aldringen – who owned 8,000 hectares of Sudetenland real estate near Teplice

– had recently described as 'deep, heartfelt joy' and an 'overflowing feeling of thanks for our great Führer'. Thanks to Masaryk's democracy, aristocratic landholdings were half what they had been twenty years earlier, and the shadow of Bolshevism threatened a future that was still worse. Nazism – if you didn't look too closely – seemed to promise a return to the old order: more civilisation, not less.

This interpretation became harder to sustain in September 1939, when Hitler's stormtroopers marched into Poland. Britain and France finally responded. Europe was once again at war; civilisation's certainties were once again in doubt. Yet most nobles in the Protectorate still saw the Nazi Reich as a force for conservatism, and Prince Alfons Clary-Aldringen's two sons were among many well-born young men who rushed to enlist with the Wehrmacht.

As the fighting began, tolerance of dissent in the Protectorate was sharply reduced. So it was both surprising and brave when, on 7 September, the Protectorate's puppet president, Emil Hácha, was presented with another declaration from a group of Czech nobles. There were eighty-five signatories this time, represented by sixty-nine signatures and representing thirty-three different aristocratic families. Ra was once again among the ringleaders, and is once again assumed to have implicated Lata with his signature. The letter spoke of the nobles' 'inherited identification' with the Czech 'national community' and their 'shared history, fate, and responsibility for future generations of the nation' – and stated emphatically that, 'whatever happens' their loyalty was Czech: 'With the conviction of the unity of all parts of our nation … we want always and under all circumstances to identify ourselves with the Czech nation.'

This was even bolder than the previous declaration. It could serve no conceivable purpose except as a gesture of defiance: a signal that, even at this darkest moment, there were Czechs who had lost neither their courage nor their pride. They knew they would pay for it. They did it anyway. The jolt of hope it delivered to the despairing nation was as thrilling as it was brief.

The Nazis took note and waited for their revenge.

# 25.

# The reckoning

The early months hardly felt like war. Konstantin von Neurath, the Reichsprotektor, governed Hitler's new province cautiously. Dissent was purged, anti-Semitism encouraged and slavish sycophancy towards the Third Reich demanded; but the aim was to keep the population submissive – not to provoke general rebellion. Atrocities occurred: notably the execution of nine students, with 1,200 others being sent to concentration camps, following anti-Nazi protests in Prague in October and November 1939. But these were still rare enough to shock.

Most people did what Lata did: kept their heads down and hoped for better times. Travel was difficult and public gatherings were discouraged, but some strands of normality were unbroken. Racing continued at Velká Chuchle and continued to be popular. Lata went when she could, especially to help Šmejda. But time was scarce. Gabriele was spending extended periods in Austria, Alžběta was living in Prague, Markéta had her young son to attend to – and the workload at Řitka wasn't getting smaller. Among other things, Lata was responsible for three horses; at least one of which, a bay gelding called Holomek, was a gift from Ra. These kept her busy and sane but also tied to Řitka. They didn't alter the fact that her nation was sinking into a moral abyss.

Different people responded to the changed realities in different ways. In Pardubice, the new Reich-approved authorities melted down the town's commemorative statue of Tomáš Masaryk in April 1940 and gave the metal to the German war effort as a 'birthday present' for Hitler. František Aubrecht, by contrast, was already working for the Czech resistance, among other things by helping to distribute the illegal magazine, *V boj* ('In battle'), in Pardubice and Prague. In Velká Chuchle, Willibald Schlagbaum had taken a break from horse racing to join the German army, while Eberhard Mauve was among a number of prominent figures who signalled their acceptance of the new status quo by contributing a prize for a new race. Mauve became prominent in the new Jockey Club of Bohemia and Moravia – which replaced the Prague Jockey Club as Czech racing's governing body. The Prague Jockey Club's considerable assets appear to have gone straight into Nazi coffers or pockets. Mauve was eventually judged sufficiently 'German' in outlook to be made deputy to the club's president, SS-Brigadeführer (later SS-Gruppenführer) Count Carl Friedrich von Pückler-Berghaus, whose other responsibilities would soon include being in charge of the Waffen-SS (the military version of the SS) in the Protectorate.

Then, in the summer of 1941, the realities changed again. In June, Hitler launched Operation Barbarossa. The Wehrmacht advanced on Russia with devastating speed; the Waffen-SS mopped up resistance and Jews in its wake, savagely. Some of the worst atrocities were committed by the SS Cavalry Brigade, under the leadership of

Hermann Fegelein. In a two-week period starting at the end of July, the SS Cavalry Brigade slaughtered at least 15,878 men, women and children in the Pripet Marshes in what is now Belarus. According to the historian Paul J. Wilson, it was 'perhaps the first of Himmler's murder brigades to receive and follow orders to shoot women and children'.

In July, Hitler formalised his plans for a Final Solution to the 'Jewish question'. Berlin, Vienna and Prague were identified as the first cities to be completely cleared of Jews. In September, Reinhard Heydrich – who even Hitler referred to as 'the man with the iron heart' – was put in effective charge of the Protectorate as acting Reichsprotektor. His mission, he told an aide, was to 'Germanise the Czech vermin'. It also involved creating a holding camp for the Protectorate's Jews in the Bohemian town of Terezín. More than 77,000 people eventually passed through the camp: nearly 90 per cent of the Protectorate's Jews. Most were then sent for extermination in the east.

Amid so much evil, it hardly seemed worth grumbling when, that July, the estates of ten noble families who had associated themselves with the declaration of Czech national loyalty in (especially) 1938 were abruptly taken into administration. (Another fifty-five estates were seized over the next eighteen months, generally from owners who had signed the 1939 declaration.) The confiscation barely amounted to a hill of beans in the wider landscape of catastrophe, yet it did make a difference, especially for the struggling Brandis sisters – who were among those singled out for that first wave of punishment. All revenues earned by the Řitka estate would henceforth go to the Protectorate's Land Office – leaving the sisters, theoretically, with nothing to live on. A German commissar, Herr Eickhart, was placed in overall charge of the administration, and a new manager, Josef Satorie, was installed on the estate.

Reluctantly, Lata dismissed the remaining chateau staff (who seem to have included a cook, a maid and a coachman). The estate still employed up to forty agricultural workers, but they now worked for Eickhart and Satorie, not for the contessas.

Luckily, Satorie, who set up home in part of what had been Řitka's servants' quarters, proved a more sympathetic manager than expected. The Brandis sisters were able to feed themselves, mostly from their own little patch of vegetable garden. The farm continued, just, to function, although the tenant farmer, Vladimír Daneš, would later be evicted as well. Occasionally, Satorie would pass on a sack of flour or potatoes to its original owners. The rest of the village struggled by as best they could. There were no round-ups of Jews in Řitka: the only Jewish family had left the village in 1937. But there were whispers about what was happening elsewhere. In neighbouring Mníšek pod Brdy, twenty-eight Jewish men, women and children were eventually deported to Terezín and other camps, mostly en route to Auschwitz. In Řitka, meanwhile, the vigorous malice of Heydrich's regime made itself felt in lesser ways. That October, for example, the village Sokol was dissolved and all its assets confiscated.

Lata and her sisters responded, in the first instance, by refusing to speak German. This was awkward: German was their first language, and their mastery of Czech was imperfect. But they stuck to their resolution stubbornly, to the irritation of Protectorate representatives who had dealings with them.

'It does not cross my mind at all to complain,' wrote Lata to Lori Kinský, soon after the administration was imposed. 'I can only say that my love for my fellow humans is not growing.'

§ - § - §

On 27 May 1942, a team of British-trained Czechoslovak paratroopers tried to assassinate Reinhard Heydrich in Prague. The acting Reichsprotektor died of his wounds eight days later. The reprisals plumbed the foulest depths of organised savagery. The villages of Lidice and Ležáky were obliterated; thousands of civilians were summarily shot; hundreds of women and children were deported to Ravensbrück concentration camp – and later murdered.

Pardubice suffered, too. The paratroopers who killed Heydrich were part of a larger team, some of whom had based themselves in and around the town where Lata and Norma had sparked such celebrations five years earlier. Their operation, code-named Silver A, was helped by the local resistance, including František Aubrecht, who lived in the nearby spa town of Lázně Bohdaneč. Another resistance member, Arnošt Košťál, was the latest owner of the Hotel Veselka – by then a popular drinking haunt for the Gestapo. Košťál gave one of the Silver A agents, Josef Valčík, a job in his wine cellar. When word reached Košťál that Valčík was under suspicion, he tipped him off – and persuaded him to drop, very publicly, a large pile of plates. Košťál, equally publicly, sacked him while he was still picking up the pieces, providing an innocent excuse for Valčík's sudden absence. It didn't help for long. The wave of arrests and torturings that followed Heydrich's assassination eventually resulted in the whole Silver A network being exposed, along with most of the local resistance. The subsequent slaughter took place at the Zámeček. Over a nineteen-day period in June, 194 men, women and children, including the Silver A conspirators and much of the population of Ležáky, were murdered in the grounds where Poldi, Ra and Lata had practised their jumping skills. Most were kept beforehand in what had once been Poldi's well-stocked wine cellar.

Four months earlier, in exile in Brazil, the novelist Stefan Zweig – Lata's erstwhile compatriot – had taken his own life, overwhelmed by the barbarism that had engulfed what was once Austria-Hungary. Like Lata, he had lived his formative years in the peaceful, cultured prosperity of 'a great and mighty empire, in the monarchy of the Habsburgs. But,' he wrote bleakly in his final work, 'do not look for it on the map; it has been swept away without trace... All the bridges between our today and our yesterday and our yesteryears have been burnt.' Lata was a very different character from Zweig: simpler and more trusting in traditional values. Yet no one who had enjoyed the best of Austro-Hungarian civilisation – and who now contemplated the orgy of murder the Nazis had set in motion – could dissent very much from Zweig's despairing verdict in *The World of Yesterday*, which he completed the day before he killed himself: 'Europe ... has torn itself apart suicidally in a war of brother against brother ... Against my will I have witnessed the most terrible defeat of reason and the wildest triumph of brutality in the chronicle of the ages. Never ... has any generation experienced such a moral retrogression from such a spiritual height as our generation has.'

For eighteen years before the Nazis came, every October, the brave young riders of Czechoslovakia and Germany – and Austria, France and Italy – had shared danger and adrenaline and fierce rivalry, peacefully. They had drunk together, frequented the same hotels and grand houses, admired one another's horses. Now they shared only the horrors and depravities of total war.

Some did so for longer than others. Oskar Lengnik, who had eventually reached the pre-war rank of SS-Obersturmführer but had a military rank of Leutnant, was killed in action on the eastern front ('fighting the Bolsheviks', in the words of one SS journal) in 1942. Similar fates would in due course befall Curt Scharfetter, Hans Schmidt and Heinz Lemke (missing presumed dead in Russia in 1944). The records are incomplete, but as far as I can tell no Velká Pardubická jockeys were among the approximately one-in-three members of the pre-war Equestrian SS who were hand-picked by Fegelein to serve in his wartime Waffen-SS cavalry divisions. Lengnik fought in the 1st Cavalry Regiment of the main Wehrmacht, yet remained close enough to the SS to be awarded the Totenkopfring – the SS Death's Head ring – in December 1941. The others were in artillery or infantry regiments. Given their prowess as horsemen, this is slightly surprising. Perhaps it counted against them that, being based in East Prussia, they were not part of Fegelein's main SS riding school in Munich; or perhaps it was just a mundane matter of the Wehrmacht enlisting them first. But it is not inconceivable that their credibility as potential members of an elite killing force had been undermined by their humiliating defeat by a woman in 1937. I like to think that this was the case, because it would mean that Lata had inflicted on the Nazis' paramilitaries precisely the dishonour that Czechoslovak officers had been so reluctant to risk in 1927; and, with gratifying further irony, that this dishonour then spared them complicity in the many atrocities committed by Fegelein's horsemen. That is not to say that they were not complicit in other atrocities; but perhaps we can hope that death kept their hands relatively clean.

Poldi von Fugger also fought in the east, with the Luftwaffe. By the end of the war he would be a major general and a prisoner of the Soviets (who captured him after driving the Germans back into Czechoslovakia and did not release him until 1955). Willibald Schlagbaum fought in Russia, too. He was badly wounded in 1942 and eventually lost a leg; he then set up a bookmaker's business in Prague, receiving his licence from the Reich authorities in April 1943. He lived in a flat that (his daughter believed) had been seized from a Jewish family, and kept a large swastika flag hanging from one wall. After the war he returned to Germany and became a successful and relatively contented innkeeper – although he never fully came to terms with the fact that he had lost the most important race of his life to a woman. He died of a heart attack in 1971. Helmut Böttcher never saw the war, having died in a motorcycle accident in 1937, mourned for his 'gentle, modest' nature. Heinrich Wiese continued to sit, notionally, in what was by then the Greater German Reichstag. On 26 April 1942 he helped pass a decree proclaiming Hitler 'supreme judge of the German people' – confirming the Führer's right to overrule all other institutions, including the judiciary. Soon afterwards, he was awarded the War Merit Cross, a decoration for civilians who had performed valuable service in furtherance of the war effort. But there is no evidence that, after the Reichstag's term expired for the last time in January 1943, Wiese then did his bit as a soldier. All we know is that he somehow survived the war (and, briefly, raced again).

Of the Czechoslovak jockeys, Hynek Býček was still helping the resistance – for example, by distributing food tickets – from his stable in Velká Chuchle. František Aubrecht – who had somehow avoided arrest – was trying to do much the same in the Pardubice region, although after June 1942 there wasn't much of a resistance network left for him to help. Josef Charous had been sent to Terezín. He would soon be transferred to Auschwitz, where he died in August 1943 – just one among fifty former Olympic competitors to die in Nazi concentration camps, but as far as I know the only Velká Pardubická veteran to do so.

Karel Šmejda, Norma's notional trainer, quietly continued his work at Velká Chuchle. He was one of fourteen trainers (counting Býček) who maintained stables there throughout the war. Hanuš Kasalický applied for German citizenship and membership of the Nazi Party. By 1942 he was said to be consorting with the Gestapo and to be insisting on 'Heil Hitler' greetings from visitors to his chateau in Všenory; he was also reported to have boasted of his connections to the Nazi branch of the Kinský family. Tried for collaboration after the war, he argued that he had not been collaborating, merely trying to preserve his property. The court was not convinced, yet the argument was perhaps not as flimsy as it seems.

Most people did what they deemed necessary for the preservation of life as they knew it, and would have told themselves that the choices they made were more innocent than they appeared to others.

But some were more careless of their safety. Josef Soukup, the groom who had escorted Norma from the Pardubice finishing line with the V-for-victory sash across his chest, was still employed by Ra – who, like Lata, continued to inhabit part of the property the Germans had taken from him. Soukup was the main operator of Ra's high-risk scheme to spare his horses conscription to Fegelein's cavalry – a fate that would otherwise have awaited them. Taking advantage of the fact that Chlumec and Obora were now in different administrative districts, Soukup would lead the most valued Kinský horses from one estate to the other at night, so that the requisitioning officers (visiting at different times) never actually saw them. Norma herself may have benefited from this ruse. She gave birth to five foals in the course of the war and may even have survived until its end. Yet the risks, to Soukup and to Ra, were enormous: getting caught would have led them at best to a concentration camp, at worst to summary execution.

Somehow the risks don't seem to have bothered Ra. Even now, he saw life as a game, to be played with spirit and ingenuity. When the Nazis began to conscript young Czechs as forced labour for their war industries, he was able to wangle exemption for sixteen-year-old Génilde by threatening to tell his 'good friend' Major General von Fugger. Soon afterwards, when the Nazis tried again, Ra breezily approved Génilde's whirlwind marriage to František ('Toši') Dobrzenský, on the grounds that Toši's mother's Hungarian citizenship (and with luck Génilde's pregnancy) would help him to protect her from further danger. The marriage proved ill advised and fell apart shortly after the birth of their second child. But Génilde did at least survive the war – and, indeed, is alive at the time of writing. Ra was unable, however, to save Génilde's brother Norbert from forced labour. And he was entirely helpless when, in 1943, the Germans occupying Karlova Koruna allowed a huge fire to break out, destroying the main domed tower and leaving most of the rest of the property uninhabitable.

Lata seems to have taken an equally happy-go-lucky approach. When the Nazis tried to requisition Řitka's horses, she managed to sweet-talk the major in charge into categorising Hostivít, wrongly, as unfit for service. She then redoubled the risk, for her and for 'the brave major', by describing the incident in a letter to Lori. Perhaps it never occurred to her that the letter might fall into the wrong hands. Perhaps she simply scorned caution.

Another time, according to family tradition, the Gestapo attempted a round-up of one or more people of Russian origin in and around Řitka – presumably including Kasian Rusniak, the former prisoner of war who lived up in the woods and worked on the (regime-administered) Brandis estate. Lata went straight to Gestapo headquarters in Prague, carrying her horse whip, and complained very forcibly (presumably in German) that 'a gentleman does not behave like this'. The Russian(s) were soon returned.

More recklessly, Lata insisted on keeping a rifle on the estate, hidden in a hay loft. This was a crime punishable by death – as Lata came perilously close to finding out when, at some point in 1942, an unidentified farmhand found it and handed it over to the Gestapo in Jíloviště. Lata was named as the assumed owner, but Hanuš Kasalický appears to have used his influence to make the case go away. If nothing else, this suggests that the bond of affection between them had not been entirely broken.

The Gestapo were not squeamish about punishing respectable ladies. Being female reduced your chances of being ordered to commit terrible acts in wartime; it did not protect you from having them done to you. Several of the First Republic's most prominent female activists, including Františka Plamínková and Milada Horáková, had already been sent to concentration camps. Plamínková was executed in June 1942; Horáková survived to be executed by a subsequent totalitarian regime. Lata may not have been aware of such details, but she must have known the kind of people she was up against, and the small value they placed on Czech lives. Yet cowed submission was not in her nature, and somehow her cheerful insubordination infected those around her.

One day, Markéta's husband, Sergej Jaroševský, defied regulations by slaughtering one of Řitka's pigs. This was illegal. Livestock belonged to the regime. But the family and farmworkers needed food, and Josef Satorie – who had by now developed a close relationship with Lata's resident cousin, Gikina – not only turned a blind eye but lent a hand with the slaughter. This turned out to be a noisy process, and reports of the squeals reached the Gestapo. Some officers came to investigate. Satorie denied everything and the Gestapo left empty-handed.

Then there was the time that the contessas decided that villagers were tired of the ban on public gatherings and needed cheering up. They organised an impromptu May Day dance in the chateau, with a gramophone playing in the kitchen. 'I'll never forget it,' said Františka Mašková, the village carpenter's daughter, more than seventy years later. 'We all went. I was just a teenager. We danced the whole night. There were waltzes, polkas, old Czech dances. I can still remember the tiles on the kitchen floor, and the cold air on my bare arms when we walked home in the early morning. It was magical.'

Spreading magic was part of what Lata and her sisters saw as their duty. Someone needed to keep morale up, and although much of their inherited privilege had vanished, their sense of inherited responsibility remained. Lata, as a local and national hero, could project the idea that all was well simply by being there. She lacked the popular touch but, instead, had what you might call the aristocratic touch. Tall, graceful, kind, upright, she never betrayed anxiety or fear. Villagers watched her riding to church on Holomek, and noted that the horse, despite spending the rest of the week working in Řitka's yard, was as beautifully turned out as its rider. Somehow it felt as though, despite Heydrich, the village life they had always known was still intact, and would endure.

Sometimes, however, there was a price to be paid. On a cold May evening in 1944, Markéta, unexpectedly soaked by rain, insisted on fulfilling a commitment to read the litany for a service outside Řitka's little roadside chapel. The next day, she had a fever; a few days later, it was pneumonia. They managed to get her to a hospital in

Prague, but there were no antibiotics. A few weeks later she was dead.

Lata, Kristýna and Johanna immediately assumed responsibility for bringing up her seven-year-old son, Petr. His father, Sergej Jaroševský, had had to find work some way outside the village, and had been coming home only at weekends. So the sisters, reeling from their own loss, had to find it within themselves to provide, between them, all the mothering their distraught nephew needed. 'They always made me feel loved,' Petr remembers tearfully today. 'I was never lost, with them.'

As if that wasn't enough to worry about, Alžběta's twenty-three-year-old son Jan was soon in hospital as well, suffering from pleurisy. He spent much of that winter being treated. Lata shared her concerns with Lori Kinský. 'You know Lori,' she wrote, 'when my heart becomes very heavy, then I think to myself: the dear Lord God knows best how he arranges things, after all. One must trust in him ... But Lori, despite all my confidence, I am still very anxious about the boy ...'

A fortnight later she wrote again: 'I would like to wish you with all my heart a good and merry Christmas and a happy 1945. In these hard times, however, it seems almost like a mockery ...'

§ - § - §

In fact, it was the most hopeful new year the world had seen for a while. The old year had already brought hints that the tide was turning: the relief of Leningrad (January), the D-Day landings (June), the (failed) Slovak National Uprising (August); and the liberation of Rome

(June), of Paris (July), and, in September, of Kalinov, near the Dukla Pass on Slovakia's eastern border. But you didn't hear much about such Nazi reversals in the Protectorate's mainstream media; and in most places, including Řitka, there were more local troubles to worry about. The Allies were still disembarking on Normandy's beaches when Markéta breathed her last.

By 1945, however, it was hard not to notice the change. The Nazis were worried, which made them more dangerous but also less terrifying. At Velká Chuchle, the regime's new insecurity had resulted, since September 1944, in racing being closed to the public. Horses still raced, but only in Saturday 'breeding tests', accessible only to Jockey Club members, stable owners and licensed racing personnel. Lata is unlikely to have had anything to do with these, although she did still exercise horses sometimes for Šmejda. Like most people, she had gradually lowered her horizons in the interests of sanity and survival. But she must have sensed the new atmosphere. And it must have occurred to her that, if she could hang on for just a few more months, the Nazi nightmare might end – and things might return to how they had once been.

One spring day, patrolling the woods with horse and dog, Lata came across a wounded man. If family accounts are accurate, he was a Russian soldier, hurt in battle and on the run. Lata told no one but Kristýna. The fewer people who knew, the fewer there were who could be caught and punished. They managed to treat his wounds – Lata is said to have made use of her stock of horse medicines – and provided him with food until he was well enough to link up with local partisans, who were hiding out in the woods near Mníšek pod Brdy.

As the year progressed, the number of Czech partisans increased. Across the Protectorate, there may have been as many as 7,500. Their hideouts moved closer to Řitka. Lata ensured that food was made available to them. A row of potatoes in the vegetable garden was left in the ground, so that they could be taken at night. Lata took additional supplies up to the woods in a churn, returning with the churn filled with water from a hill-top well. To the casual observer, she appeared to be fetching water; none the less, villagers seemed to know about it. This, again, was high-risk behaviour: getting caught meant death. But perhaps now it felt as though it might not be a purposeless death.

People felt much the same all over what remained of occupied Europe. Men and women who had been keeping their heads down sensed that, if they seized the moment, they could liberate themselves. Those who had thrown in their lot with the Nazis began to fear that they had backed the wrong side. Some decided that it was not too late to switch. In Berlin, Hermann Fegelein, whose work with the SS Cavalry had helped him become one of Hitler's very closest henchmen (he had even married Eva Braun's sister), made hurried plans to desert but was caught red-handed. Hitler had him shot on 28 April, drunk and strapped to a chair. Two days later, the Führer took his own life.

The Red Army had reached Zlín by then, in the south-east, and was advancing slowly towards Prague. In the north-west, the Americans had reached Pilsen. Rumours were swirling about uprisings in various parts of the

Protectorate; some of them were true. In Řitka, hopeful young men were drifting into the woods, keen to associate themselves with the partisans. Finally, the Czechs of Prague decided that their time had come. On 5 May, two announcers on the official radio channel defied Nazi censors by speaking only in Czech and playing only Czech music. The Waffen-SS – whose leader in the Protectorate, Jockey Club president Count von Pückler-Berghaus, had promised to drown any revolt 'in a sea of blood' – moved in to stop them. Soon there was fighting in and around the radio building on Vinohradská street. At 12.33 p.m., a desperate broadcast went out: 'Calling all Czechs! Come to our aid immediately! Come and defend Czech radio!' People responded. Word spread. This time, the Czechs were going to fight. They were going to liberate themselves.

By the time rebels had secured the radio building, seventy-nine people had died in that battle alone. But the fire they had lit could not be put out. A full-scale uprising was in progress. The Gestapo headquarters were occupied, hundreds of barricades were erected. The Germans must have known that the Protectorate was doomed. Nonetheless, they fought back fiercely: Poldi von Fugger, whose unit's retreat from the east had briefly brought him all the way back to Prague, was among those who did so. Count von Pückler-Berghaus even tried to call in airstrikes on the city. The gunfire and the explosions could be heard in Velká Chuchle. Those who heard knew immediately what it meant.

Lata heard. She got on her bicycle and headed for Prague. Reaching the River Vltava, she was stopped by rumours that the Germans had booby-trapped the bridges. Instead she found a boat to take her across. She then found her way to the big Sokol gym near Vyšehrad, where for the next three days she worked more or less non-stop, nursing the wounded. Her sisters had no idea where she was.

Karel Šmejda remained in Velká Chuchle, keeping an eye on his horses. The fighting continued, and spread south and west from Prague as German forces fought for survival – or, if they could get far enough west, for the opportunity to surrender to the Americans rather than the Russians. By 7 May, there was a large, heavily armed Waffen-SS presence in and around Velká Chuchle. A curfew was imposed.

Many villagers had fled by then, along with a number of horses, to a small settlement on the far side of the hill. Other horses were trickier to move and thus remained in the stables. That evening, the gunfire grew so loud that Šmejda became concerned for their wellbeing. 'That's all he wanted,' says Jan Zágler, Eduard Zágler's son: 'to make sure his horses were all right. He was such a gentle, kind man.' Ignoring the curfew, Šmejda walked to the stables to feed, water and reassure them. He was shot dead by a German machine-gunner before he could get back to his place of safety.

That morning, at 2.41, Germany had surrendered unconditionally to the Allies. The ceasefire took effect the following morning, at one minute after midnight.

# 26.

# Brave new world

It proved harder than expected to celebrate. After more than six years of Nazi tyranny, Prague was officially liberated on 9 May. The Red Army claimed the credit, although the Czechs had done most of it themselves. Even then, fighting continued outside the city. That same day, a train carrying ammunition exploded near Velká Chuchle station, setting fire to the nearby stables. Despite heroic rescue efforts, three horses could not be saved from the inferno.

The last Germans surrendered on 11 May. The following day, SS-Gruppenführer Count von Pückler-Berghaus, under house arrest in Čimelice, killed first his family and then himself. The Jockey Club president had been apprehended with the help of Norbert Kinský, now working for the Americans as an interpreter. His suicide has been described as 'the last shot fired in the war in Europe'. By then, more than 3,000 Czechs had lost their lives in the Prague area in less than a week. No one counted the German losses, but many Czechs took savage revenge.

The woods above Řitka were soon full of Soviet soldiers. Thousands camped there until June. Locals greeted them with garlands, but were glad to see the back of them when they left.

Then, sooner than anyone had expected, it was back to the grind of survival. Czechoslovakia had got off lightly compared with most of Europe. Yet there were still so many loved ones to mourn, so much material loss to be made good, so much wrong to forgive.

Edvard Beneš's restored government, ruling mainly by decree for the first five months, decided to keep forgiveness to a minimum. Czechs deemed to have collaborated with the Nazis had their property confiscated. (Kasalický lost half of his. His wife was eventually allowed to keep the other half, on the grounds that they had been living more or less separate lives.) The justice was rough: the local People's Courts that administered it often had private agendas to pursue. Some felt that it was better than no justice at all.

The nation's remaining German minority were presumed guilty of collaboration and stripped of their citizenship. Those who could prove that they had resisted the Nazis were allowed to apply to become citizens again. The rest had to leave. Reliable figures are impossible to come by, given the post-war chaos, but by the end of 1947 more than two million people had been expelled, mostly to Germany. The ethnic cleansing was enforced so harshly that anything between 10,000 and 30,000 people died in the course of it. The rest of the world barely noticed, so numb had people become to atrocity.

But they noticed in Řitka. Lata's German-born cousin, Gikina, was among those eligible for expulsion – a threat that may have encouraged Josef Satorie, already probably her lover, to propose marriage. Soon afterwards, the newly-wed Satories moved to the eastern Sudetenland, where the state employed Josef to protect the estates of expelled Germans from looting and degradation. Meanwhile, the National Land Committee was considering confiscating two-sevenths of the Brandis estate to reflect the fact that Marie Therese and Gabriele had, in effect, identified themselves as German: the former by living in Austria, the latter by spending much of the war there and, now, moving there permanently. (It was even alleged that she had become a Reich citizen in 1941.) The local committee that initially proposed this action may not have been entirely disinterested: most confiscated land was divided into small lots and allocated to small local landowners.

The case took time to resolve, but the newly restored Řitka estate appears to have been placed almost immediately into provisional administration. This was partly an emergency measure. The departing German administration had left the estate with nothing: even the harvest and seeds had been taken away. That was the price Lata had paid for being among the minority of aristocrats who stood by the Czech nation in the face of Nazism. Now there was a new price to be paid. The plundered estate had too few resources remaining to it to support a workforce big enough to put things right. Some labourers were reported to be moving instead to the Sudetenland, seeking newly vacated properties with which to make a fresh start. At the same time, Lata and her sisters found themselves on the receiving end of an obscure claim relating to the question of what had happened to the non-fixed assets of Řitka's tenant farmer, Vladimír Daneš, following their confiscation in 1941 – and who, if anyone, had ultimately benefited from them. The arguments were confusing, and we will not get bogged down in them. But we have not heard the last of this claim, and nor had Lata.

It barely needs adding that, whatever the rights and wrongs of these cases, it cannot have been pleasant for Lata to have had them hanging over her, so soon after the liberation. Even now, it feels slightly shocking. She had done her bit for her country before and during the war. She must have been looking forward to a time in which, once again, she could enjoy 'the feeling that, far and wide, there was no one who did not like me'. Instead, with the blood barely dry on the streets of Prague, her fellow Czechs seemed to be turning on her.

§ - § - §

In 1946, elections were held. The Communists, who by now had more than a million members, were the most successful single party, with 38 per cent of the vote but no overall majority. The next two years were marked by bitter, dirty political infighting between Communists, social democrats (many of them in the party known as the National Socialists) and smaller parties. The Communists insisted on control of the ministry of the interior. This allowed them to make ruthless use of the security services. It also meant that land reform remained high on the political agenda.

All this cast a shadow over Lata's life. She probably wasn't too bothered about ceasing to be rich; and she was used to being considered a class enemy. What must have hurt was the fear of losing her past. Řitka was all that remained of that lost period of innocence, half a lifetime earlier, when her parents had been alive and well, her days had been full of laughter and outdoor play, the pains of adulthood were unimagined, and a benign, whiskery Emperor had embodied the promise that the world would never change. She had never left home. To have all that torn from her now would be like losing a part of herself. That's the trouble with idyllic childhoods: it's hard to let them go.

She tried to pick up the pieces of her past regardless, and to enjoy some kind of return to the way things had been before the Nazis came. It wasn't easy. With Šmejda dead and Kasalický out of reach or out of bounds, Velká Chuchle was no longer the attraction it had been. But Orlík was still there, and for a while Lata resumed her visits, when Ra and Lori were in residence. She rode there, naturally, and sometimes she took Petr Jaroševský with her, tucking her ten-year-old nephew onto the saddle in front of her.

There was also Obora. Lata went there at least once after the war – the seventh prince Karel Schwarzenberg, son of Ra's stepson Karel (and a significant figure in twenty-first-century Czech politics), remembers seeing her there. It would be nice to think that, while she was there, she was reunited with Norma. Sadly, there is no proof that Norma survived the war. We know that she was alive in 1943, and by one account until April 1944; after that, the trail goes cold. Perhaps she and Lata did indeed meet again. But the golden heroine of 1937 was already so forgotten, her glory so submerged in subsequent history, that no one kept a record of how, where or when her life ended. It was a sad prefiguring of the fate awaiting her rider.

§ - § - §

In October 1946, Pardubice racecourse reopened for business. The Nazis had converted it into an airfield;

their overthrow had resulted in forty-two bomb craters. Yet two months of frantic repairs had made the course ready for the first Velká Pardubická since 1937. Huge crowds descended on the town, which was decked out as if for a festival: one account mentions 'specially illuminated historical buildings, decorated shops, social evenings, fashion shows and a crowded theatre'. Many officers of the Allied armies, notably the English and French, had promised to attend, and did so. So did more than 50,000 other people – far more than the course could safely accommodate.

There was, of course, no question of East Prussian involvement. Even ignoring the fact that Germans were not welcome in Czechoslovakia, there was no East Prussia left. The frontier land of the Trakehners and their riders had been utterly obliterated in the post-war settlement. More than two million civilians were forcibly evacuated to Germany, and at least 300,000 people (along with around 18,500 out of 20,000 Trakehner horses) had died in the course of a westward journey so cruel that, even now, it hardly bears thinking about. But I doubt if many people thought about that in Pardubice in October 1946.

Instead, a race-day ceremony paid tribute to the Czech war dead associated with the race, including Karel Šmejda, trainer of the last winner; Josef Charous; and Arno Košťál, executed owner of the Hotel Veselka.

The organisers struggled to contain the crowds within their allotted areas, and the chaos, though cheerful, caused delays. Eventually, however, the Velká Pardubická runners appeared on the course. Lata rode Nurmi, a four-year-old stallion who lacked the placid temperament of his mother, Norma. When it came to the trial jump, Nurmi refused – but in time-honoured tradition was allowed to race anyway.

It was hardly worth it. Nurmi ran strongly for three jumps but fell badly at Taxis. Lata, catapulted ahead as he hit the ditch, was lucky not to be crushed as he somersaulted after her. Nurmi was unhurt; Lata suffered a broken collar bone and a severely bruised shoulder. There was no point in carrying on: this was no life or death struggle between nations and ideologies. While the rest of the field charged into the distance (Titan, ridden by Captain Miloš Svoboda, was the eventual winner), Lata was escorted from the course by some French army officers – a well-meant gesture that she is said to have found patronising and irritating.

§ - § - §

Lata's injuries healed slowly: she was now fifty-one. Her convalescence cannot have been helped by an increasingly fraught political atmosphere. A nationwide drought in 1947 caused a crisis in food production. To ease it, the government introduced a 'millionaires' tax' – a one-off levy on those with assets of more than a million crowns – to be paid into a Fund for National Renewal. That same summer saw the enactment of Law 142/1947, a legislative attempt (overseen in the Czech lands by the Communists) to complete the unfinished business of land reform. The First Republic's programme had confiscated around four million hectares of land – roughly half of big landowners' landholdings – but attempts to expropriate more had ground to a halt thanks to a combination of patient lobbying and practical difficulties. Now, with the Communists in charge of the ministry of the interior, a more aggressive programme was introduced. Broadly speaking, private holdings were limited to fifty hectares, which meant that, once the administrative wrangling had been completed, all the woods above Řitka would pass into new ownership. Ironically, the expulsion of all those Germans had meant that the supply of land now exceeded demand, but the Communists were determined to destroy large landholdings anyway, as a matter of principle. Most woodland ended up with the State Forest Administration. At around the same time, the burned remains of Ra's Karlova Koruna were taken into state ownership – in due course being converted into a museum. And although he retained Obora for a little longer, the state soon seized the vast forests around it.

Lata tried to carry on as before. So did Ra. It was hard to see any other way of clinging to normality. So it was that, in July, fully fit once again, Lata rode Ra's temperamental stallion, Otello – father of Nurmi – in the Velká Poděbradská steeplechase in Poděbrady. They were unplaced but, on the bright side, Lata was uninjured. A few weeks later, she, Ra and Génilde all rode in the Kunětická Hora steeplechase in Pardubice. Jan Masaryk (by then foreign minister) was among those who watched Lata win on Nora, another Norma foal. Ra came second on Nurmi while Génilde – twenty-two and married – came third on her own favourite mare, Puszta. It was, commented Masaryk, 'a bit of a family affair'.

But it was clear that this kind of comfortable exclusivity could not continue. Lata's world was under attack again, and this time the attackers weren't going away. All through that year, politicians such as Masaryk and Milada

Horáková (once she had recovered from what the Nazis had done to her) fought stubbornly to preserve the traditions of First Republic democracy. But the Communists had the momentum. They were backed by Moscow, but there was also wide popular support for the idea that it was time to govern for the many, not the few. Traditional capitalism had delivered two catastrophic wars in three decades. Could a new system really do worse? As for the pre-war ruling class, hadn't they failed the nation and, in many cases, betrayed it? Why should they not be stripped of their privileges? This last argument was a little unfair on those who hadn't betrayed anyone but, on the contrary, had risked life and property to defend their nation. That didn't stop the champions of change from making it. This was not a time of nuanced debate.

In October 1947, Lata returned to Pardubice. It was an even bigger occasion than the previous year, although this time the organisers were better prepared for the vast crowds. The prize money for the winner had been almost doubled – to 150,000 crowns – and the number of foreign visitors reflected this. The sixteen runners included five French horses, with officers from the French, Bulgarian and Czech armed forces among their riders. Lata rode Otello, the most exciting of Ra's horses but also the least governable and most aggressive. (He was put down a few years later after killing his groom with a bite to the neck.)

By the time they reached the start, Otello was in his most volcanic, hellraising mood. Even Lata struggled to control him. After much bucking and rearing, he bolted. Lata could only sit tight as Otello charged towards a distant corner of the course. Meanwhile, the frenzy had spread. Vítěz bolted, too, and refused to stop until he had gone all the way back to the military riding school in the centre of Pardubice. His jockey, Zdeněk Widner, never lived down the embarrassment – and never stopped blaming Lata for his involuntary gallop through the streets. Lata took fifteen minutes to get Otello back to the start, whereupon the race began.

Otello set off like a rocket. He was well ahead at the approach to Taxis, which Lata hoped to jump on the right. At the last minute he veered left. He cleared the jump but left a nine-horse pile-up behind him. All but two remounted, and in due course Otello was overhauled. He had already squandered half his energy; by halfway he had lost his enthusiasm. At the Irish Bank, he refused. Lata could not persuade him to change his mind and, indeed, may not have tried too hard to do so. Otello was not going to win anything that day. It was a relief to get back to the stables, but also a deep disappointment: another year, another failure to complete the course. How many more chances would she get?

§ - § - §

Four months later, Czechoslovakia became, in effect, a one-party state. The Communists provoked their coalition partners into resigning from government, then intimidated President Beneš into letting them govern alone. Formerly democratic ministries were occupied by the secret police; the army was confined to barracks; a general strike was organised; people's militias roamed the streets. By the end of 'Victorious February', Czechoslovakia's Communist era had begun. There would not be another free election for over forty years.

On 10 March, Jan Masaryk died mysteriously, falling out of a window. Losers of political battles in the Czech lands have often suffered from such accidents. (The Defenestrations of Prague of 1419 and 1618 are the two most famous examples.) For the Communists' opponents, Masaryk's death epitomised their methods: backed by Moscow, they used violence and intimidation to achieve their ends, then denied everything. By May, when a new constitution formalised the Communist takeover, there wasn't even any need to deny. There were no opposition parties, no free press; soon there would be no one who dared to accuse the Party of wrongdoing. Beneš, broken, resigned in June. He died three months later. Czechoslovak democracy had predeceased him.

In Řitka, nothing changed. Ivy still clung to the chateau's long front wall. The farm girls still sang as they worked in the fields. The same ancient forest covered the hills beyond, irrespective of ownership. In the stables, three six-year-old mares rubbed shoulders with twenty dairy cows. Lata probably still rode in the woods, and on Sundays she certainly rode to church. A young village boy, Jiří Mudr, whose parents lived in Prague but had just begun to build a weekend cottage in Řitka, used to wave at her. After a while, Lata began to pause and greet him: 'Hello, boy from Prague.' Then, as they became friends, she would lean down, scoop him up and put him on the saddle in front of her. They would ride together through the village. 'She was very elegant, always beautifully dressed, but she always remembered me,' says Mudr, who still lives in Řitka today. 'She would ask me questions: did I go to school? Did I like Prague? I'll never forget her voice. Sometimes she'd give me a sweet.' Then she would set him down and ride on alone to Líšnice, where her sisters would be waiting in the family pew.

This was life as Lata understood it. Her role was to serve God and to serve her community, to be kind to children and animals, and to keep up traditions that had served her family well. But tradition could no longer be relied upon; and what replaced it might prove harsh, if you were an aristocrat. The previous August, Law 143/1947 Sb – widely known as the Lex Schwarzenberg – had provided for the confiscation of all the property of, specifically, the Schwarzenberg family, including Orlík. A special law was needed because, in contrast to most confiscation victims, the Schwarzenbergs could not be faulted for their wartime conduct. Ra's stepson Karel was considered a hero of Prague's liberation (although his worst injuries resulted from accepting a lift from a drunken motorcyclist). But he was still an obscenely privileged aristocrat. In 1945 and 1946 he was often guest of honour at events celebrating the liberation. By 1947, such invitations had dried up. Orlík was taken over by the state, and by 1948, according to Karel's son (then aged ten), 'People were crossing the street to avoid him.' The Schwarzenbergs fled to Austria.

For the rest of the former nobility, it was just a matter of waiting to see how bad the worst would be. Most of them could still inhabit the homes they had grown up in and enjoy the familiar estates around them – for now. But their world was being dismantled, with upsetting enthusiasm. At some point soon – perhaps within weeks, perhaps within months – all those memories and comforts would be wrenched from them. This may have been fair. Even so, it must have felt a little bit like waiting for a loved one to die.

The Kinskýs' remaining estates were seized as 1948 unfolded, along with their horses. That June, Ra's son Norbert married in Italy. Ra and Lori went to the wedding and never returned. Norbert's younger brother Radslav, a brilliant geneticist who was then doing military service in Pardubice, remained in Czechoslovakia and would eventually find menial employment as an unskilled worker on a state farm at Slatiňany. Génilde, too, stayed behind, but soon found herself in trouble with the secret police, the Státní bezpečnost (StB). Her hastily arranged marriage was all but over; her soon-to-be-ex-husband, (ex-)Count Dobrzenský, was abroad; and the StB felt that the young Génilde was ripe for exploitation as an informant. Génilde was approached but refused to cooperate, at which point threats were made that involved her two young children (then close to their fifth and second birthdays). 'I realised,' she says today, 'that I would have to escape.' She made enquiries, found a people smuggler, and prepared a high-risk escape plan.

§ - § - §

That October's Velká Pardubická was a low-key affair, with only eleven runners. Foreign visitors were notable by their absence. Lata did not attend either. Instead, on the weekend of the race, she cycled to Prague, where Génilde still had her marital home. This was not prudent, given the political climate. But it was a visit that Lata was determined to make.

Her relationship with Génilde had always been a close one. The disappearance of so many family members on both sides had made it closer: Lata was almost a stand-in mother. So Lata knew that this was the night on which Génilde planned to leave Czechoslovakia. 'She was in on the secret,' says Génilde. 'So she came in the evening to say goodbye. She was very kind.' In addition to saying fond farewells, Lata gave her some sleeping pills – which may have been a herbal concoction made from a family recipe. (It is conceivable that they were originally intended for horses …) 'She told me to give them to my baby.' This was good advice, up to a point. Czechoslovakia's Communist paradise was barely eight months old, but already a two-mile exclusion zone had been established on the border to block the flood of people wanting to leave. Génilde had to find her way undetected to a certain abandoned cottage within the zone, on the north-western border near Cheb, and wait there, in silence and darkness, until the people smuggler came for her. If a cry from twenty-three-month-old Harry alerted the border police, a lengthy prison sentence was the best that Génilde could expect. 'We had to stay there most of the night, waiting. We couldn't have any light and we couldn't make any noise.' Harry also had to be kept quiet during the final walk across the border into Germany. 'Lata gave me four pills,' says Génilde. 'But when it came to it I was worried that it might kill my baby. So I only gave him one.'

This was probably just as well. Young Harry – whom Génilde carried in a blanket while leading his brother Václav by the hand – spent the entire escape in the profoundest of sleeps. Anything profounder might have been irreversible. Yet his silence did at least allow the young family to make their way undetected through the hills on foot, on a black autumn night, into the safety of the US zone of occupied Germany. Later, after a spell in a refugee camp, they reached Switzerland, where Génilde found work as a chambermaid. Later still, in 1949, she was able to join Ra and Lori in Italy.

By then, the message had got back to Lata that the escape had been successful. Initially, however, she had no way of confirming that her beloved Génilde was safe. Yet she did have faith that all was well: partly because she would probably have heard about it had things gone wrong but also for a more personal reason. 'She gave me a medallion,' says Génilde. 'It had a picture of the Virgin Mary on it. She said: "I wore this medallion in every race I rode, and it kept me safe. So I hope now you will get safely over the border."'

They never saw one another again, but I have no doubt that Lata comforted herself with the thought that her gift had helped protect Génilde and her children from the many dangers they faced. But there was danger in Lata's life, too.

# 27.

# The fall

Lata's world was emptying. In ones and twos, in different ways, those who had meant most to her had departed: Ra, Lori, Génilde; Šmejda; Kasalický; the Schwarzenbergs, the Satories. Her family was dwindling, too, with three siblings dead and two living permanently in Austria, beyond the newly drawn Iron Curtain. Alžběta and her children were in Prague; Sergej Jaroševský had moved with Petr to Moravia. Life in Řitka continued in its familiar rhythms, more or less. But it sometimes felt ghostly.

She still had Kristýna and Johanna. Apart from that, little could be relied upon. She still had her home, but for how much longer? As for horses – in whose unfailing good nature she had always placed so much faith – it was hard to feel confident that they would be part of her world for much longer. The Communists didn't approve of horses, sensing, correctly, that they were a crucial component of the world they had come to destroy. It wasn't just that the privileged classes kept horses and employed the less privileged to help them do so. In the pre-war world, as we have seen, there had barely been a Czech or Slovak life in which horses played no role. The rural economy was built around them. Small, independent farmers – neither privileged nor collective-minded – were synonymous with horse-ownership. So, in a sense, was Czechoslovak democracy. Tomáš Masaryk, coachman's son, often rode in public and sometimes wandered into crowds on horseback to chat. His habitual closeness to horses was seen as entirely consistent with his preference for the company of ordinary people: it emphasised his ordinariness, not his importance.

The horse, in short, could be seen as a symbol of bourgeois individualism as well as feudalism. What it didn't symbolise was Communism. In the first decade of Czechoslovakia's Communist regime, 300,000 horses are thought to have been sent to the slaughterhouse. Estates that had once kept horses became agricultural collectives, in which tractors replaced horsepower. Racehorses, studs and stables were mostly taken into collective or state ownership. (The Kinskýs' horses, perhaps including Norma, ended up at the state farm at Slatiňany – where Radslav did his best to ensure that the breed was not wiped out entirely.) The Prague Jockey Club was abolished and replaced by the partly state-run Czechoslovak Racing Association. Racing continued, but the days in which the rich and fashionable gathered at the track to see and be seen – and 'gentleman' owners rode their own horses when they chose, or allocated them to favoured cousins – were over. This was a less frivolous kind of racing. There wasn't much place in it for Lata.

§ - § - §

But even the Communists did not dare to come between Czechoslovaks and their Velká Pardubická, and Lata, in turn, was not prepared to abandon her favourite racing event without a struggle.

The 1949 race was another quiet one. The foreign visitors continued to stay away; so did some domestic ones. A number of long-serving racecourse staff were absent, too: starter, judges, course inspector, handicapper and course vet had all been replaced by more politically acceptable appointments. Of the eighteen runners, all but four were owned by state farms rather than private individuals. Two, Nora and Čingischán, were Kinský horses, owned and trained by the state farm (strictly speaking the State Experimental Horse-breeding Institute) at Slatiňany.

Lata was unable to get a ride on either, or on any other Velká Pardubická horses. At fifty-four, she probably didn't seem like the asset in the saddle that she had once been – even though the standard of those who did ride does not appear to have been particularly high. But what she stood for – old-world privilege and First Republic self-belief – probably counted against her as well.

Even so, she had persuaded the Slatiňany state farm to give her a ride in the last race of the day, the soon-to-be-renamed Kinský Memorial Steeplechase. On a five-year-old bay mare called Naďa – Norma's daughter – she lined up at the start with five other runners at around 4 p.m. One of them was Génilde's brother Radslav Kinský. He had not attempted to escape himself because someone had to stay behind in Czechoslovakia to look out for the children, if Génilde was caught and jailed. He was riding a dark buckskin Kinský horse called Nella on behalf of its new owners, the military riding school at Stará Boleslav.

Učeň, owned by the Pardubice military riding school and ridden by Captain Oldřich Dostál, had won the

Velká Pardubická about an hour earlier, but there were still plenty of spectators, many of them not in the stands but at strategic vantage points around the course. The Memorial race includes most of the key Velká Pardubická jumps, apart from Taxis, but is about half the distance, without all the ploughed fields. The conditions were challenging, however. It was 23 October, about a fortnight later than usual, and heavy rain, possibly coupled with mishandling of sluice gates, had left the water obstacles filled to overflowing. In the Velká Pardubická, only five out of eighteen runners had reached the finish. In the Memorial race, most of the twenty-two horses which had originally been entered had dropped out before the start. Of those that remained, Naďa and Lata had as good a chance as any.

It was the first time Lata had started a Pardubice race without wearing the Kinský colours. It was the first time she had started without wearing her Virgin Mary medallion, which she believed had kept her safe in all her steeplechases so far. Yet she must have felt confident, because she also started without a helmet. Shortly before the race she had lent hers to one of the other jockeys – a young man who for some reason had been unable to obtain one. According to Lata, he was 'afraid to ride without it'.

The race began. For the first two obstacles, Coura-Iris led from Nella and Naďa. Then Rival, Petar and Viking II moved up to challenge. All six horses approached the Snake Ditch in a bunch, with Lata and Naďa just at the back with Nella and Petar. Then the Snake struck. Not for the first time that day, the horses failed to decode the glistening waters of the ditch-only obstacle, whose overflowing contents merged edgelessly with the wet turf on the far side. Coura-Iris plunged in, catapulting Captain Bozděch from his saddle. Viking II did much the same with Lieutenant Král. Naďa, jumping after them through a curtain of spray, was already in the air when Lata noticed the two fallen horses below.

No one quite saw what happened next, except that Petar came to grief at almost exactly the same moment. Radslav, jumping fractionally behind, always worried afterwards that Nella might have clipped Lata with a stray hoof, but there was no evidence of that. One picture seems to suggest that Lata – if it is her – landed on her head. Other accounts suggest, plausibly, that it was the flailing horses on the ground that were her undoing.

All we can say for certain is that, after Captain Bozděch had remounted Coura-Iris and galloped off in pursuit of the other surviving runners, three horses and three riders remained at the Snake Ditch. Nella and Viking II merely needed to be helped out of the water, but Petar was dead, having half cleared the ditch but broken his neck on landing. The three jockeys were alive, but all three – Lata, Lieutenant Král and Petar's rider, J. Vágner – appeared to be seriously injured.

It took time for medical help to arrive: crowds on the course impeded the ambulance. Rumours of catastrophic injuries exacerbated the problem. By the time the ambulance reached the Snake Ditch, there were clear signs of life from Král and Vágner but Lata remained motionless. She was still unconscious when she reached the nearby hospital, half an hour or so after the accident. Král and Vágner were by then being described as having only minor injuries, but Lata's appeared to be life-threatening. Before long, rumours were circulating that she was dead.

Later, Communist propagandists are said to have added the insinuation that, knowing that she was on the wrong side of history, the former countess had deliberately tried to kill herself.

§ - § - §

Lata could not defend herself. She was still in a coma several days later, although she uttered occasional monosyllables and sometimes cried out at night. By then she had been diagnosed with injuries including a fractured skull, a broken collar bone, a complex fracture of her left leg, a fractured sacrum, a damaged spine, several broken ribs, vaginal bleeding and assorted bruises and flesh wounds, notably on her right leg. When she fully recovered consciousness, five days after the fall, additional ailments revealed themselves, such as double vision and shaky limb movements.

She insisted, quite forcefully, that she did not want to be treated by doctors. She wanted someone to summon a vet instead. She may have had a specific vet in mind: perhaps Jaroslav Drobný from Městec Králové, who worked regularly for the Kinskýs and may have been important to her. More probably it was a symptom of confusion, or of a more generalised sense that it is better to put your trust in the world of horses than in the world of men.

Her twelve-year-old nephew visited with his aunts. 'She didn't recognise me at all,' Petr Jaroševský remembers. 'I was terribly upset.' But gradually the clouds cleared. As they did so, it became clearer how much discomfort she was in. She said that her whole body ached. She said that she felt as if she had been beaten up.

Doctors removed a shotgun pellet from her head. She said that she thought she knew how it had got there, years earlier, when she and others were shooting in Řitka's woods. She had never thought it worth doing anything about it.

She also claimed to remember everything about the race up until the fall itself. One account quotes her as describing it as follows: 'There were two horses lying in the Snake Ditch. When I saw them, it was too late. Naďa had already taken off. I pulled her back, but you're not supposed to do that. She tripped over something with her front leg, we went down, and other horses fell over us.' As for not having worn a helmet, she said that she was glad that she had lent hers to the young man who needed it (presumably either Král, Vágner or Bozděch): 'Maybe it helped him – who knows? Otherwise he might have crippled himself.'

By mid-November, getting on for a month after the race, she was becoming more like herself. 'The patient does not complain of anything,' noted the doctor. A week or so later, she was able to walk, shakily. She still suffered occasionally from double vision, and she had difficulties with balance. None the less, on 3 December she was ready to go home.

The hospital's report on her injuries and treatment ran to four closely typed pages.

She was told she would never ride again. 'Oh yes I will,' she said. 'Like the Devil!'

But the Devil had different ideas.

# 28.

# Enemy of the people

Perhaps she found peace in Řitka. If so, it was short-lived. The Communist revolution – two years old in February 1950 – was entering its cruellest phase. Dissenters were being arrested; concentration camps were filling up; show trials were being prepared; the StB were recruiting informers by the thousand. Across the country, semi-spontaneous Local Action Committees had sprung up to advance and enforce the Communist agenda. Even Řitka had one.

Those familiar, ivy-clad walls could not insulate the Brandis sisters from the harsh winds: you could feel them everywhere. In May and June, for example, the entire nation heard radio broadcasts of the trial of Milada Horáková, feminist, democrat and wartime resistance activist, who was accused, absurdly, of counter-revolutionary crimes ranging from plotting to kidnap Party leaders to fomenting nuclear war. Suitably prepared by torture, she and her twelve co-defendants were supposed to stick to an agreed script during the trial, although Horáková repeatedly deviated from it. Meanwhile, the entire nation was encouraged to join in a 'spontaneous' hate campaign against the accused. Millions succumbed to the pressure. In Řitka, the Action Committee convened a public meeting on 7 June, which approved a statement calling for the 'severest possible penalty' for these 'monsters' and 'pariahs'. (Horáková and three others were hanged.) If Lata and her sisters did not participate – and I don't think they did – this will not have improved their chances of avoiding pariah status themselves.

But perhaps they sensed that they were already pariahs. A secret police report a few months earlier had described Lata and her sisters as 'downright class enemies': estate-owners with a tendency to mix in politically unsound circles whose relatives had a habit of fleeing the country. Now they began to get a sense of what it meant to be out of favour. All through that year, the confiscation of land and the collectivisation of agriculture continued; so, more distressingly, did the demands for money from the Brandis family. The details were absurdly complicated but may be oversimplified as follows. The five co-owners of what remained of the Řitka property – Lata, Kristýna, Johanna, Alžběta and Petr Jaroševský – had been deemed since December 1946 to owe 207,378.50 crowns to the Fund for National Renewal, mostly as a result of the benefits that Vladimír Daneš alleged that their estate (now under administration on behalf of the state) had received during the Nazi administration. The claim was eventually reduced on the grounds that two-sevenths of the estate had been confiscated immediately after the war. The fact that the remaining five-sevenths had been taken into administration and that the co-owners were receiving little or no income from it was ignored. The family were required to pay 145,627 crowns, plus steadily accumulating interest. By late 1949 the sisters were being threatened with the seizure of their furniture if they failed to do so. Yet they could not pay. In effect, they were guilty of two offences: being too rich and being too poor. They were being pursued for an alleged benefit (which they denied) to an estate which, with the exception of fifty hectares, they no longer possessed. Their income was in any case so pitiful that they could barely afford to live, let alone make six-figure payments to the state. Yet they remained aristocrats, born into unearned privilege. They could hardly expect a sympathetic hearing.

There had been a time – for most of the past forty years – when Lata could have been relied upon to take charge of such a situation. But she was not yet healed; and her incapacity made the problems worse. Months after her discharge, she was still troubled by memory disorders, mood swings, depression and mental weariness. Monthly payments that were supposed to reduce the family's liabilities were missed; letters may well have gone unread. There was also the question of a bill from the hospital in Pardubice, for 5,670 crowns, which Lata appeared unable to pay. Eventually, Alžběta's son, Jan Pospíšil (father of the current Jan Pospíšil), attempted to sort things out on the sisters' behalf. Now a lawyer in his late twenties, he corresponded tirelessly with the authorities, explaining that Lata was incapacitated and that she and her sisters were unable to pay and were, in effect, being taxed on income that they no longer had. He succeeded in delaying the inevitable, but the authorities were implacable.

By the end of 1950, the estate had been incorporated into a collective state farm that also included the village's 'upper farm' and another property just up the hill at Černolice. The three resident sisters were banished to a few rooms at end of the chateau. The rest of the building became a hostel for agricultural workers.

Lata and her sisters accepted their fate. They had little choice. Lata's unaccustomed apathy added to their helplessness. In November 1950 a Prague neurologist declared her unfit for work. She still struggled with her balance and needed a stick to help her walk, and there was no question of riding a horse or even a bicycle. The fate of the estate's remaining horses was in any case unclear. They seem to have ended up in Černolice. Řitka's stables became a giant cowshed. Lata spent much of her time indoors – although she did make friends with several of the new farmworkers.

§ - § - §

The months turned into years. Lata recovered her strength, both mental and physical. The grip of the Communists grew tighter and harsher. You can get a sense of how harsh from the story of Vladimír Hejmovský, who in 1951 became the oldest ever winner of the Velká Pardubická when, at the age of sixty-one, he rode Salvator to victory. He did not return to attempt a second victory in 1952 because the security services had by then realised that, during the Russian Civil War of 1918–21, he had been a colonel on the White (anti-Communist) side. He died during interrogation by the StB. Needless to say, he fell – or 'jumped' – from a window.

The same grip could be felt in Řitka. In early 1953, a CIA plane managed to scatter a batch of propaganda leaflets over the area. Some curious villagers picked them up; a few were rash enough to keep them. 'My father was jailed for three and a half years,' remembers Alena Brabencová (then Mašková). 'I think there were five or six in the village arrested altogether. I was at elementary school at the time. When the time came for me to go to high school, I wasn't allowed to go.'

Around the same time, in March 1953, Miloslav Sléha, son-in-law of Lata's former gamekeeper, Jan Běhal, was arrested for supposedly subversive activities and sentenced to eighteen years' imprisonment. For the next seven years – after which he was released under an amnesty – his wife, Jana, was left to raise two daughters alone, while earning a precarious living as a seamstress. Spare moments were spent travelling with her daughters to remote corners of the country, to visit Miloslav in various camps, including the notorious Jáchymov uranium mines.

At a time when Communism still had popular support, Řitka showed less enthusiasm for the cause than most villages. 'We were a Sokol village,' insists Jana Sléhová, who still lives in the village. 'The Communists were mostly in Černolice.' Even so, it was the Communists who wielded all the power now in Řitka, and there were more than enough of them to ensure that dissent was spotted, reported and punished. The climate of fear was suffocating. Altogether, around 130,000 Czechoslovaks – 1 per cent of the population – were sent to prisons, camps and mines under Communism, most of them in the 1950s. Former aristocrats were not immune: Arnošt Schwarzenberg, Karel's uncle, spent four years in custody from 1953 to 1957, including two years of hard labour in Jáchymov. Nor did sporting fame protect you: several leading athletes were in camps, along with most of the world-beating national ice-hockey team. Lata and her sisters, in debt to the state and visibly unsupportive of the regime, were at obvious risk. None the less, they did what they could to support villagers who were in trouble: for example, with commissions for Jana Sléhová (usually delivered via Kristýna). But they could not do so for long.

In June 1953, the last vestiges of inherited aristocratic wealth in Czechoslovakia were vaporised by a radical reform of the currency. The old crown was replaced by a new one, whose value depended on how many you possessed. You could exchange five old crowns for one new one, up to a maximum of 1,500 old crowns; beyond that, each new crown cost you fifty old ones. Most private savings were erased by the reform, which also involved the nullification of insurance stock and assorted state-backed financial obligations. There were widespread protests, but few turned violent and all were successfully suppressed.

It was at around this time that the Brandis sisters' financial problems overwhelmed them. Their aristocratic origins made it almost impossible for them to find paid employment – employers who knew what was good for them didn't hire class enemies – and Lata was in any case unfit to work. But deriving an income from their land was no longer an option either. With no way of paying what they owed the state, they were effectively bankrupt. Eventually, after months of acrimonious correspondence about the valuation and seizure of assets, they were evicted. A small cottage was found for them in Klínec, a tiny settlement three miles to the east. To describe it as basic would exaggerate its comforts. There was just a small main room, with two tiny bedrooms and a toilet tucked away to the side. The steep slope below created space for a log-cellar underneath, and there was a small verandah. There was no upstairs, no running water, no electricity and, since the hillside was thickly wooded, not much light. But Lata was no stranger to physical hardship. The frightening new pain she had to bear would not be the absence of material comforts but the loss of the home and the village to which all her family memories were attached.

They took what possessions they could, in a large cart. One cartload was more than enough to fill their new home. Everything else, they abandoned.

An agricultural training college was soon based in the chateau in their place, in addition to the state farm and the workers' hostel. Some say that furniture was flung out of the window in preparation for the conversion. Everyone agrees that there was looting. 'There are many homes around here where you'll see pieces of furniture which used to belong in the chateau,' one old villager told me, correctly. (In May 2018 I actually saw one such piece returned, when a man from a neighbouring village, after half a century of being nagged by his conscience, appeared at Řitka with a big Venetian-style silver mirror in the back of his car.) Even if you question the fairness of the Brandis family's having had so many possessions in the first place, you can imagine the sense of violation: like being burgled by a large group of local people who share your possessions among themselves and make little effort to conceal it. But no matter how much it hurt, and regardless of the affection that most villagers still felt for the Brandis family, 'No one would stand up for them,' says Františka Mašková. In some cases, people felt that they were safeguarding things on the sisters' behalf. In others, according to Jaroslava Orolová, grand-daughter of a former Řitka estate manager, 'People who had cause to be grateful to the family didn't show them much gratitude.'

Some fine china was initially kept in the cottage of a former estate worker but ended up scattered around the village. 'Children used to use the plates and dishes for making mud-pies and things like that,' remembers Alena Brabencová. 'It used to make me sad, to see that beautiful china cracked and muddy, just lying around where the children had played with it.'

Petr Jaroševský watched Lata and her sisters leave their home for the last time. 'When they left Řitka, they walked away beside the cart with their heads held high and never once looked back,' he remembers. 'They never returned. They never complained. They never even talked about it.' Just as they had refused to speak German, so they now refused to speak the language of victimhood.

# 29.

# In the woods

The story of the next twenty-five years can be told in a few pages. The cartload of possessions was unpacked. Lata and Kristýna took the larger bedroom; Johanna the smaller. You could barely see the floor in either room.

Johanna and Kristýna, both in their fifties, found jobs, with difficulty. Most employers wanted nothing to do with them, given their origins; but they had to earn a living somehow, and they were eventually allowed to start work on the production line of the vast Orion chocolate factory in Modřany, on the edge of Prague. This may have been intended as a humiliation. If so, they bore it quietly, and over the next few years – for nearly a decade, in Johanna's case – they appear to have fitted in reasonably well. They were not the only members of the formerly privileged classes to do manual labour in 1950s Czechoslovakia, and they were probably more used to physical work than many. Occasionally, one sister or both would be hauled off the shop floor to undertake interpreting duties for visiting foreigners.

Lata, unfit to work, stayed at home. She received a small disability pension. None the less, she spent most of each day working, unsteadily, with her hands. There was water to be fetched, in a bucket, from a well more than a hundred metres down the steep hill. There were logs to be chopped, too, and chickens to be fed, and an unreliable septic tank to be maintained, and clothes to be washed, and a tiny, cluttered house to be cleaned. Johanna usually cooked the evening meal, but Lata made sure that everything was ready for her. For someone who struggled to stay upright without a stick, it was a heavy workload. It was also lonely. Kristýna and Johanna used to leave at 6 a.m. for the railway station at Bojov – nearly a mile up the hill – to get to their shifts at the factory; they did not return until the end of the afternoon.

Sometimes, there would be visitors: Alžběta, or one or more of her children, from Prague; or the Satories (Josef and Gikina), who were now living just north of the capital, working on a pig farm. But visits were confined to weekends. As for neighbours, the only other habitation in sight was a weekend cottage further down the hill. Its owners, the Breyer family, were friendly, but they spent their weeks in Prague. From Monday to Friday, all through the 1950s and into the 1960s, Lata spent her days alone.

She kept herself sane through discipline and ritual: each task performed at its allotted time, each meal consumed formally and correctly, at the same invariable point in the day. She was not the sort to sit around feeling sorry for herself, and she would not have wanted to feel that she was not doing her bit, relative to her sisters. So she got on with it. She usually had a dog to keep her company: there was a succession over the years, of which the ones most often mentioned are Harryk, a large hound, and Jenka, a fousek (a Czech breed not unlike a pointer). There were, however, no horses, which saddened her.

But she did have God. That thought had always meant a lot to her. Now, as she grew older, it seemed to mean more. Every Sunday, unfailingly, she and her sisters would walk to Líšnice, making their slow way over the hill, dressed in black. It was a long slog for an invalid with a stick, yet Lata seemed happy to continue, at her own pace, indefinitely. If they reached the village in time (as they usually did, since they always started out at the same time), they would stop for coffee with a church warden's wife, Růžena Pojerová, before the service. Then they would continue to church, where their attendance was probably noted by an StB informer or two. (Religion was not quite illegal but was highly suspect politically.) They sat in their usual place, always in the same positions, and worshipped as their parents had taught them, oblivious to the congregation's curious gaze.

Lata, in particular, always seemed to concentrate intently, both hands neatly raised together in prayer. A few feet away, on the wall, a painted statue – a crucified Christ, grotesquely skewered with a large spear – emphasised the creed of redemption through suffering. Its relevance to her own journey – from worldly riches and glory to a life of poverty, disgrace and obscurity – hardly needed spelling out.

After the service, the sisters would talk briefly to the priest, Father Josef Javůrek, and perhaps to the church wardens, but rarely to anyone else. Johanna was chattier than the others. After a brief diversion to buy provisions, they would then walk home: spread out this time in a long line, each deep in her own thoughts.

Back in the cottage, the observance of ritual continued. Each meal was eaten, usually in silence, at its allotted

time; each sister sat in her invariable place. A grandfather clock from Řitka, known as 'Big Ben', dominated
the room. Afterwards, they went on the verandah and
smoked. In the evening, they listened to the news on the
radio: not the official radio, but a Czech-language broadcast – presumably Voice of America – transmitted from
the West. Sometimes, depending on who was present,
they spoke German to one another. They probably found
it easier. It may also have occurred to them that their loyalty to the Czech nation had not been well rewarded.

§ - § - §

While Lata and her sisters adapted to their new lives, the
Velká Pardubická underwent its own metamorphosis.
The carnival atmosphere ceased. The wealthy no longer
drank and shopped and showed off their cars and their
finery; nor was there any celebration of the race's aristocratic origins. Lata, its most famous Czech victor, was
all but unmentionable. Instead, the race became a celebration of the friendship and sporting prowess of the
nations of the Soviet bloc.

Like the English and the Germans before them, the
horsemen of the Soviet nations developed their own special relationships with Europe's most notorious steeplechase. The Czechs generally spoke of them as 'Russians'.
In fact, they were more likely to come from less central
parts of the Soviet empire such as Uzbekistan or Georgia.
Whatever their origins, they appeared to be under the
strongest of incentives to win. Many adopted the dangerous practice of tying themselves to their horses with
ropes around the wrist. This meant that, if they fell,

they wouldn't have to worry about their horse bolting but, instead, could remount quickly. Did it work? You can judge for yourself from the names of the winners, carved on a stone plaque on the back of the main Pardubice stand. The decades before the First World War are dominated by English and Irish names: Moore, Fletcher, Williamson, Buckenham, Geoghegan. As the Second World War approaches, the Germans dominate: Schmidt, Schwandt, Wiese, Lengnik. The 1950s and early 1960s have a different geographical flavour: Fedin, Prachov, Avdějev, Makarov. Once again, the Velká Pardubická had reinvented itself.

Yet Lata still had her admirers in the racing world, even if fewer than before occupied positions of influence. One of these was a young woman called Eva Vítová – future wife of 1953 Velká Pardubická winner Ferdinand Palyza and subsequently celebrated under her married name of Eva Palyzová. Eva was just old enough to have seen Lata race in Pardubice and had been inspired by her achievements to become a steeplechase jockey herself.

The racing world accepted her quickly. That would not have happened without Lata's example – although Palyzová's exceptional talent obviously helped. By the early 1960s she had won most major steeplechases in Czechoslovakia, some repeatedly; but the Velká Pardubická eluded her. She first started in the race in 1959, but failed to finish. Then, in 1965, she came back to Pardubice to try again.

Czechoslovakia was a slightly less frightening place by then. The apparent permanence of Communism had reduced the need for terror. The concentration camps had been closed, the show trials stopped, and the first hints

were appearing of a political thaw that in 1968 would cul-
minate in the 'Prague Spring'. Lata was still unacceptable
as a national hero; but she was not quite so hopelessly
beyond the pale.

With Palyzová considered to have a realistic chance
of winning, someone had the bright idea of inviting Lata
to watch Palyzová try to join her in Pardubice's female
hall of fame. She was tracked down, driven over, introduced to her young imitator and seated in a VIP box: a
stooped, seventy-year-old figure who had to be helped
by Palyzová on the steps. Many people left their seats in
order to get a look at her. Jiří Kocman, a former Chlumec
stable lad and Velká Chuchle apprentice who had ridden
in the Velká Pardubická himself (and who later became
a world champion carriage driver), was among those
who spent time talking to her, mainly about horses. He
found her 'very friendly'. 'The Bolsheviks had tried to
suppress the memory of her,' says František Vítek, the
jockey. 'But people still remembered, and it was great
that she could come.'

The thirteen-horse field that year included four Soviet
horses, three from Romania and two from Hungary,
but the finish was fought out by two horses from
Czechoslovak state farms: Cavalet, ridden by Palyzová,
and Mocná, ridden by Vítek. Cavalet had looked strong
all race, apart from a knock at the fourteenth, and for
much of the second half the six-year-old seemed poised
to win, especially after Vítek almost fell at the Big Water
Jump. 'At one point I was two hundred metres behind,'
remembers Vítek. 'I thought I was going to come second.' So, presumably, did Lata. But Vítek kept Mocná in
touch, and as they rounded the Popkovice woods Cavalet

began to seem catchable. Vítek let Mocná go. 'As we passed the trees, she was flying. There were frozen leaves on the ground: I can still hear the sound of them crunching underfoot as we caught up.' At the last, they were almost neck and neck. Cavalet took off first but brushed the top and Mocná landed fractionally ahead. This was all the encouragement Vítek needed. Mocná won by half a length.

She was the first mare to win since Norma, much to Lata's delight. Afterwards, Vítek chatted with Lata; and whereas Palyzová (who rode in six subsequent Velká Pardubickás) docs not seem to have been particularly impressed with her warmth, Vítek was. 'She was very friendly to me,' he says. 'She told me that I had ridden a very clever race. I said I had just followed Palyzová. Then Lata said that she was very glad it was me who won, and not Eva Palyzová, because it meant that she was still the only woman ever to win the Velká Pardubická.'

The next day, a photograph of Lata and Palyzová together appeared in some newspapers, but readers seeking explanatory text were disappointed. In the words of the Czech sportswriter Pavel Kovář: 'There was no way that an article about the life of the woman who won the Velká Pardubická could be published. No editor found the courage to do that.'

§ - § - §

As time passed, Lata diminished. The tough, agile warrior who had ridden helmetless in Pardubice in 1949 had lost her cat-like resilience. Two decades after her last race, she had the hesitant shuffle of a frail-boned old woman.

Perhaps she was never entirely free from pain. Yet something in her bearing still suggested a sporting champion. There was a firmness in her gaze: a lack of apology for herself. For all her weakness, she never spared herself physically. She was still a natural leader.

The Brandis sisters' legal difficulties were over by now. They had lost everything. There was nothing else to argue about. Instead, within the constraints of their poverty, they lived as they saw fit. A small circle of friends and family kept in touch – in an increasingly watchful capacity. Lata's cousin Gikina Satorieová was perhaps the most regular visitor, especially after her husband's death in 1971. But there were also Alžběta's children, Jan and Eva; and, in due course, Jan's wife and son (the current Jan Pospíšil). Petr Jaroševský used to visit, too, and eventually he too brought a wife and children with him. If a visiting family stayed overnight – as tended to happen – the children would share a room with Johanna, while the parents slept on the floor of the tiny dining room. By day, however, adults took precedence. Children were expected to behave impeccably indoors, even if – like the young Brandises – they were allowed to run amok outside. Similar rules applied for dogs.

Lata exchanged occasional letters with Ra, although her side of the correspondence is lost. Both knew that their letters were intercepted and read by the security services, so meaningful exchanges were minimal. But the letters told her that she was not forgotten. They petered out, however, following Lori's death in May 1967. As for the other man who had once filled much of her life: Hanuš Kasalický had died in 1959, disgraced, dispossessed and bitterly resentful of both facts. His last years were spent barely ten miles from Klínec, in a small villa in Černošice. Lata may not even have known that he was there. Unlike him, she had moved on. 'We closed the book,' she explained once, when asked about her past life in Řitka, 'and we never opened it again.'

Instead, the sisters tried to make the best of the new chapter in their life. They were helped in this by the friendship they developed with their weekend neighbours, the Breyers. The families used to visit one another for evening tea. Sometimes, too, at the Breyers' house, they would stay and listen to German-language radio (again, broadcast from the West). Lata got on particularly well with their son, Petr, who was six when they first met in 1953. By 1965 he was eighteen and, encouraged by Lata, had become seriously interested in horses – so much so that, to Lata's delight, he bought one, Lacík, which he kept nearby. Lata loved to watch Lacík and be close to him. There was no question of her riding again, although she must have been tempted. (She had occasionally tried to ride a bicycle – 'like a man with a bellyful of beer', according to Jan Pospíšil – but her sisters had hidden it to prevent a recurrence.) But, even without riding, she thirsted for the company of horses. It was as if they refreshed her spirit. When farmers brought working horses to help mow the meadows above the woods, Lata used to go up and offer to lend a hand. The offer was absurd – there was nothing she could usefully do – yet she found it comfortable to be close to the creatures; and perhaps, too, they found it comfortable to be close to her. She still greeted each horse with a friendly pat, and it was clear from her body language that, even now, she felt entirely confident and relaxed in their company.

Frail-boned or not, 'I simply do not believe that a horse could ever deliberately do something bad to me.'

§ - § - §

One winter in the early 1970s, Lata was ill. Father Javůrek visited her in the cottage. A former political prisoner who had partially atoned for his crimes by driving a tractor on an agricultural cooperative, he felt a natural sympathy for those who had fallen foul of Communism. Parishioners used to warn him when they spotted StB informers at his services: 'Hold your tongue, Josef!' He and Lata got on well.

According to one account of their conversation, she expressed relative contentment with her lot: 'They've been taking our property all our lives. First after the establishment of the republic, then Hitler and now the communists. But things could always get worse ...'

She refused to talk about what she had lost: 'Communism took everything we had but our pride – they couldn't take that.' In any case, she added: 'You know what the Bible says: the ones who are first shall be the last.'

She did, however, admit to having one remaining wish – although 'not even our Lord can grant it'. Father Javůrek asked her what it was.

'If only I could, at least for a while, sit in the saddle again.'

# 30.

# The show goes on

Each October, the three old ladies would listen to the Velká Pardubická on the radio. Lata and her sisters were listening when Nestor won in 1966 – the last horse of Kinský descent to do so. They listened to Eva Palyzová's unsuccessful attempts in 1967, 1969, 1970, 1971 and 1972. The last of these races also featured Jana Nová, who came eighth and last after falling twice but did at least finish.

They did not listen in 1968 because there was no race. The official reason was the weather, but everyone knew the real reason: Czechoslovakia was under military occupation. Eight months of joyous liberalisation had angered the Soviet Union, which in August had led a Warsaw Pact invasion to extinguish what the world called the Prague Spring. Months of brave but ultimately futile passive resistance followed, as Czechoslovaks tried to defend what Alexandr Dubček, the Communist Party's reforming First Secretary, called 'socialism with a human face'. In Řitka, several people got carried away with the anti-Soviet graffiti ('Brezhnev = Hitler' was painted on a road) and Pavel Liška, manager of the Řitka part of the state farm, eventually lost his job for having painted the provocative word 'Neutrality' on the chateau gates.

But it took time for the reimposition of orthodoxy – 'Normalisation' – to take effect, and erstwhile political outcasts remained at least partially rehabilitated. In early 1969 Lata was among a group of prominent racing figures who were invited to a meeting at the State Racecourses organisation to discuss the commemoration of what would have been Rudolf Popler's seventieth birthday. She didn't contribute much, beyond saying how saddened she had been by Popler's death. But it would have meant something to her to be included again, however briefly, among racing's great and good.

Thereafter, her world continued to shrink. In January 1970, Gabriele died in Graz; Marie Therese died in Reiteregg the following year, on Christmas Day. Both sisters were buried in Austria. There was no question of going to either funeral – even assuming that the news reached Lata in time. Each loss will have grieved her, notwithstanding any tensions there had been over the years; and it will not have escaped Lata's notice that she now had more dead siblings than living ones.

By October 1973, Petr Breyer – who with Lata's encouragement was on the way to becoming a successful event rider – was sufficiently concerned about Lata's morale to decide that she needed a treat. So he drove her to Pardubice to watch the Velká Pardubická. She was not a celebrity this time: just an ordinary, unrecognised racegoer. But she was clearly delighted by the experience; and, in addition to the relief of seeing Eva Palyzová fail to finish on Metál, she must have been intrigued to see the first English victory in the race since 1906.

Seven months earlier, the British ambassador to Prague, Ronald Scrivener, had written an article for

*Country Life* magazine evoking the glorious traditions – long forgotten in the West – of continental Europe's most extreme steeplechase. Christopher Collins, a thirty-three-year-old amateur National Hunt jockey and event rider from Buckinghamshire, read the article and decided, in the same adventurous spirit that had brought Popler to Aintree forty-two years earlier, that he would try to win the race. The Cold War was in one of its chillier phases, and visits by Westerners behind the Iron Curtain were tortuously difficult to arrange. But the Czechoslovak racing authorities were eventually won over, and Collins was able to make a summer reconnaissance trip. He was horrified by what he saw – he initially assumed that Taxis was not a jump but 'a sort of giant boundary between different sections of the course' – but decided that 'having got so far, I had better have a go'. He returned in October with one of his own horses, Stephen's Society, a seven-year-old Irish-bred gelding who was slow – his steeplechasing career had largely lapsed into hunting and eventing – but could at least be trusted to jump whatever he found in front of him.

The language barrier added to the strangeness of the trip. Collins recalls a series of incomprehensible pre-race briefings, and he initially felt that he was seen as a 'degenerate capitalist'. But the locals were clearly impressed by Stephen's Society, who was bigger than the other horses; and once the race began, they were all in it together. Collins – who had no idea that among the spectators was an old woman who had conquered these obstacles many times, in far more intimidating circumstances – began cautiously. But once Stephen's Society had made it (just) over Taxis, both horse and rider began to relax and, gradually, worked their way up the field. There was a difficult moment when a loose horse forced Stephen's Society out so wide that Collins had to bring him to a halt; but even then, after resuming in last place, the pair never looked uncomfortable. They regained the lost ground easily, the gelding's stamina and jumping ability more than compensating for his lack of pace. They won by between eight and twelve lengths, depending on whose account you believe, and Collins was suddenly a local hero.

'They were very friendly,' remembers Collins. 'They seemed particularly pleased that I wasn't Russian.' He won 100,000 crowns and a motorbike, but, this being the Cold War, was unable to get the money out of the country (and even in Czechoslovakia, he says, 'there was nothing to spend it on'). But money wasn't really the point: 'It was about the adventure.' And, if nothing else, he had triumphantly rekindled the English love affair with the race.

Lata and Breyer returned the following year. So did Collins and Stephen's Society. The latter pairing was greeted with an unexpected warning: foul play was planned. It was the Velká Pardubická's centenary, and it seemed that, while everyone had been happy to see a plucky English adventurer win once, a repeat victory would not be acceptable. The warnings came from multiple sources, including a waitress at Collins's hotel who drew a diagram on a napkin showing how two Russians planned to obstruct him at Taxis. An anonymous phone call to the British embassy identified two suspects. The ambassador arranged a meeting with them, along with the director of the State Racecourses organisation (who according to Collins 'looked as though he spent most of his life interrogating people in a basement'). Through an interpreter, Collins warned the trio that Stephen's Society was big enough to look after himself and that any attempt at interference would be met with a robust response.

In the event, despite some minor jostling in the early stages, the race proceeded without foul play. Collins fell at Taxis 'without any assistance from anyone'. He then remounted, against his better instincts but in keeping with what he realised was 'the spirit of the race'. He fell again at the Big Water Jump; remounted again; and eventually finished a distant and dispirited third. But his gameness had been noted, and at the post-race dinner that same director of the State Racecourses organisation made a point of coming up to him to say: 'Mr Collins, you are sportsman.' The compliment seems to have delighted him almost as much as the previous year's victory – 'like a cloud … yielding place to a blue sky'.

For Lata, this subplot is unlikely to have registered. Just being there was enough. A photograph taken that day shows her in her overcoat, sitting in the stand. She is gazing intently, alone: rugged and inscrutable as an Easter Island statue. Her lips are slightly parted. What she sees is clearly absorbing her. But you cannot be sure if what she sees are the horses and riders in front of her or those inside her head, from long ago.

§ - § - §

That was Lata's last visit to Pardubice. The journey was too daunting. Her eightieth birthday approached and passed. So did the fiftieth anniversary, in 1977, of her first appearance in the Velká Pardubická. So Lata missed the opportunity to see, that year, another landmark: the first attempt at the race by an Englishwoman.

The story would have interested her. Charlotte Brew's journey to the starting line had been little easier than Lata's. A twenty-one-year-old councillor's daughter from Coggeshall, Essex, Brew was one of several British women to take advantage of the Sex Discrimination Act (1975) to exercise their right to compete as equals in steeplechases. (The Jockey Club, so helpful to Lata in 1927, had hitherto taken a less relaxed attitude to women in British racing.) In the spring of 1977, Brew had taken this right to its logical conclusion and become the first woman ever to ride in the Grand National.

Like Lata fifty years earlier, Brew was inexperienced: she had ridden in her first point-to-point three years before. Unlike Lata, she rode her own horse: a big twelve-year-old chestnut gelding called Barony Fort on whom she had won several point-to-points before coming fourth in the 1976 Liverpool Foxhunters Chase, which brought qualification for the next spring's Grand National. As April 1977 approached, it dawned on the racing world that Brew actually intended to ride in the big race. The savagery of the collective response was shocking. Journalists, jockeys, trainers, male and female – everyone seemed to want to pile in. Brew was criticised for being too young, too weak, too reckless, too lacking in basic competence; and, by implication, too lacking in a sense of feminine decency. Her appearance was 'ridiculous' and 'shouldn't be allowed', according to a group of female jockeys interviewed on television the night before the race; a group of male trainers threatened her with dire consequences if her incompetent riding interfered with their own horses' efforts. The trainer David Nicholson denounced her attempt as 'a complete horlicks'. The *Racehorse* magazine accused her of 'courting disaster'.

The hostility began to affect Brew's riding. She dealt with it by cutting herself off from all media coverage. (Her mother had already been hiding the worst of it.) On the positive side, the villagers of Coggeshall were supportive, and there was a flood of encouraging letters and telegrams. The women of the BBC typing pool informed her that they were so outraged by the cruel remarks of Julian Wilson, the racing correspondent, that they were refusing to do any more typing for him.

On race day, the *Sun* devoted its front page to the participation of 'the dark-haired filly from Essex', bumping Elvis Presley's soon-to-be-terminal health problems on to page 3. The Aintree racegoers who mobbed Brew on the way to the start seemed on balance more supportive than hostile – although she could have done without some of the 'mansplaining' from well-wishers. The race itself was a disappointment, though. Fearful of humiliating herself, Brew started cautiously, and Barony Fort was never able to make up the lost ground. He spent most of the race bringing up the rear before refusing at the fourth from last. By normal standards it was a respectable first attempt, but Brew felt bitterly disappointed. And so, six months later, she found her way with Barony Fort to Pardubice, to attempt a challenge that was arguably harder still.

It was a frightening journey for a young woman with little experience of foreign travel, let alone of life behind the Iron Curtain. Yet what she immediately realised was that she was welcome. She was provided with an interpreter, escorted, entertained: the Czechoslovaks seemed delighted that another foreigner should be brave enough and crazy enough to attempt their great national challenge. Her gender was relevant only insofar as it was another thing to admire her for. 'They were very welcoming. And they made no distinction between the sexes, which was great.'

She was a little unnerved when a man who looked like a priest delivered what she assumed was a pre-race blessing. (It is more likely to have been a pep-talk from the starter.) And she initially assumed, when first shown Taxis, that those who said that it was a jump were joking. Yet the early stages of the race, at least, went well for her. 'It was all a bit of a blur. We started slowly, and before I knew it we were at Taxis. I just closed my eyes and hoped for the best.' They landed safely and were very comfortable over the next dozen obstacles. 'We could easily have won,' she says now. 'He was running well within himself.' But an unexpected encounter with a fallen horse at the Big Water Jump resulted in a spectacular fall, and although Brew remounted, Barony Fort – who had briefly disappeared under the water – had lost his zest. Little Taxis brought their race to an end two jumps later.

Afterwards, Brew was made to feel more welcome than ever. Like other foreign visitors before and since, she discovered that, in the mad world-within-a-world of the Velká Pardubická, all that really counts is a have-a-go spirit. Demonstrate that, as Brew did, and – irrespective of your origins – your hosts will want to claim you as one of their own.

Brew – who now goes by her married name of Budd – responded to their warmth. For many years she remained in friendly contact with her interpreter, Vladimír Šabata. But there was one aspect of the race's heritage that she didn't discover until four decades later, either because everyone had already forgotten, or because no one had thought it worth mentioning.

'I never realised,' she told me in 2017, 'that a lady had ever won the race.'

# 31.

# Journey's end

A part from a few faded newspaper cuttings, Lata had nothing to remind her of her triumphs. There had been trophies and rosettes once. Not now: not in the long, lonely days of the late 1970s. Even the silk scarf that Ra had given her in thanks for Norma's victory had somehow been lost. As for Ra, he had died in 1975, in Rome, on New Year's Day.

By 1978, she herself was fading. Younger relatives had slipped gently from the role of cared-for to that of carer. Friends joined them in visiting when they could and contributing what they could. When electricity finally reached Klínec, at around this time, Petr Jaroševský helped Petr Breyer's father dig a ditch up the hillside, so that water could be pumped up to the cottage. Jan Pospíšil the elder continued to keep an eye on the sisters' financial and legal affairs. Jan Pospíšil the younger used to bring Lata packets of her favourite cigarettes – Gîtanes and Gauloises – and then redoubled her pleasure by smoking them with her.

In November 1978, Petr Breyer organised a fox hunt near Líšnice. This didn't involve any foxes: just a dragged scent and thirty dressed-up riders. It was, in part, a consciously anachronistic gesture of defiance: a celebration of a half-imagined Bohemian tradition that had more to do with the Kinskýs' flamboyant world than with Communism's grey orthodoxies. Its highlight was a visit to the meadows above Klínec, where Lata and her sisters, and Gikina Satorieová, and Harryk the hound, were waiting to watch them pass. Breyer brought the hunt to a halt and introduced them to Lata. The huntsmen sounded a fanfare in her honour, Breyer made a short speech, and then everyone applauded Lata. 'It seemed to make her very happy indeed,' says Breyer.

§ - § - §

By 1979 it was hard to see how the elderly sisters could continue. All three were weak. Visitors worried that they weren't eating properly.

Thamar Kinský, Radslav's wife, was allowed to pay a quick visit to Czechoslovakia while on holiday in Austria and found a few spare hours to go and see Lata. She was shocked by what she saw. 'She seemed frail and unwell and hardly seemed to know what was going on. But when I mentioned Radslav, her face lit up.'

Another visitor was Michal Horáček, then a journalist but later a politician (and in 2017 a presidential candidate). He thought the sisters seemed not only 'frail' but 'obviously struggling to make ends meet'. Lata talked to him for quite a long time, but only about racing personalities of the 1920s and 1930s. 'That was the world she found pretty and dignified,' says Horáček. 'What came after that was not worth even mentioning.'

In June, Lata was invited to make a guest appearance at Velká Chuchle with Eva Palyzová and Míla

Hermansdorferová – a pioneering flat-racing jockey who in 1972 had become the first woman rider to win the Czech Derby. Illness prevented her from attending. By then, the sisters rarely even made it to church. Instead, Father Javůrek went regularly to the cottage to give them mass.

In the autumn of 1979, Kristýna fell ill. She died of pneumonia on 25 November. This may have been the moment when her eighty-four-year-old twin began to lose the will to live. It proved too complicated to bury her in the family tomb: the land was no longer the family's and the tomb had, in any case, been damaged (some said vandalised) in 1974. Instead, Kristýna's ashes were buried in the new cemetery at Líšnice.

The remote cottage was no longer a viable home for Lata and Johanna. Arrangements were set in motion for Johanna to live with Gikina Satorieová. (They eventually found a couple of rooms to rent from a Líšnice farmer, Mička Kaščák.) Meanwhile, Lata received a visit from Ernst Haan, her nephew (Gabriele's son) from Austria. He, too, was shocked by the state she was in and tried to persuade Lata to move with him to Reiteregg.

Lata was reluctant: why would she want to move to an unfamiliar country after a lifetime on Czech soil? In any case, she hated having a fuss made over her. But Haan had a special inducement: at Reiteregg, he explained, Lata would be among horses. According to Saša Jaroševský, 'When she agreed to go to Austria, horses were the magnet that drew her. She loved horses more than anything.'

It took time to arrange the migration. There was still an Iron Curtain to cross. Eventually, in September 1980, Haan was able to come and fetch Lata. She was smiling as he helped her into his car. Eva Pospíšilová waved her off. Then came the long drive to Austria. It felt, perhaps, like the beginning of a longer journey. It was.

At Reiteregg, Lata found what has been described as a 'horse paradise'. Not only were there stables and riding horses and carriage horses, but her new home – a big, solid castle with stuccoed walls and a turreted clock tower – was set on a wide, green, peaceful hill-top. Rich pastures sloped gently all around, grazed by horses, with roll after roll of receding hills stretching out beyond. It is hard to imagine a more elegiac place for a horse lover to sit and watch the sun going down over what used to be the Habsburg heartlands. On a clear day you can see half of Austria. Perhaps Lata wondered if, somewhere on the dissolving horizon, the Řitka of her childhood might somehow be visible as well, waiting for her to spot it.

A few minutes' walk from the castle walls stood a small private chapel, where prayers could be said. Family members were buried here. For the first time in years, Lata's deepest thirsts, for horses and for God, could be satisfied with relative ease. As an extra mercy, Kristýna's remains were transferred to Reiteregg and reinterred at the chapel. The thought of being separated from her life-long companion and twin would have been hard for Lata to bear.

All that remained was to wait.

Perhaps she missed home. I doubt she missed the cottage in the woods, but she must have thought sometimes of Řitka. She did not share any such yearnings with her hosts. According to her (late) niece, Dorothea Haan, she still never said a word about the loss of her family home or the way she and her sisters had been treated by the

Communists. Horses, church, family, the great horsemen of days gone by: that was what filled her spoken thoughts. The rest she kept to herself.

She died peacefully, on 12 May 1981. When news reached Czechoslovakia, it was marked by a down-page sentence on one or two sports pages. There were no obituaries. She was buried at Reiteregg. Her name can still be seen in the little chapel, on a stone plaque, directly beneath Kristýna's. For some reason the sight of that carved name makes me think of the sentence carved in stone on the tomb of Pope Gregory VII – Saint Gregory – in Salerno Cathedral. The words, supposedly the eleventh-century pontiff's last, are adapted from Psalm 44. I am sure they would have been familiar to Lata. And I can't help imagining her saying them quietly to herself, as she gazed northwards over the Austrian hills towards her distant homeland: 'I have loved justice and hated iniquity; therefore I die in exile.'

§ - § - §

Perhaps I am underestimating her resilience. Many people did. A less troubled version of her story can be found in two photographs from that final six-month sojourn in her dead sister's castle: the last surviving snapshots of Lata's life.

In one, probably taken in 1981, she sits upright in a broad, straight-backed armchair, in a warm brown cardigan, in a room flooded with evening sunlight, rich as a blood orange. There is no suggestion of pain, physical or mental. Instead, she gazes calmly at the camera: enigmatic, unflinching; but also untroubled.

The other picture was taken outdoors, on a wide track near the castle. Ernst Haan is driving a four-wheeled carriage, drawn by a pair of what look like Haflinger ponies, an Austrian breed not unlike the Kinský horse in colouring, with rich golden-chestnut hides and long, flaxen manes and tails. Lata is sitting in the carriage, alongside a lady who may be Dorothea Haan, Lata's niece. The green slope behind them is lightly planted with young trees. Beyond, indistinct highlands blur into a pale blue sky. Lata is wrapped in a long coat. It must be autumn; perhaps October. We cannot tell what Lata is thinking: we never could. But she is laughing.

# 32.

# The right stuff

In 1987, two leading Czechoslovak sportswriters, Ivan Hanousek and Jiří Lacina, published a 416-page compilation of mini biographies called *Our Famous Sportspeople*. It featured 156 of the most notable sporting personalities in Czechoslovak history, including nearly thirty women. There was no room in it for Lata Brandisová. Fifty years on from her unparalleled triumph in Pardubice, her glory had been erased from her nation's collective consciousness. It has yet to be fully restored.

The Velká Pardubická, by contrast, has thrived without interruption, all through the greyest days of Communism and through the capitalist free-for-all that succeeded them in November 1989. The latter left Pardubice's streets spattered with coffee shops and garish shopping malls; the return of tourism persuaded some of the town's hotels to modernise. But the spirit of its famous race endured, barely changing, no matter how many contrasting regimes came and went. Josef Váňa, the most celebrated Czech racing hero of modern times, won his first Velká Pardubická in 1987 and was still being celebrated for his barely sane disregard for pain and danger when he won his eighth in 2011. He was by turns a hero of the Czechoslovak Socialist Republic; a hero of the democratic Czechoslovakia of 1989–92; and a hero of the new Czech Republic that came into being on New Year's Day 1993. He won at least one Velká Pardubická as a citizen of each nation, and each time his compatriots understood what it meant: he had won a terrifying steeplechase, heroically simple in the rawness of its challenge, in which only the bravest and the best could hope to win but anyone bold enough to attempt the challenge could win friendship, respect and a lifetime of warm welcomes in Pardubice.

Many British riders tried their luck in the same period. Those who did so in the 1980s included George Saunders, an SAS veteran of exotic lineage who rode in 1982 and 1983, part-funded by the generosity of Christopher Collins, who wanted to put his still unretrieved prize money from a decade earlier to good use. Saunders was respectively sixty-two and sixty-three years old and left both times on a stretcher. This failed to deter others from following in his footsteps, among them George Goring (a London hotelier); and William Sporborg (an accountant from Hertfordshire); and, after the Velvet Revolution, high-profile jockeys such as Charlie Mann, Marcus Armytage, Gavin Wragg, Richard Dunwoody and Ruby Walsh. There is no space to describe all their adventures. Mann's story can stand for them all.

Oktavian Kinský would have recognised Mann as a kindred spirit: someone for whom the boundaries between riding and partying are indistinct. 'I rode in six [Grand] Nationals,' says Mann proudly, 'and was pissed for three of them.' He first went to Pardubice in 1989, not to ride but to support some fellow jockeys. The

Communist regime was still in place. Pre-race celebrations got out of hand, and the group spent a night in the cells of one of Eastern Europe's most feared security services. They made it to the race, even so, and Mann was impressed. He resolved to come back and win it – and in 1994 he reappeared in Pardubice with that in mind. This was madder than it sounds. Mann had been unable to obtain a jockey's licence since breaking his neck in a fall at Warwick in 1987. Unable to race without one, he scoured the world for countries whose racing authorities might be less picky, but not even the Bahamas would touch him. So he printed his own licence, figuring that no one would ever check, and presented himself at the start of the 1994 Velká Pardubická on his nine-year-old chestnut gelding, It's A Snip ('as slow as a hearse', according to Mann, but an utterly reliable jumper). The plan might have worked had Mann not made the mistake of coming second. The resulting headlines alerted the Jockey Club, who fined him £1,000, perhaps hoping that it would teach him sense. The following year, wanting another go, he once again printed his own licence, calculating (correctly) that 'No one would believe I'm that stupid.' He not only got away with it but won the race – and, like Christopher Collins before him, found himself a local hero. 'I'm a legend out there', he still likes to boast.

Mann's irresponsible antics are not to everyone's taste, yet his spirit somehow feels closer than most to the original spirit of the race: wild, macho, reckless, stubborn, and possibly a little unhinged. But he's not the only one. In 1994, he wasn't even the only jockey to have shrugged off a broken neck to get to the start line. You could still see the scars on André Bocquet's neck, left by emergency surgery after the Frenchman fell badly at Taxis two years earlier. And both men seemed relatively sane compared with Josef Váňa, who, as previously mentioned, had been clinically dead a few months earlier, but was now having another shot at the world's most dangerous steeplechase.

Is it right to celebrate the spirit that inspires such recklessness? Probably not. Yet Velká Pardubická enthusiasts find it difficult not to – because that is what the race really inspires: celebration. 'I have a theory,' wrote the journalist Alastair Down about the Irish Pardubice regular Ken Whelan, 'that Ken is locked up somewhere very secure for 364 days of the year and on the 365th they let him out. If he flies out to Pardubice for yet another crack at it they know it's right to lock him up again for the next year.' That caught the spirit of the race perfectly. So did Marcus Armytage, when he told readers of the *Daily Telegraph* how his own days as a Velká Pardubická jockey had ended. Armytage, who rode Mr Frisk to victory as an amateur in the 1990 Grand National, started three times in Pardubice, in 1990, 1991 and 1992. But, he explained, he had seen the light – 'actually, the flashing blue light' – after sharing a post-Taxis ambulance ride with a fellow jockey who was receiving emergency heart massage to keep him alive. 'He spent three weeks in a coma,' wrote Armytage cheerfully. 'But five years later he was back riding in the race.' The note of admiration was unmistakeable. Some detected a hint of lingering doubt as well – as though Armytage still felt tempted to have another go himself.

That's a crucial part of the Pardubice mindset: an inability to contemplate a challenge without wanting to rise to it. That was true in Oktavian Kinský's time and it is true today. Velká Pardubická jockeys are people who look at footage of Taxis and, instead of wincing, see something life-affirming in it – and feel like having a go themselves. The danger is part of the point.

In fact, there is a lot less danger in the race than there was in Lata's day. The obstacles have been repeatedly toned down, especially following demonstrations from animal rights protesters at the 1992 race. (Some of the protesters were later alleged to be professional agitators. Even so, it's hard to look at historical footage of the race and not see what they were getting at.) Today's Taxis ditch is half as deep as the one Lata jumped. The number of runners is strictly limited, fallen riders are forbidden to remount and there is half as much ploughed land to be crossed in the course of the race – which means far fewer horses attempting jumps when they have no strength left. The result has been a race that is faster, less lethal and, overall, more like an ordinary steeplechase. A few traditionalists complain that this has sapped the race of its drama. Most people feel that there is still more than enough drama and danger to justify the much-repeated claim that the Velká Pardubická is the world's 'most dangerous' and 'most extreme' steeplechase. Some dispute the continuing accuracy of that claim; crucially, however, the extremity remains the central point. Like mountaineering or sky-diving, this is a sporting niche defined by its dangers. Velká Pardubická jockeys attempt the challenge not because they consider it prudent, but because they know that it isn't. And that in turn creates a special bond between them: a community of shared thrills.

Of course, it is neither big nor clever to expose yourself to gratuitous risk. Yet there is arguably something noble about the way that these riders accept the possibility of injury and even death with a casual cheerfulness that eludes most of us. None of us has more than a temporary hold on life, no matter how tightly we cling. Those who relax their grip reveal, in doing so, a form of wisdom.

There may still be Velká Pardubická jockeys who, like Lata, 'don't feel all that attached to life'. Others just prefer to focus on what might go right rather than what might go wrong. That doesn't make them mad, in either case. They are drawn to the challenge because it's there, and so are they, and that might not always be the case; so they might as well have a go. This is what feeds the graveyard camaraderie of the starting line, and the wild *joie de vivre* of the post-race celebrations. (Czechs were still talking about Gavin Wragg's exuberant encounter with an equestrian statue at Slatiňany a decade later.) The occasional excesses of the partying are in close harmony with the spirit of the race's founders. The shadow of death sharpens participants' appetite for life.

§ - § - §

Perhaps that all sounds ridiculously macho. But the jockeys who celebrate their shared enthusiasm for the Velká Pardubická are no ordinary community of elite sporting performers. If they sometimes get carried away, there is nothing boorish or intimidating about them: none of the testosterone-fuelled disdain for outsiders (and women) that we associate with words like 'jock' and 'locker-room'. In Pardubice, anyone willing to submit themselves to the great ordeal-by-steeplechase can expect to be toasted as a kindred spirit, irrespective of background. It doesn't matter if you're professional or amateur, old or young, rich or poor, Communist or capitalist, Czech, Slovak, German, Russian, British, Irish or French. If you're up for it, you can join the club. It is, if you like, a brotherhood; except that, thanks to Lata, that word no longer applies. It's not about gender. It's about spirit. To put it crudely: you need balls, but not a penis.

None of the British Velká Pardubická veterans I spoke to when researching this book had heard of Lata Brandisová before I mentioned her. But the race they experienced would have been a very different thing without her. Like most of the rest of the racing world, and like much of Czech society, it would have been an event in which all the most important roles were taken by men. Its toughness and its maleness would have been interwoven. It would have been what it began as: a test of manhood. Instead, thanks to Lata, it has become what it is today: a battlefield on which any woman who is brave enough can fight on equal terms with men, and be judged on her performance, not her gender. Women do still get their own changing room, as stipulated by the English Jockey Club; but that is the only special treatment they can expect.

Only a few women have attempted the challenge, but enough have done so for the point to have been made: Eva Palyzová in the 1960s, Jana Nová and Charlotte Brew in the 1970s; then, after a gap, Renata Charvátová (who got as far as Taxis on Monka in 1990) and Lucie Baluchová (who came third on Gretty in 1997 but failed to finish when she tried again on Ligretta in 2010). Above all, there has been Martina Růžičková (now Růžičková-Jelínková), whose obsession with the race has been a recurring subplot in the story of the Velká Pardubická in recent decades. She first started the race in 1991, on Monka. In 1998, she had another go, on Damion. Then there was Chailand, in 2006, followed by Rubín, in 2010. Each attempt ended with a painful fall (two at Taxis), leaving her with a list of Pardubice-related breakages (shoulder, hands, spine, collar bone, legs, arms) that makes you wonder how she found the courage to keep coming back.

Finally, in 2014, Růžičková tried again with Rubín. They tailed off badly at the end, but still managed to finish in fifteenth place. Her sheer doggedness had made her a Pardubice favourite, and she was rewarded with the kind of applause that must have greeted Lata's last place in 1927. Her fellow jockeys were delighted, too – she was fifty by then, and had known some of them as children. ('I'd raced against their fathers. I used to say to them: "Boys, if you lose, I won't buy you ice-cream."') No one seemed more thrilled by her achievement than the great Josef Váňa.

'Now I can die peacefully,' said Růžičková-Jelínková. In fact, she then began to concentrate on being a trainer, and in 2016 one of her horses, Charme Look, actually won the Velká Pardubická, fulfilling her lifelong wish to win the race, although not exactly as she had hoped. ('My advice,' she says, 'is that if you make a wish, you should be specific.') Meanwhile, she has played a significant role in the fact that, over the past decade, Lata has begun to enjoy a partial rehabilitation.

'Lata's story is a very important one,' she says – and twenty-seven years of wrestling with the Velká Pardubická's challenge have made her unusually interested in it. 'It's important not just in sport, but politically, and in terms of women's rights and liberation.' In today's world, she explains, 'women can drive cars, they can choose careers. I think Lata Brandisová was a model for the kind of lives we have today. Women spectators loved her. They didn't want to spend all their time in the kitchen. She showed that they could do other things instead.'

For a long time, she has been trying to raise money to make a film about Lata's life. It has yet to come to anything, but her enthusiasm for the story has encouraged the Velká Pardubická's organisers to take more interest in the Brandisová legacy. In October 2017, eighty years on from Lata's most glorious day and ninety years on from her first, controversial attempt, they organised a reunion of women who had ridden in the Velká Pardubická. There were only five: Eva Palyzová died in 2011. But Nová, Brew, Charvátová, Baluchová and Růžičková-Jelínková were warmly welcomed and enjoyed an ebullient eve-of-race dinner. In the paddock on race day, they were chatting and laughing like old friends. Brew was on Czech soil for the first time since 1977. She had flown from Bristol with EasyJet, sharing the flight with a spectacularly drunk and offensive stag party (two of whom ended up spending much of the weekend in custody). Instead of cringing like the other passengers, Brew stood up, ticked off the swaggering stags one by one and shamed them into quietening down. It seems an apt embodiment of the strength of character required by a woman who wants to make her mark at the highest level of a rough, male-dominated sport; and, for that matter, by a woman who wants to make her mark in any way in a rough, male-dominated world. In both cases, the same qualities are required: self-confidence; principle; a calm contempt for male boorishness; a willingness to stick one's neck out; a refusal to be constrained by fear.

Each of the five guests of honour at the 2017 Velká Pardubická had encountered discrimination; each, in her different way, had beaten it. Baluchová spoke wearily of the many times she'd patiently schooled a horse to realise its potential, only to see the ride snatched from her and given to a man. 'I only got to ride Gretty in the Velká Pardubická because it was my own horse.' Růžičková-Jelínková encountered disparagement when she was starting out, but, again, believed in herself. 'People might say "She rode badly because she's a woman." Some even claimed that I was only getting rides because I was sleeping with trainers. But it was usually just journalists or bookmakers: people who'd never achieved anything themselves.' The jockeys themselves were never hostile, and prejudice was mainly encountered at small provincial meetings. As she progressed to a higher level, the shared severity of the tests seemed to engender respect. 'The harder the race, the better they treated me,' says Růžičková-Jelínková. 'We always joked at the start, and made fun of each other. Everyone knew that in a couple of minutes we could be half-dead or leaving in an ambulance. And, yes, there was partying afterwards, even though I'm not much of a drinker. There is friendship between Velká Pardubická riders – much greater than in flat racing.'

What she doesn't add is that there is also more genuine respect between the genders in the Velká Pardubická than in almost any other major sporting event, anywhere. That's not to say that the playing field is entirely level.

Crucially, prejudice persists further down the horse-racing food chain. I can't find a comparable set of statistics for the Czech Republic, but a recent set of UK figures will, I suspect, strike a chord for women in horse racing (and other sports) in many nations: women account for 74 per cent of people who ride horses, 51 per cent of stable staff, 11.3 per cent of professional jockey licences and 5.2 per cent of actual rides in races. The figures barely need dissecting. The story tells itself, as you watch the opportunities diminish in proportion to their increasing attractiveness. Yet a fourteen-year study at the University of Liverpool, whose findings were published in 2018, concluded that the gender of the jockey had no significant effect on the outcome of races, once you took into account the quality of the horses they were given. To put it crudely again: the only thing between your legs that has any real bearing on the outcome is the horse.

Slowly, the broader picture is changing. In the 2018 Grand National, three out of forty jockeys were female: Rachael Blackmore, Katie Walsh and Bryony Frost. There was much talk in the days leading up to the race about whether this might be the year in which, finally, a woman won the National. In the event, Frost's fifth place on Milansbar was the best any of the trio could manage. But it can only be a matter of time – perhaps it will have happened by the time you read this. Walsh, who has now retired, had previously won the Irish Grand National (in 2017) and come third in the 2012 Grand National. If women could get a fairer share of the best rides, of course one of them could claim the big prize at Aintree; just as one could – again – in Pardubice. Change is happening. What slows the process down is lingering prejudice among trainers and owners. What speeds it up is each headline-making female breakthrough, which weakens the grip of those who keep women down while simultaneously inspiring more women to strive to work their way up.

No female jockey has changed more attitudes with the headlines she made than Lata Brandisová. Her name was subsequently expunged from her nation's sporting history, thanks to her knack of getting on the wrong side of totalitarian regimes; as a result, it dropped from the world's, too. But the ripples of change that began with her achievements never stopped spreading. Her metamorphosis – in one glorious decade – from scandalous intruder to national treasure enabled a wider process of change, as breakthroughs in elite sport often do. Male domination of horse racing continues to recede, while her nation's ultimate symbol of sporting manhood – the steeplechase she was accused of dishonouring when she first tried to compete in it – is now honoured in many nations for its mature, inclusive approach to gender, and for the encouragement its story offers to all women with sporting dreams.

§ - § - §

A few minutes before the start of the 2017 Velká Pardubická, the runners and riders walked past the main stand in a long line, in the traditional pre-race parade. At the head of the line, in Lata's honour, rode a young woman in Kinský colours on a golden isabella Kinský horse. A commentator explained, for the benefit of mostly baffled spectators, that she symbolised Lata Brandisová:

*'první a jediná žena, která vyhrála Velkou Pardubickou'.* It was a phrase that even an inept language learner like me could recognise: I've encountered it so often, I know it by heart. It's her label, attached to her, with minor variations, whenever her story is introduced. Tomáš Masaryk was *'prezident-Osvoboditel'*: the 'president-liberator'. Lata Brandisová was 'the first and only woman to win the Velká Pardubická'.

It remains her label, and until her story finishes finding its way back into the collective consciousness it will continue to be widely used. After more than eighty years, it is still a glorious descriptor, summarising a sporting achievement as awe-inspiring as it was improbable. Yet perhaps a greater achievement is the certainty that, one day, part of the label will cease to be true. She will always be the first. She will not always be the only.

# Epilogue

## The good and faithful servant

On a bright May morning in Řitka, on the rough green slope behind the house, the crisp air shivers with the thud of hoof on turf. Some recent recruits to the Prague police are undergoing essential training. Their teacher is Gabriela Křístková. Their classroom is a patch of cool field, just beyond the garden wall, sheltered by clusters of high, tilting sycamores. Their lesson is in jumping: a valuable skill, it seems, in a modern urban force whose duties include crowd control.

Lata used to practise her jumping on much the same patch a lifetime ago. Today's tuition is delivered with the help of giant logs, arranged into a course of equestrian obstacles: simple jumps, wider jumps, sloping jumps, uphill jumps, ditches, and an up-and-down 'table' to be jumped onto and then off again. Lata's course was probably quite similar.

But these students are struggling. They are Kladruby horses: heavy, placid animals – some black, some grey; solid in body and nature. Their muscular flanks are twitching with exertion; puffs of their warm breath steam in the bright air. But their faces are what you notice. Long,

convex foreheads and tufty forelocks make them startlingly expressive, and there is no mistaking the young
horses' thoughts: the jumps both fascinate and baffle
them. Anything resembling a normal jump they leap
with relish. Less familiar obstacles, such as the ditches
and the table, unnerve them.

The challenge for the police officers on their backs is to
show them what needs to be done and to coax them into
believing they can do it. For some, this takes all morning.
Horse after horse lopes eagerly towards the first ditch,
which drops slightly from take-off to landing but lacks
an above-ground obstacle. Horse after horse shudders to
a frightened halt as it realises that there is an unexpected
item in the jumping area. Some seem frightened; others merely overwhelmed by puzzlement. Most, having
refused once, are more suspicious than ever when asked
to try again. Yet somehow, as the morning wears on,
each horse is gradually persuaded, until all six have mastered this and several other initially daunting obstacles.
Different officers take different approaches: some soothe,
some chivvy, some get off and lead. Others find that it
helps to let the horse watch while others negotiate it successfully. The common factors are trust and tenderness,
used to empower each horse to make that first, frightening leap of faith. It is like watching children learning to
ride bicycles.

Actually, there is another common factor. All the riders are women. The observation is worth making because
it is unusual to see that kind of gender balance in a group
of police officers, in any country. In another respect, it
is unremarkable: among riders, all-female is the norm.
Gabriela teaches riding skills across a whole spectrum

of ages and abilities: to eager child novices, awkward teenagers, experienced equestrians, the sick, the disabled, and to competitive eventers at everything up to international level. Right across that spectrum, an overwhelming majority of her pupils are female.

'It's funny,' she says. 'I wonder what those army officers would have felt – the ones who didn't want Lata to race against them – if they looked at what's happening today. All the people learning to ride are girls. In twenty years' time there probably won't be any male riders.'

She exaggerates only slightly. The trend is overwhelming. The 74 per cent figure quoted earlier errs on the low side; in many countries it is nearer 80 per cent. And that, remember, covers all age groups. Focus on young riders starting out in the sport and the gender imbalance is even more pronounced. You can speculate endlessly about the reasons. (For example: boys prefer football and fighting; boys can't handle commitment; boys are emotionally immature; etc.) You probably shouldn't. The stereotypes of the modern world can be as limiting as those of the old. Yet not every stereotype is entirely baseless. And this morning I cannot keep a new one out of my head: maybe, when it comes to horses, girls and women are just *naturally better at it*.

The observation almost makes itself. As the police horses wrestle with their insecurities, the field seems to glow with empathy and nurturing. Each horse has its own learning style, its own quirks and insecurities. The teaching style is feminine. Each officer senses her horse's needs, then finds ways of delivering the appropriate help. At times it is moving to watch: there is something maternal about the solicitude. The fact that the child figure in the relationship is ten times the size of the mother figure somehow accentuates the vulnerability and tenderness. I can't help wondering how many men would show such patience or sensitivity.

Such thoughts are simplistic and, probably, patronising. They are unfair, too. There is no law of nature that says that men must be brutish and women sensitive. Yet we talk, sometimes, about masculine and feminine management styles, and people of both genders understand what is meant. Riding is similar. An approach based on domination could be described as a 'male' approach, whoever employs it; an approach based on empathy – seeing things from the horse's point of view – could be described as 'female'. Ask a female jockey about riding in the Velká Pardubická and the chances are her answer will incorporate the horse's point of view. 'You have to let the horse choose the pace it's comfortable with,' says Lucie Baluchová; 'He hates guidance that's too firm,' says Martina Růžičková-Jelínková, referring to her favourite Velká Pardubická horse, Charme Look. Ask a man, and in my experience you're more likely to get an answer with 'I' in it. But each gender is capable of either approach. Cutting-edge champions of natural training methods, such as Monty Roberts and Pat Parelli, could be said to deal with horses in a 'female' way, yet are no less male for that. The question is: which is more effective – especially when it comes to ultra-tough challenges such as the Velká Pardubická? Most experts would say that it depends on the horse. 'There are lots of horses who don't run well with men, and a lot for whom girls are too weak,' says Růžičková-Jelínková. Stallions often respond better to men. Yet a woman, she believes, 'puts more spirit in it – and a kind of responsiveness.' Charlotte Budd agrees. 'A woman might be more tactful,' she says, tactfully. 'A horse might think, "Well, you're not going to get me to do things by brute force." But a more subtle approach might work.' Once again, the horse's viewpoint is in the foreground.

At the very least, the question is worth looking at with an open mind. Traditionally, a trainer considering using a female jockey for such a race asks himself (it is usually a 'himself'): 'Is she man enough to ride in an extreme steeplechase?' But perhaps it is male jockeys who should prompt the question; and the question should be: 'Is he woman enough to ride in an extreme steeplechase?'

Lata, asked by a journalist for the secret of riding successfully in the Velká Pardubická, was clear about what was required. 'The craving for glory alone is not enough,' she said. 'There must also be love for the horse.' This may seem counterintuitive: if you love the horse, why would you ask it to participate in such a dangerous exercise? Her point, I think, was that if you ask in good faith, with love, the horse will do it gladly; if you seek merely to dominate, it will keep something back. 'With goodness,' she added, 'one achieves everything with a horse.'

Every horse understands the dangers of jumping: you have only to watch the novices on the Řitka jumps course to see that. Yet if the right person asks them, in the right way, and is willing to share the danger, a horse will attempt almost anything.

§ - § - §

As the lesson draws to an end, the young police horses assemble with their mostly dismounted riders near where I am standing. They seem exhilarated: buzzing with achievement. The nearest horse is close enough for me to feel his warm exhalations and, momentarily, the brush of his silk-soft nose against my ear. I glance up to the nearest of his big brown eyes, expecting curiosity, but he is not looking at me. His gaze is settled on his rider, just in front. It is a gaze of trust and adoration.

Lata's formula – 'love for the horse' – left something out. There must also be love *from* the horse. You see that in all the most successful pairings: the empowering empathy comes as much from the ridden as the rider. You could feel it here this morning, too, in the renewed courage with which these police horses responded to each brisk pat or leaning whisper, and in the obviously shared delight of horse and rider at each new break-through. Pardubice, similarly, has seen many mutually empowering love affairs between rider and horse: Popler and Gyi Lovam!; Lengnik and Herold; Lata and Norma. So has Aintree, from Bruce Hobbs and Battleship to Bob Champion and Aldaniti. The races are brutal. They are also demonstrations of what love between species can achieve.

Love, wrote Lata towards the end of her life, should involve 'a complete trust, one to another – then the love and affection cannot disappear'. That strikes me as a pretty good description of what passed between her and her horses. But that trust was also tied up with another idea. The horse, she believed, 'is the noblest animal' – to be won over 'like a noble man, through love'. I'm sure she wasn't thinking of nobility in the dull sense of aristocratic pedigree, any more than Jiří Kocman was when, sharing his memories of Chlumec, he described Lata as 'a noble lady of rare character'. Rather, each was referring to a more elusive idea: nobility in the sense of that which is best in us. This was the sort of nobility that Socrates had in mind when (according to Plato) he used the image of an immortal horse to embody the better half of the human soul: 'a lover of honour and modesty and temperance, and a follower of true glory.' Flesh and blood horses sometimes seem to do the same. They appear stoical, brave, unselfish; wisely contented. In a greedy, agitated world, some people find solace in their profound inner stillness. Yet there is also nobility in the honest joy that a horse takes in doing the things it does best – galloping, jumping, racing; and in the fact that it is both the toughest and the gentlest of creatures; and, often, in the fact that it is great-hearted enough to spend every last ounce of its powers in the heat of battle.

One mystery remains: if the horse is so noble, why is it so biddable? Why does it submit to the constant diversion of its gifts to serve human ends? Is it stupid? Is it servile? Some would say so. Yet the same evidence can be interpreted in the opposite way: perhaps the horse submits because this capacity for patient, loyal, uncomplaining service is another facet of its nobility – perhaps even its essence.

Lata understood that. She understood the paradox of what used to be called horsemanship: the fact that the horse must *choose* to do as it is asked. She knew that, whether it is the exhaustion of the plough or the terror of the steeplechase, the horse will not only endure beyond all reason but will do so willingly; but only if there is love between human and horse.

§ - § - §

Inside the Lata Brandisová mini museum at Řitka, Gabriela guides me through the memorabilia in the glass cabinet. She takes out Lata's old Communist-era identity card, issued when she was sixty-seven. We flick through its pages. One has a question about military service: 'Soldier or not a soldier?' 'Not a soldier,' states the handwritten answer.

'But,' says Gabriela bitterly, 'she was more of a soldier than half the men in our army today.'

I have no idea if this is a fair assessment of the fighting men of the Czech Republic. She is right about Lata, though. In the trenches, you would be happy to have someone like her at your side. Any soldier would. There are, of course, still men who insist that women have no place in battle. They have rarely seen active service themselves. Men under fire are generally less concerned with their comrades' gender (or sexuality) than with whether or not they are brave and true. Lata, to her core, was brave and true.

Yes, she was born into privilege. What made her life memorable was the grace with which she endured hardship. All through her life things were taken from her. She suffered hurt after hurt, physical and emotional, and spent the last thirty years of her life hungry, poor, despised and rejected. Yet she never asked for pity. She had a soldier's heart.

But her heart was also full of love: the kind of love that, in St Paul's words, 'beareth all things, believeth all things, hopeth all things, endureth all things'. That, in a dozen words, was what she did.

'There are so many people today who complain about absolutely anything,' Martina Růžičková-Jelínková told me once. 'Yet this woman, who had so much to complain about, never did. I find it very moving.' So, suddenly, do I. Lata was extraordinary not just in what she achieved but in how she lived. She gave what she had to give, dreamed and chased improbable dreams, suffered what she had to suffer, and did what she believed was her duty. Each time she encountered a setback, she picked herself up and resumed her journey. She never complained: just quietly endured what was asked of her, as a soldier does; or – in another biblical phrase that must have been familiar to her – as a good and faithful servant does.

Perhaps this was the key to her mystery: the parable of the servant who made the most of the talents entrusted to him. Lata did the same, in a world in which women were constantly encouraged not to use their talents but to bury them. Yet she did so not in a self-seeking way, but dutifully, sticking faithfully to her path with quiet courage.

My eyes wander again to that faded photograph, mentioned much earlier, of Lata and Norma, head by head, radiant in the glow of their great triumph. It is, I realise, a picture of two friends: equals; perhaps even kindred spirits. Lata's gift for seeing the world through equine eyes was not simply a means to an end. In some ways, I suspect, it was more basic than that: the worldview of the horse actually overlapped with her own.

Horses, for Lata, were her 'dearest and most faithful friends'; Norma was a 'good and loyal horse'. But the trust and affection flowed in both directions. She had her faith; the horses had theirs – in her. Both pointed to the same thing: the duty to be a good and faithful servant. And the resulting bond empowered horse and rider to do things together that others said could not be done.

Lata Brandisová was indeed, as Kocman said, 'A noble lady of rare spirit.' But the nobility that defined her was not that of a countess. What would be the point of telling her story, if that were all? She was noble in a rarer, more precious way. Hers was the same brave, loyal spirit that animates the great heart of a horse.

# Sources & Notes

This is a work of non-fiction. There is occasional speculation in it (always identified as such) but there is no invention. Each statement about what happened is based on evidence. Some of that evidence is less specific or less certain than I would have liked, but is used on the basis that, in the absence of anything firmer, it is a reasonable basis for provisional belief. An early draft of this book included notes identifying the source of every single factual assertion. There were more notes than book. Since most of the sources identified were in Czech or German, and few are available to UK-based readers, it seems more helpful to identify my principal sources in general terms, with the remaining itemised notes being restricted, as far as possible, to points that may be of use or of interest to English readers.

The boxes bequeathed to Jan Pospíšil's aunt Eva (Eva Pospíšilová), mentioned in my opening chapter and referred to hereafter as the Pospíšil Papers, will ultimately be accessible in the state archive of the Czech Republic. (At the time of writing, they are still being sorted and catalogued in the state archive in Dobřichovice.) Statements about the Brandis family's history and financial affairs and the ownership and management of Řitka can be assumed, if not otherwise stated, to have their source in these papers. So, usually, can anything involving family memorabilia (letters, memory books, etc.) – although Lata's correspondence with Lori Kinský is preserved only in the Kinský archive in Zámrsk.

Direct quotations from Lata, unless otherwise stated, come mainly from one of three sources. One is a long interview she gave in late 1927 or early 1928 to a German-language newspaper, published under the heading 'Die Dame im Rennsattel'. The cutting is in the Kinský archive. The newspaper looks very much like *Neues Wiener Tagblatt*, but I have been unable to trace the article to its original context. The second source is a long first-person account of her life that Lata provided for the book *Berühmte Reiter erzählen*, ed. Wilhelm Braun and A. R. Marsani (Wilhelm Limpert-Verlag, 1941), pp. 181–7. I assume that she wrote the account (in German) herself; and, for obvious reasons, that she did so a long time before the book was published. The third is a fifteen-minute radio interview for Český rozhlas ('Jak jsme letos vyhrály Velkou Pardubickou'), broadcast on 10 November 1937. The actual recording appears to be lost but a transcript, possibly incomplete, survives. In all three cases, Lata talks mostly about her childhood, her early experiences of riding and racing, and her attitude to horses; although the radio interview also deals with the 1937 Velká Pardubická. Her accounts are quite consistent between the three sources.

Lata also gave a flurry of interviews to the Czech press in late 1937. I have listed the most important of these in the note to page 236 (on page 389). These provide a number of details (again, sometimes duplicated) about Lata's lifestyle in Řitka in the 1930s, and, to a lesser extent, about her experiences at the 1937 Velká Pardubická. 'V sídle amazonky' by Vladimír Štědrý (from an unidentified Czech newspaper, October 1937) is particularly good about the former; 'Vítěz Velké pardubické, slečna Brandisová, vypravuje' (an un-bylined interview in *Svoboda-Brno*, 22 October 1937) is better on the latter.

My descriptions of the Brandis family's day-to-day life in Řitka and, in particular, of their interactions with villagers, draw heavily on the accounts of people who still live locally. Their names can be found in the fifth paragraph of the Acknowledgements on page 403. Several could speak directly of memories from the 1930s onwards, while their testimony grew denser and more convincing as the story approached the present day. A number also supplied second- or third-hand testimony, based on accounts they had heard from parents or grandparents.

Much the same can be said of the testimonies of the family members listed in the second and third paragraphs of the Acknowledgements (page 402). Their accounts of events before the 1930s are second- or third-hand; thereafter, they grow more confident and reliable with each passing year. Génilde Kinsky was born in 1925 and saw Lata regularly for the next twenty-three years. Petr Jaroševský lived with Lata from his birth in 1937 until 1950, and continued to see her often thereafter. Petr also has his own large album of family photographs, which offer priceless evidence of what Řitka looked like from the inside (even before he was born).

Another very helpful resource has been *Řitka v minulosti*, František Šírl's meticulously typed, unpublished, ten-volume local chronicle, available in the National Archive (or, if you know who to ask, in the village itself). This is particularly valuable as a record of the details of day-to-day village life, even before the Brandis family arrived. Statements about such details in *Unbreakable* should be assumed, unless otherwise stated, to be drawn from this chronicle. Šírl also devoted a couple of pages to Lata, whom he interviewed in the 1970s. These writings were also published (posthumously) in *Rodopisná revue* ('Lata Brandisová – vítězka Velké pardubické v roce 1937', 14 March 2012). I have quoted from his interview selectively. He was a meticulous chronicler, but it is clear that horse racing was not his special subject.

I should acknowledge two influential pieces of writing by the sportswriter Pavel Kovář: a long article in *Reflex* magazine ('Lata Brandisová', *Reflex*, no. 40, pp. 72–4); and a longer, related chapter ('První vítězka Velké pardubické') in his book, *Šampaňské s příchutí pelyňku* (Secret Partnership, 2000). There is much duplication between the two pieces, and in citing them I have treated them as one (referred to as 'Kovář'). Many details that I have subsequently traced to other sources initially came to my attention via Kovář.

There is, similarly, much overlap between the 'O Latě Brandisové' chapter in *Příběhy předmětů*, by Jiří Střecha and Václav Žmolík (Česká televize/Albatros Media, 2012) and the television programme *Příběhy předmětů: Podkova Laty Brandisové*, dir: Vlastimil Šimůnek, first broadcast on Česká televize in 2011. Again, for citation purposes I have treated these as one (referred to as *Příběhy předmětů*); and, again, I acknowledge an influence much greater than the small number of specific citations below implies. I have also benefited greatly from the exhaustive research undertaken by Lenka Gotthardová for her long article 'Perličky vzpomínek na Latu Brandisovou' (*Farmář*, 5/2015, pp. 49–51); and, indeed, have also benefited from the author's generous advice.

When it comes to the world that Lata Brandisová lived in, I am heavily indebted to the work of many other authors. Specific d ebts a re c ited i n t he d etailed notes below. A few are large enough to deserve broader acknowledgement – even though many of the works in question are, unfortunately, unavailable in English.

My understanding of the Velká Pardubická and its background is founded in John Pinfold and Kamila Pecherová' s wonderfully authoritative and readable *Velká pardubická a Velká Národní Liverpoolská* (Helios, 2010) – which, despite its title, has text in English as well as Czech. Equally essential, although not available in English, has been *Od Fantoma po Peruána*, by Jaroslav Hubálek and Miloslav Nehyba (Jezdecký spolek Kolcsa, 2001) – an encyclopaedic, year-by-year chronicle of the race from 1874 to 2000. Miloslav Nehyba is also the author of *Dostih s Taxisovým příkopem* (Helios, 2017), which brings the story closer to the present day. (These books represent only two tips of the iceberg of Mr Nehyba 's private archive, which he has been kind enough to share with me.) I have also made extensive use of *Taxis a ti druzí: Velká pardubická steeplechase*, by Vladimír David (Kraj, 1987); *100 ročníků Velké pardubické steeplechase*, by Miloš Svoboda (Státní zemědělské nakladatelství, 1990). I also recommend *Království za koně*, by Michal Horáček (Olympia, 1983); *Život mezi překážkami (příběhy hrdinů Velké pardubické)*, by Petr

Feldstein (Secret Partnership, 1999); and *Velká pardubická: příběhy z dějin, současnosti a zákulisí slavného dostihu,* by Pavel Kovář (2011). None of these is available in English. Velká Pardubická-related books with a focus on specific jockeys include: *Tisíc a jeden skok: životní steeplechase Rudolfa Poplera,* by Josef Pávek (Olympia, 1969); *Pojďme na dostihy,* by Hynek Býček (Melantrich, 1941); and *Baroness Daisy – The Jockey's Wife,* by David Dunford (Russell Press, 2015). Fascinating details about the world of Czechoslovak horse racing during Lata's lifetime can also be found in *Velká Chuchle dostihová,* by Jiří Zlámaný (Secret Partnership/Filip Trend, 2003), and – with more of a Chlumec focus – in Pavel Fiala's *Mistr opratí Jiří Kocman* (Nakladatelství Lenka Gotthardová, 2017).

Farewell to the Horse: The Final Century of Our Relationship,* by Ulrich Raulff (Penguin, 2017), is a superb account of the changing relationship between human beings and horses. Lenka Gotthardová's *Od trójského koně po Váňu* (Nakladatelství Lenka Gotthardová, 2014) explains the importance of the horse in Czech culture. *The History of Steeplechasing,* by Michael Seth-Smith, Peter Willett, Roger Mortimer and John Lawrence (Michael Joseph, 1966), is good on the British roots of steeplechasing. *The Principles of Riding* (Kenilworth Press, 1983) provides a fascinating insight into traditional German approaches to horsemanship; Alois Podhajsky's *The Complete Training of Horse and Rider* (Wilshire Books, 1967) gives the inside view from the Spanish Riding School in Vienna. *Slavní koně,* by Zdeněk Mahler (Orbis, 1992), celebrates individual equine heroes. *They're Off! The Story of the First Girl Jump Jockeys,* by Anne

Alcock (J. A. Allen, 1978), has a particularly good chapter on Charlotte Brew.

For the history of the nobility under the Habsburgs I learnt from *Das Leben adeliger Frauen*, by Martina Winkelhofer (Haymon Verlag, 2011); *Twilight of the Habsburgs*, by Alan Palmer (Phoenix Giant, 1997); *The Glory of the Habsburgs*, by Princess Nora von Fugger (Harrap, 1932); *The Sporting Empress*, by John Welcome (Michael Joseph, 1975); *The Decline and Fall of the Hapsburg Empire 1815–1918*, by Alan Sked (Routledge, 2001); and from reference books such as *Český biografický slovník XX. století*, ed. Josef Tomeš (Petr Meissner, 1999); *Biografický slovník českých zemí*, by Pavla Vošahlíková et al; *Almanach českých šlechtických rodů* (Martin, 1999), by Vladimír Pouzar et al.

The troubled history of the Czech nobility in the First Republic is dealt with superbly in *Noble Nationalists: the Transformation of the Bohemian Aristocracy*, by Eagle Glassheim (Harvard University Press, 2005); and also in *Šlechta střední Evropy v konfrontaci s totalitními režimy 20. století*, by Zdeněk Hazdra, Václav Horčička, Jan Županič (Ústav pro studium totalitních režimů, 2011). I also recommend 'Šlechta ve službách Masarykovy Republiky', by Zdeněk Hazdra, in *Šlechtické rody Čech, Moravy a Slezska* (Lidové Noviny, 2014); *Ve znamení tří deklarací*, by Zdeněk Hazdra (Ústav pro studium totalitních režimů, 2014); and *European Aristocracies and the Radical Right, 1918–1939*, by Karina Urbach (Studies of the German Historical Institute London, 2007).

For the more specific history of the Kinský family I have relied mainly on *Zu Pferd und zu Fuss: 70 Jahre aus den Erinnerungen*, by Zdenko Radslav Kinský

(L. Heidrich, 1974); *Sága rodu Kinských*, by Karel Richter (Zámek Karlova Koruna/Hrad Kost, 2008); and *Dějiny rodu Kinských*, by Aleš Valenta (Veduta, 2004). For anyone interested in Karel Kinský, I also recommend *Liverpoolský triumf Karla knížete Kinského*, by Kamila Pecherová (Nakladatelství Lenka Gotthardová, 2018).

A *History of the Czechoslovak Republic, 1918–1948*, ed. Victor S. Mamatey and Radomír Luza (Princeton University Press, 1973), is a good starting point for an overview of the First Republic. Similarly, for an introduction to Tomáš Masaryk's life and thought, *T. G. Masaryk: Against the Current, 1882–1914*, by H. Gordon Skilling (Pennsylvania State University Press, 1994), and *Thomas Masaryk*, by Robert Birley (Athlone Press, 1951), have both stood the test of time; as, on a related theme, has *Land Reform in Czechoslovakia*, by Lucy Textor (Allen & Unwin, 1923).

The literature of Nazism is too vast to summarise here. But Richard J. Evans's Third Reich trilogy – notably *The Third Reich in Power* (Allen Lane, 2005) – and *The Third Reich: A new history*, by Michael Burleigh (Macmillan, 2000), have both been important to my understanding of the rise of National Socialism. *Stormtroopers*, by Daniel Siemens (Yale University Press, 2017), demonstrates the importance of paramilitary groups in Hitler's Germany. For tensions between Germans and Czechs in Czechoslovakia, you can find vivid first-hand reportage in *German and Czech: A threat to European peace* by Sheila Grant Duff (NFRB Research Pamphlets, 1937) and – repackaged with hindsight – in *The Parting of Ways*, by Sheila Grant Duff (Peter Owen, 1982). *A History of Eastern Europe: Crisis and Change*, by Robert Bidleux and

Ian Jeffries (Routledge, 1998), is also good on this period (as well as on the post-war triumph of Communism); as is *The Czech Fascist Movement: 1922–1942*, by David Kelly (East European Monographs, 1995). *Documents on British Foreign Policy 1919–1939*, ed. E. L. Woodward and Rohan Butler (Her Majesty's Stationery Office, 1949) is a valuable resource for those interested in the UK's role in the story, while David Vaughan's *Hear My Voice* (Jantar, 2018) – a 'documentary novel' – is a vivid and impeccably sourced account of the propaganda battle between Czechs and Germans in 1938.

For the Nazis' use of sport as a weapon of propaganda, Nele Maya Fahnenbruck's '. . . *reitet für Deutschland': Pferdesport und Politik im Nationalsozialismus* (Verlag die Werkstatt, 2013) looks specifically at horse racing – but not at steeplechasing, and not in English. *High Society in the Third Reich*, by Fabrice D'Almeida (Polity, 2008) and *The Nazi Conscience*, by Claudia Koonze (Belknap Press, 2003) offer valuable insights into this theme, as do *Max Schmeling and the Making of a National Hero in Twentieth-Century Germany*, by Jon Hughes (Palgrave Studies in Sport and Politics, 2017) and *How Hitler Hijacked World Sport*, by Christopher Hilton (The History Press, 2012).

Hard-core students of steeplechasing in inter-war Germany will find plenty of details in *Berühmte Reiter erzählen; Das Hohelied des deutschen Amateur-Rennsports 1827 bis 1938*, by O. Christ (M. & H. Schaper, 1938); *150 Jahre Amateur-Rennsport*, by Wilhelm Kauke (Ahnert-Verlag, 1977); *Rehers Jahrbuch für den Pferde-Sport 1936* (Verlag von August Reher, 1936); and *Die Rappen-Reiter*, by Wilhem Fabricus (Mellinger, 1970) – although they might find it slightly harder to track down the books themselves. They will also find vivid accounts of the glory days of East Prussian steeplechasing and horse-breeding in *Trakehnen*, by Martin Heling (BLV Verlagsgesellschaft, 1959); in *Menschen, Pferde, weites Land*, by Hans von Lehndorff (C. H. Beck, 1980); and in *Pferde und Reiter in aller Welt*, by A. R. Marsani and Wilhelm Braun (Wilhelm Limpert, 1939).

For a more general introduction to the story of East Prussia, I recommend *Forgotten Land*, by Max Egremont (Picador, 2001), and *From Prussia with Love*, by Roger Boyes (Summersdale, 2011); or, for German-speakers, *Ostpreussen für Anfänger: Ansichten, Einsichten und Vergnügliches für Spurensucher*, by Brigitte Jäger-Dabek (Edition Jäger-Dabek Media, 2013). Or, if you read only one book about the East Prussian tragedy, read *The Flight Across the Ice*, by Patricia Clough (Haus, 2009): a heart-breaking account of the forced migration of the exclave's people and horses in 1945.

When it comes to the grotesque story of Hans Fegelein and the Equestrian SS, I strongly recommend two works: *Fegelein's Horsemen and Genocidal Warfare*, by Henning Pieper (Palgrave Macmillan, 2015), and *Himmler's Cavalry: the Equestrian SS, 1930–1945*, by Paul J. Wilson (Schiffer Military History, 2000). Additional details can be found in *Riding East: SS Cavalry Brigade in Poland and Russia 1939–1942*, by Mark C. Yerger (Schiffer Military History, 2004), and *Axis Cavalry in World War II*, by Jeffery T. Fowler (Osprey Publishing, 2001).

On the more uplifting story of women's struggle for equality in Czechoslovakia, I have learned a great deal from *Elusive Equality: Gender, Citizenship, and the Limits of Democracy in Czechoslovakia, 1918–1950*, by Melissa

Feinberg (University of Pittsburgh Press, 2006); and from *Czech Feminisms: Perspectives on Gender in East Central Europe*, ed. Iveta Jusová and Jiřina Šiklová (Indiana University Press, 2006) – especially Karla Huebner's chapter, 'The Czech 1930s through Toyen'. *The Feminists*, by Richard J. Evans (Croom Helm, 1979), is also helpful, and there are excellent contributions from Melissa Feinberg and Jana Osterkamp in *New Perspectives on European Women's Legal History*, ed. Sara L. Kimble & Marion Röwekamp (Taylor & Francis, 2016). *Women and Sports in the United States: A Documentary Reader*, ed. Jean O'Reilly & Susan K. Cann (University Press of New England, 2007) has a good chapter on 'Olympic Women: A Struggle for Recognition' by Jennifer Hargreaves. *Příběh české rekordwoman*, by Pavel Kovář (Pejdlova Rosička, 2017), tells the remarkable story of Zdeněk Koubek.

*Prague in Black: Nazi Rule and Czech Nationalism*, by Chad Bryant (Harvard University Press, 2009), is a thorough and horribly compelling account of life in Czechoslovakia under the Occupation. More vivid still is *Mendelssohn is on the Roof*, by Jiří Weil (Penguin, 1992), a fictional work so deeply grounded in fact that it is hard to think of a better introduction to the experience of Czechoslovakia's Jews from 1938 to 1945. For more on the Occupation, I recommend: *A German Protectorate: The Czechs Under Nazi Rule*, by Sheila Grant Duff (Frank Cass, 1942); *Life with the Enemy: Collaboration and Resistance in Hitler's Europe 1939–1945*, by Werner Rings (Doubleday, 1982); *Czechs under Nazi Rule*, by Vojtech Mastny (Columbia University Press, 1971); and Jiří Padevět's *Průvodce protektorátní Prahou* (Academia/

Archiv hlavního města Prahy, 2015). *The Journey*, by Cecilia Sternberg (Častolovice, 1999), describes events from the perspective of a Prague-based noblewoman; *The Hitler Kiss*, by Radomir Luza with Christina Vella (Louisiana State University Press, 2002), tells the inside story of the Czech resistance. *The Encyclopedia of War Crimes and Genocide*, by Leslie Alan Horvitz and Christopher Catherwood (Infobase, 2014), is a sadly necessary accompaniment.

I have also drawn heavily on several meticulous studies of Pardubice's history, notably *Kniha o městě Pardubice*, ed. Dagmar Broncová (Milpo Media, 1999); *Český fašismus v Pardubicích a na Pardubicku 1926–1939*, by Jiří kotyk (OFTIS, 2016); *Všední život na Pardubicku v období nacistické okupace a druhé světové války*, by Karla Jará et al (Krajská knihovna, 2012); *Pardubický Zámeček a jeho osudy*, by Jiří Kotyk (Klub přátel Pardubicka, 2015); *Silver A a Heydrichiáda na Pardubicku*, by Radovan Brož, Jiří Štěpánek and Jiří Kotyk (Evropské vydavatelství, 2012). Several of the authors also advised me personally. On a smaller scale, Vladimír Hellmuth-Brauner's *Všenor z minulosti blízké a vzdálené* (Spolek pro zvelebování Všenor, 1937) was an essential starting-point for the story of Hanuš Kasalický.

The closer Lata's story approaches to the present day, the more I have relied on eyewitness accounts and personal memories rather than published sources. However, some of the following might prove useful for readers wanting to learn more about specific aspects of Czechoslovakia's post-war story: *The Transfer of the Sudeten Germans: A study of Czech-German relations, 1933–1962*, by Radomir Luza (Routledge & Kegan Paul,

1964); *National Cleansing: Retribution against Nazi Collaborators in Postwar Czechoslovakia*, by Benjamin Frommer (Cambridge University Press, 2010); *The Collectivization of Agriculture in Eastern Europe*, ed. Irwin T. Sanders (University of Kentucky Press, 1958); *The Lost World of Communism*, by Peter Molloy (Ebury, 2009); *Reform Rule in Czechoslovakia*, by Galia Golan (Cambridge University Press, 1973); *The Prague Spring '68*, ed. Jaromír Navrátil (Central European University Press, 2006); *The Prague Spring and its Aftermath*, by Kieran Williams (Cambridge University Press, 1997).

Remarkably little about Lata Brandisová has been published online; less still is reliable or original. However, it would be wrong not to acknowledge the wealth of meticulously researched background material on the website of the venerable racing magazine (now online only) *Dostihový svět*. Much of this material has been translated into English by Robin Healey.

I have already mentioned Česká televize's 2011 documentary, *Příběhy předmětů: Podkova Laty Brandisové*. I also recommend Petr Feldstein's made-for-television film, *Velká pardubická koňská opera* (Česká televize, 1999). There is of course also plenty of Velká Pardubická footage on YouTube, some of it quite sickening; but I don't think there are more than a few seconds in which Lata appears – in Pathé News reports from 1937 and 1946. As for radio, Český rozhlas has broadcast a number of brief items relating to Lata over the years. I will not list them: most simply retell the same basic story. But I must acknowledge one ten-minute episode about Lata in Český rozhlas: Dvojka's 'Příběhy slavných' series, first broadcast on 8 October 2013. I happened to hear this on a podcast in late 2016 – which was when I encountered Lata's story for the first time.

I hope that, in addition to clarifying various arcane points, the notes below acknowledge all my other significant debts. If I have left any out, I apologise for the oversight. It should at least be clear that, in assembling this story, I have taken advantage of the prior work of many people, living and dead. I am grateful to them all.

# Notes

Title page: **the World's Most Dangerous Horse Race**

Some in the Czech racing world dispute this designation. They prefer 'toughest' to 'most dangerous' and argue that the Grand National is at least as severe. Traditionally, the Velká Pardubická was often described as 'the toughest steeplechase in mainland Europe' – thus avoiding a direct challenge to Aintree. But the Pardubice race is frequently described as 'the most dangerous' (for example, in 'Jump off at the deep end', by Erlend Clouston, *Guardian*, 10 April 1999; or 'The Velká Pardubická is the most dangerous horse race in the world', by Rob Sutherland, *Daily Telegraph* (Australia), 30 September 2015); and, as I argue in chapter 32, the Velká Pardubická is unique in the sense that the danger is usually presented as its raison-d'être.

p. 3: **Emil Zátopek, the runner ... the near-invincible national men's ice-hockey team of 1947–49**
Zátopek and Čáslavská supported the liberal reforms of the Prague Spring of 1968 and publicly opposed the resulting Soviet-led invasion. Both were excluded from public life and prevented from working in their chosen fields. Fikotová-Connolly was denounced as a traitor after marrying an American, Navratilová after seeking asylum in the US as an eighteen-year-old. The ice hockey team, whose crimes included allegedly considering defection and singing anti-Communist songs, received gaol sentences of up to fifteen years.

p. 6: **under 'restitution'**
Following the fall of Communism in November 1989, a series of laws from April 1990 onwards allowed property confiscated in Czechoslovakia between 25 February 1948 and 1 January 1990 to be reclaimed by its original owners or their heirs. This often proved more complicated than it

357

sounds, especially since many owners had gone into exile. Czech citizenship was required in order to benefit; and the millions who lost their homes in the three years following the Second World War are still excluded.

p. 11: **three villages, two farms, several fish-ponds**
Like many details in my account of the Brandis family's life in Řitka, these are derived from a combination of three sources: *Řitka v minulosti*; Kovář (who draws heavily on Šírl's chronicle); and local memories. I am grateful to Petr Breyer for the information that the other two villages were Čisovice and Bojov. The brewery, which was in Řitka, appears to have been closed soon after the family acquired the estate.

p. 12: **swam across the Danube for a bet**
'Dame gewinnt "Grosse Pardubitzer"', *Prager Tagblatt*, 19 October 1937.

p. 12: **tutoring princelings ... in ... horsemanship**
According to Lata, he was a graduate of the Riding Teachers' Institute in Vienna.

p. 12: **the resulting quarrel ... was so violent that shots were fired**
The version of the incident passed down in family tradition is quite lurid, and is partly supported by the local chronicler of Křesetice, the village next door to Úmonín. I have exercised restraint to maintain consistency with known dates of birth, marriage and death.

p. 13: **later accused of tampering with Christian's will**
This and other salacious details were recorded in the Křesetice chronicle.

p. 13: **whose grand friends included at least one royal archduke**
Leopold was on friendly terms with Archduke Ferdinand Karl Habsbursko-Lotrinsky of Austria, younger brother of the Archduke Franz-Ferdinand whose assassination sparked the First World War. Ferdinand renounced his dynastic rights in 1911, after marrying inappropriately, and thereafter called himself Ferdinand Burg; see correspondence in the Pospíšil papers.

p. 14: **Johanna borrowed money to fund the purchase of Řitka**
The money was borrowed from an order of nuns in Austria, the Daughters of Charity of Saint Vincent de Paul, to which Leopold's elder sister, Maria Theresia, belonged. See Pospíšil papers.

p. 14: **allegedly rapacious vendor**
*Řitka v minulosti* implies that previous owner, Dr Karel Klaudy, used legal trickery to enrich himself at villagers' expense.

**p. 15: those three villages would dwindle to one**
This may be an over-simplification. *Řitka v minulosti* suggests that the family may still have owned a brickworks in Bojov and a farm in Čisovice in 1917 (when Lata was twenty-two), at which point they sold them off along with their other land disposals (see page 64).

**p. 15: not entirely banned from contact with village children**
This was certainly true in Úmonín (according to Josef Vepřek) and there are indirect reasons – such as the number of village children who saw inside the château grounds – for supposing it to have been true in Řitka.

**p. 16: 'dogs barking from every window'**
'Kazí sport ženy', un-bylined interview with Lata published in *Pražanka-Praha*, 10 November 1937.

**p. 16: a very formal kind of German**
This way of speaking, in which the third person ('he', 'she', 'they') is used instead of the second ('you'), is now obsolete; but the Brandis sisters are remembered in Řitka as having used it. Lata did not, however, use it in correspondence in later life.

**p. 16: German forms of each other's names**
Strictly speaking, this part of the story should describe the Graf and Gräfin von Brandis, and their children Maria Theresia, Gabriela, Leopold, Nicolaus, Maria (Lata), Christiane, Elisabeth, Margarete and Johanna. In fact, the siblings usually used nicknames: for example, 'Velká' for Marie Therese, 'Mur' for Gabriele, 'Utzle' for Lata, 'Zecko' for Kristýna, 'Peprl' for Alžběta and 'Michle' for Johanna. Even Lata's descendants sometimes find the variations confusing, so I have spared readers this challenge.

**p. 16: expected to be fluent in French**
For a comprehensive account of what was expected of daughters of the nobility, see *Das Leben adeliger Frauen*. The most rigorous demand was simply to stick with your own kind. William D. Godsey, Jr. ('Quarterings and Kinship: The Social Composition of the Habsburg Aristocracy in the Dualist Era', *Journal of Modern History*, Vol. 71, No. 1, pp. 56–104) calculated that there were 474 families in the Habsburg 'court circle' during this period, including the Brandises. In terms of future spouses and future friends, this was supposed to constitute Lata's entire world.

**p. 18: our knowledge of her siblings**
In addition to villagers and other family members, I am particularly grateful to Petr Jaroševský, Lata's nephew, for his detailed recollections

of the sisters' lives and habits. These were however formed at a slightly later stage in their lives and include nothing about Lata's two short-lived brothers.

### p. 20: **walls bristled with hunting trophies**
There are several photographs in the Pospíšil collection, and also in the collection of Petr Jaroševský, which show walls bristling with trophies to a quite shocking degree.

### p. 24: **'would have given her life for her horses'**
The friend was Jiří Kocman, best-known today as a world champion harness racer, who worked at Chlumec as a stable lad from 1949 to 1951 and also knew Lata when, before that, he was an apprentice jockey at Velká Chuchle.

### p. 25: **more horse-focused**
See: *Farewell to the Horse*; the first chapter makes a persuasive case that, because of slow uptake of technology and growing populations, the 'last century of the horse' – from 1815 to 1914 – 'witnessed not only the exodus of the horse from human history, but also its historical climax: never before had humanity been as heavily dependent on horses as when Benz and Daimler's internal combustion engines began rattling away ...' Today, by contrast, to quote Cyril Neumann, co-founder of Prague's Equestrian Club Ctěnice, 'We have many more people who ride, but we have far fewer "horsemen".'

### p. 28: **Wealthy Hungarians such as Count István Széchenyi**
For a full and fascinating account of the early history of English-style steeplechasing in the Habsburg lands, see *Velká Pardubická a Velká Národní Liverpoolská,* from which many of the details in chapters 3 and 4 are taken.

### p. 31: **riding his horses ... up the grand staircase**
I am grateful to Count Francesco Kinský dal Borgo, whose branch of the family now owns the castle, for giving me a detailed tour of the scenes of Oktavian's excesses. Some versions of Oktavian's stunts seem implausible, given the width of the stairs – but presumably he knew what he was doing.

### p. 32: **the more flamboyant Count Karel Kinský**
A definitive account of Karel Kinský's remarkable life can be found in *Liverpoolský triumf Karla knížete Kinského,* currently available only in Czech but unlikely to remain untranslated for long.

p. 33: **'It is impossible that we had such apes in our family!'**
See: http://www.hrad-kost.cz/en/history-of-kinsky-family.php. In fairness
to Oktavian, Norbert was referring to other forebears as well.

p. 36: **'If I want to kill myself in Czechoslovakia'**
Quoted in *Velká Pardubická a Velká Národní Liverpoolská.*

p. 37: **insisted that half of the race be run through ploughed fields**
The most detailed and accessible accounts of the many changes in route,
terrain and obstacles of the Velká Pardubická course can be found in *Od
Fantoma po Peruána.* The current proportion of ploughed land is closer to
a quarter and the ploughing is much less deep.

p. 38: **the start of the first Velká Pardubická**
My detailed accounts of individual runnings of the race, of which
this is the first, are mainly based on contemporary newspaper reports
(especially in *Národní listy*); on *Od Fantoma po Peruána*; and on the
vast private archive of Miloslav Nehyba, much of which has found its
way into his own writings. But the fullest account of this particular race
is probably that in *Velká Pardubická a Velká Národní Liverpoolská*
(pp. 34–40).

p. 41: **twenty-nine horses have died**
This was the grim running total as of 2018. The vast majority of the deaths
occurred before the Second World War; there have been four in the past
twenty years.

p. 42: **'the love child of Becher's Brook and The Chair, on steroids'**
'Czech Grand National makes its European cousins look like a stroll in
the park – as I learnt to my cost', by Marcus Armytage, *Daily Telegraph*, 5
October 2016.

p. 42: **'Horses will often do a jump of that size in training'**
Quoted in *Taxis a ti druzí.*

p. 42: **'largely a question of letting the horse go'**
Kratochvíl was being interviewed on *Všechnopárty*, Českà televize, 19
January 2018.

p. 44: **Sisi … made endless visits to Britain**
For a full account of these visits, including the Empress's romance with Bay
Middleton, see *The Sporting Empress.*

p. 47: **Leopold did not approve … more time with horses than trying to
find a husband**
See: Kovář; and *Příběhy předmětů.*

p. 48: **one of the world's first private cinemas**
Strictly speaking, this was not so much a cinema as a viewing-room for an improvised three-dimensional image-viewer. See: 'Měl baron Kast na zámku v Mníšku pod Brdy domácí kino?', by Marie Charvátová (Novinky. cz, 25 February 2015).

p. 48: **Lata was shy, and disliked dancing**
Many people have testified to Lata's shyness. It was Countess Génilde Kinský, whom I interviewed in Žďár nad Sázavou in October 2017, who emphasised her dislike of dancing.

p. 50: **A photograph in the family's collection**
The particular picture I have in mind is in the Pospíšil collection. Petr Jaroševský has another one, depicting the aftermath of a different 'officers' race'.

p. 50: **a woman was obliged to do the housework**
See: 'Equality at Stake: Legality and National Discourses on Family Law in Czechoslovakia, 1918–1931', by Jana Osterkamp, in *New Perspectives on European Women's Legal History*, pp. 97–121; and *Elusive Equality: Gender, Citizenship, and the Limits of Democracy in Czechoslovakia, 1918–1950*, p. 69.

p. 53: **Archduke Franz Ferdinand ... had a reputation for being a demanding critic**
See *Twilight of the Habsburgs*, p. 321.

p. 53: **spend three times as much on beer, wine and tobacco**
*A History of Eastern Europe: Crisis and Change*, p. 398; *The Decline and Fall of the Habsburg Empire 1815–1918*, p. 262.

p. 54: **'That was how things were back then ...'**
Quotations from Joseph Roth's *The Radetzky March* are from Michael Hofmann's 2002 translation for Granta.

p. 55: **'in even rhythm, leisurely and quietly'**
Quotations from Stefan Zweig's *The World of Yesterday* use Benjamin W. Huebsch and Helmut Ripperger's 1943 translation.

p. 55: **she wasn't allowed to take her seat**
The Bohemian diet was little more than a local assembly. None the less, when the Czech nationalist writer Božena Viková-Kunětická was elected to it in 1912, the Habsburg-appointed governor declared the result void. The diet was finally dissolved the following year. See: *The Feminists*, p. 98; 'Equality at Stake', p. 97; and 'Czech Feminists and Nationalism in the Late Habsburg Monarchy: "The First in Austria"', by Katherine David (*Journal of Women's History*, Vol. 3, No. 2), pp. 26–45.

p. 57: 'Whatever happens we two will always remain the same friends ...'
Letter to George Lambton, quoted in *Velká Pardubická a Velká Národní Liverpoolská*.

p. 57: There is reason to believe that Lata's mother ... did not cope well
The details of this supposition are vague: it is an item of family tradition, which in some parts of the family (for example, among Zdenko Radslav Kinský's children) extended to the firm conviction that the Countess had permanently moved out, abandoning her family. Documentary evidence among the Pospíšil papers makes this hard to believe: she appears to have been on the premises in 1917 and 1918, at least. But she certainly had health problems, so perhaps she was incapacitated.

p. 57: **left nineteen-year-old Lata in charge**
See: Lata's account in 'Die Dame im Rennsattel'; Pavel Kovář's accounts in *Reflex* and in *Šampaňské s příchutí pelyňku*; and Jiří Střecha's in *Příběhy předmětů*. But the same caveats apply as for the previous note. It is possible that Lata's responsibility related mainly to the horses and the stables.

p. 60: **apprehended a notorious poacher at gun-point**
Lata's account is from František Šírl's interview in *Řitka v minulosti*.

p. 60: **Her father preserved a coin, dented in the middle by a bullet**
The five crown piece is now in the possession of Petr Breyer.

p. 60: **She habitually carried her father's revolver around**
*Příběhy předmětů* claims that Count Leopold spent a long time searching for the revolver on his return from war and eventually found it in the back of the carriage in which Lata had abandoned it. The story is attributed to Petr Jaroševský.

p. 60: **history's last true cavalry battle**
Other contenders for this title include the Battle of Beersheba (1917); the Battle of Komarów, in 1920 (in the Polish-Soviet war); the Polish cavalry's charge at Tuchola Forest in 1939; and the Battles of Poloj and Izbushensky (both in 1942). Jaroslavice was a proper large-scale cavalry vs. cavalry confrontation, with the Dragoons and Ulans of the Imperial Army's 4th Cavalry Division taking on Cossacks, Dragoons, Hussars and Ulans of the Russian 10th Cavalry Division. It's hard to describe the outcome succinctly, beyond the observation that lots of men and horses were killed.

p. 61: **Linguistic barriers between the Emperor's subjects**
Mobilisation posters are said to have been printed in fifteen different languages.

p. 61: **Half of the regular army had been killed before 1915**
*A History of Eastern Europe: Crisis and Change*, p. 398; *The Decline and Fall of the Habsburg Empire 1815–1918*, p. 258.

p. 61: **shot … while rescuing a wounded comrade**
Norbert, a three-time winner of Pardubice's officers' steeplechase, was killed on 13 October – around the time the Velká Pardubická is usually run. He was in the 11th Uhlan regiment (in Czech, 'Hulán').

p. 61: **considered by many to be the deadliest arena of all**
The Italian campaign would cost more than 30,000 Austro-Hungarian lives before end of 1914.

p. 63: **began to recruit tens of thousands of young women**
See: 'Becoming Austrian: Women, the State, and Citizenship in World War I', by Maureen Healy, *Central European History*, Vol. 35, No. 1, pp. 29ff.

p. 64: **Countess Brandisová … sold about 150 hectares**
The plots sold were all in an area called Násada. Villagers who already lived on the land were given priority. Local families who took advantage of the sale included the Mudrs, the Mašeks, the Šírls and the Sobotkas. See: *Řitka v minulosti*.

p. 66: **daily per capita consumption of flour**
See: *A History of Eastern Europe: Crisis and Change*, pp. 399–401.

p. 68: **'Don't be afraid and don't steal'**
In Czech: 'Nebát se a nekrást.'

p. 69: **more than a third of Bohemian land had been owned by 362 families**
Like other startling statistics in this chapter about aristocratic land ownership, this one is taken from *Noble Nationalists: the transformation of the Bohemian aristocracy*. Glassheim's much-cited book offers a definitive account of the nobility's contrasting experiences in the First Republic, with a particular focus on land reform and its ramifications.

p. 69: **Řitka would be exempt from confiscation**
The reason for the exemption is not clear from the correspondence (in the Pospíšil papers) but presumably related to the estate's relatively modest size. The exemption did not prevent the loss of a small amount of land – the 'Mnišecka' field – in 1933. (See: *Řitka v minulosti*.)

p. 70: **'not a single lady … who speaks or writes correct Czech'**
Quoted (along with the other quotes in this paragraph) in Glassheim. Mayer's remark about 'settling accounts' was made some years earlier,

in 'Die Nationalen und sozialen Verhältnisse im böhmischen Adel und Grossgrundbesitz', *Čechischen Revue* 2 (1908), but was no less chilling for being old.

**p. 71: 'enemies of the people' were being executed at a rate of about 500 a week**
See: *Lenin's terror: the ideological origins of early Soviet state violence*, by James Ryan (Routledge, 2012), p. 114.

**p. 71: bequest to a long-time servant, Václav Širl**
Johanna actually used the German form of his name, Wenzel; I have used the Czech form in the interests of consistency.

**p. 72: 'first and foremost the equality of woman and man' ... etc.**
The first three quotations in this paragraph are from, respectively: *Appeal to youth*, 1906; *Masaryk a ženy*, p. 130; and a talk given in Boston in October 1893, printed in *Naše doba, I*, No. 1, pp. 46–9. The fourth is from an anonymous Moravian activist writing in 1905. All four are quoted in *T. G. Masaryk: Against the Current 1882–1914*.

**p. 72: Czechoslovak declaration of independence**
Published in Paris on 18 October 1918, this is also known as the Washington Declaration. The full text can be found at: https://archive.org/details/declarationofindooczec.

**p. 72: Františka Plamínková ... rejoiced**
Quoted in 'Democracy at Home', by Melissa Feinberg, in *New Perspectives on European Women's Legal History*, pp. 76–96.

**p. 74: a large dung heap, packed around the water pump**
It was Petr Jaroševský who pointed this out. It subsequently emerged that the tenant farmer (first Hugo Polák and then, from 1937, Vladimír Daneš) was contractually required to supply the necessary manure.

**p. 74: 'Today the Czech woman is free ... as if by magic'**
'Žena ve státě československém', by Krista Nevšimalová, *Ženský obzor* Vol. 17, No. 3, p. 66; quoted in 'Democracy at Home'.

**p. 75: Female civil servants ... were no longer required to be unmarried ... a quarter of women had jobs**
The landmark details cited in this paragraph are from 'The Czech 1930s through Toyen', pp. 61–2.

**p. 75: a tenant farmer called Hugo Polák**
Traces of Polák's tenancy can be found in the Pospíšil papers and (with some discrepancies) in *Řitka v minulosti*. I think Polák's family must have

comprised the three Jewish people recorded as having lived in Řitka in 1930 (but not after the Second World War). They presumably moved away when the tenancy ended in 1937. I have not been able to discover their subsequent fate.

p. 77: **Kristýna, too, seems to have spent time away**
At one point in *Řitka v minulosti*, František Šírl seems to suggest that Krístýna moved away, to Dahlem, Berlin. Family members are baffled by this: Krístýna was certainly living with Lata before, during and after the Second World War. But perhaps she made an extended trip there at some point.

p. 77: **'One should not wait for a miracle from God …'**
Letter from Lata to Lori Kinský, 22 July 1941; in Kinský archive at Zámrsk.

p. 77: **a racehorse-owning neighbour**
Lata mentions this in 'Die Dame im Rennsattel'. It is conceivable that she was referring to Hanuš Kasalický, although in her account the neighbour came from Velká Chuchle, which is several miles away from Všenory.

p. 78: **kept hens, ducks, geese, turkeys …**
Like most of my details about Šmejda, this comes from a family account, originally from Šmejda's daughter, passed on by his grand-daughter, Božena Osvaldová.

p. 78: **her head close to its as she patted it softly on the neck**
Lata's patting habit was pointed out to me by Vlasta Klabíková, now living in Líšnice, who worked with Řitka's horses in Lata's time; the point about her head position was observed from photographs.

p. 79: **the British trainer Gay Kelleway**
Kelleway gave a shocking account of the harassment she had endured to the *Daily Mirror* in 2017. At one point she insisted on travelling to races only in horse-boxes, rather than accepting lifts from potential attackers. See 'Horse racing rocked by sex scandal as female rider claims top jockey attacked her', by David Yates, *Daily Mirror*, 3 November 2017.

p. 80: **'direct, hearty smile'**
The quotes in the first half of this paragraph are either (like this one) from Vladimír Štědrý's 'V sídle amazonky'; or from 'Ein Besuch bei Maria Immaculata Brandis', a 1937 interview by Hilde Hojer in an unidentified German-language newspaper.

p. 80: **'But of course, a female!'**
Lata quoted in 'Žena a její svět', *Express-Praha*, 20 October 1937. The term she uses is '*ženská*', a colloquial and sometimes slightly derogatory term

for '*žena*' ('woman') – which might equally be translated as 'bird', 'dame', 'chick', 'girl', etc.

p. 81: **no official records survive: just a photograph**
The photograph is in Martin Cáp's collection.

p. 81: **racing itself ... was an impossibility**
In some accounts of her life, Lata had been racing for five years by now. Search for Lata Brandisová online, and what little you find will probably include some version of the claim that she rode in three races in 1921, coming first once and second twice; and that before that she rode in a handicap in Pardubice in 1916 but fell and bruised herself badly. I don't think either claim is true. Both can usually be traced – via Kovář – to Šírl's *Řitka v minulosti*. But Šírl, though conscientious, is not infallible, especially where horse-racing is concerned.

There are all sorts of reasons for doubting the 1916 claim: racing was suspended at all the established tracks from early in the First World War; horses were requisitioned for war work; women were ineligible to compete in official races. It is arguably conceivable that Lata took part in some kind of private contest with the Kinskýs in the Lucice meadows – but most of the Kinskýs were away at war too. As for the alleged races in 1921, Lata certainly rode publicly, but I am sure that, if she did tell Šírl that she had raced, she was referring to harness-races. She herself stated repeatedly (for example, in 'Die Dame im Rennsattel', and in her Český rozhlas interview in November 1937) that she first raced officially a few months before her first Velká Pardubická attempt. Indeed, Šírl himself quotes Lata in *Řitka v minulosti* as saying that 'I had never tried a horse-race' when she was first asked to ride Nevěsta (i.e., in 1926 or 1927).

Keen students of such matters may notice that in *Berühmte Reiter erzählen* Lata does appear to claim that she took part in a women-only 'gallop race' (i.e., a flat race) at Velká Chuchle in 1921. This must be a mistake. Lata states that it was the only such race in which she ever took part – yet we know for certain that she took place in such a race in 1927, and came third, as she claims to have done in this one. She also discusses, just a few sentences later, the controversy in 1927 over whether or not it was permissible for women to participate in a public race. I assume that she hand-wrote this autobiographical account, which she would have posted to Germany, and that whoever typeset it misread her '1' as a '7' (easily done with traditional German handwriting). It is also worth mentioning that Lata appears to have had a poor memory for dates.

p. 83: **Surviving records do not portray him in a flattering light**
Papers relating to Kasalický can be found in the state archives in Prague and Dobřichovice, and in Všenory library. In fairness to Kasalický, most of them – apart from a few pages in *Všenory z minulosti blízké a vzdálené* – are from obviously hostile sources, including an aggrieved wife, and locals who stood to gain from the confiscation of his property after the war. Still, he clearly had many enemies – in marked contrast to Lata.

p. 83: **Kasalický's grand friends**
The four men appear together in a photograph in *Illustrierte Sportzeitung*, March 1925.

p. 84: **horses, tennis and parties**
The best source of information about Ra's incessant social whirl is his own memoir, *Zu Pferd und zu Fuss,* from which all my direct quotes from Ra are taken.

p. 89: **the modern Czech breeder Petr Půlpán**
Petr Půlpán, vice-chairman of the Czech Society of Breeders of Kinský Horses (Svaz chovatelů koní Kinských), runs the Equus Kinský stud at Hradištko u Sadské, not far from the Ostrov site (near Chlumec and Pardubice) where the Kinský family originally bred many of their horses.

p. 89: **In 1838 ... he bred one of his mares with a British thoroughbred**
Oktavian opened his first stud-book in 1832. The mare in question, Themby I, was bred with Whister in 1838, and the questionable isabella foal, Themby II, was born on 27 March 1839.

p. 90: **primary bloodline passes down through the female line**
Kinský horses are not unique in this; but Petr Půlpán is among those who consider it an important distinguishing feature.

p. 90: **the conventions for naming the horses reflect this**
For example – to focus on the most important bloodline in our story – the Kinský mare, Nancy, was bred with one of Themby II's eleven foals, Caesar. From this breeding can be traced the following line of mares: Nelly, Nedejse, Nepal, Norma. The "N"s continue in Norma's own female progeny.

p. 91: **Ra saw Obora as an almost spiritual haven**
At the end of *Zu Pferd und zu Fuss,* Ra makes this point explicitly in a short elegiac poem about his childhood memories of Obora.

p. 93: **a population of around 40,000**
*Demografie města Pardubice,* ed. Veronika Šindlerová (DHV CR, spol. s r.o., March 2013), p. 9.

p. 94: **'might as well be at a public hanging'**
'A race called Pardubicka', by Brian James, *The Times*, 8 October 1988.

p. 94: **'that near-death thing'**
First quoted – I believe – in *That Near-Death Thing*, by Rick Broadbent (Orion, 2012).

p. 95: **appears to have been something of a sex symbol**
Williamson features heavily in *Baroness Daisy*, David Dunford's reconstruction of the scandalous life of Daisy, Baroness de Buren – to whom Williamson was married for a while.

p. 95: **The Hotel Střebský … The Veselka**
There is a detailed description by Velká Pardubická jockey and historian Miloš Svoboda in *Taxis a ti druzí*.

p. 95: **whose owner was father of the daredevil aviator**
The Veselka was owned by František Kašpar. His son, Jan Kašpar, used Pardubice's race-course as a starting point for some of his pioneering flights, adding to his home-town's claim to be Europe's pre-eminent destination for fans of extreme sports.

p. 95: **'a constant coming and going of racegoers …'**
This and the 'disturbed ant-hill' quote in the following paragraph come from an unsigned article in *Monatliche Mitteilungen der Deutschen Reiterverbandes*, Vol. 5, No. 11, p. 215.

p. 97: **as dashing and fearless a cavalry officer as it was possible to imagine**
There is a good chapter on Rudolf Popler (in English) in *Velká Pardubická a Velká Národní Liverpoolská*. In Czech, the fullest biography is Josef Pávek's *Tisíc a jeden skok*.

p. 97: **in the process of becoming one of Europe's finest**
See: 'Mjr Franjo Aubrecht (1896–1985) a jeho boj proti totalitám', *Zprávy KPP*, 2009, pp. 7–8.

p. 99: **knocked its trainer to the ground and attacked its jockey with a whip**
The incident was reported in, among other places, the *Yorkshire Evening Post* (6 June 1893, p. 1).

p. 99: **for Czech nationalists there was a particular pleasure to be had from seeing a Czech victor**
The first stirrings of Czech nationalism at the Velká Pardubická meeting were reported in 1884. (See *Velká Pardubická a Velká Národní Liverpoolská*, pp. 58–9.) The difference in the late 1920s was that some members of the nobility had begun to share such sentiments.

p. 100: **Hector Baltazzi, an Austrian-Levantine banking heir**

Baltazzi's father is generally referred to as a Levantine Greek, but Hector, one of four sons, seems to have had most of his roots in Vienna. He subsequently owned a vast mansion at Jevišovice in Southern Moravia, near the Austrian border.

p. 102: **his favourite spruce**

The tomb is still there, but the spruce – remembered by Františka Mašková – is not.

p. 102: **the transfer of Johanna's remains**

The trouble with family tombs in the woods is that after a few decades have passed it is often impossible to determine who is in them and who is not. The nearest thing I have found to a full summary of the contents of the Brandis tomb is in the article 'Řitka', by Jan Krejčí, former parish priest of Mníšek (published on the parish website at http://farnost.mnisek.cz/historie/ritka/).

p. 103: **Růžena Mašková**

I have not been able to trace any further information about this woman. The name is far more common among Czechs than it might appear to English eyes.

p. 103: **talented women were achieving fame on a grand scale**

'The Czech 1930s through Toyen' is particularly good on this period – and, obviously, especially so on Toyen. See also: 'Olympic Women: A Struggle for Recognition'; and *Max Schmeling and the Making of a National Hero in Twentieth-Century Germany*, a biography of Anny Ondra's husband that also sheds fascinating light on her, and on the role of sport in central European politics during this period.

p. 104: **his/her birth gender**

I apologise to anyone who is offended by the combined pronoun. It seems to me that the easy modern 'their' does not do justice to the awkwardness that such self-identification involved back in the inter-war years – especially in a language that placed so much emphasis on gender (see below).

p. 104: **the Czech language's obsession with gender**

I should probably apologise for this too, since some Czechs will disagree with it. Obviously there are many languages in which gender plays a far greater role than in English. But the role seems particularly pronounced in Czech, in which actual as well as grammatical gender constantly affects the form of nouns, participles, adjectives and proper names, and in which descriptions of people that do not specify gender (for example, the fourth paragraph of the Epilogue of this book) appear to be impossible. Czech may not be unique in this, but it certainly does not lend itself to gender fluidity. It is also striking, to English eyes, that official forms in Czech never require people to specify their gender, which is self-evident from their name. (In the Communist era, however, they did have to specify their class.) Even if the charge of 'obsession' is unfair, I am not the only English-speaker to have been struck by this thought. Karla Huebner makes the same observation in 'The Czech 1930s through Toyen'.

p. 105: **'I proved that a woman can work her way up to the same level as the best of men'**
Quoted in 'Czechs in History – Eliška Junková: The Czech racing queen of the Jazz Age', by Brian Kenety, Czech Radio 7, Radio Prague, 29 September 2004; http://www.radio.cz/en/article/58631.

p. 105: **Alice Milliat**
Milliat deserves a book of her own, although little biographical information about her survives. See: 'Alice Milliat, héroïne oubliée du sport français', by Jean-François Fournel, *La Croix*, 4–5 March 2017; 'Alice Milliat and the Women's Olympic Games', by Sarah Gross, *PowerUp* magazine, 13 July 2016.

p. 105: **'to crown the victors'**
Quoted in 'Alice Milliat, héroïne oubliée du sport français'. See also W*omen and Sports in the United States: A Documentary Reader*.

p. 106: **Marie Vidláková won gold in the shot put**
It was actually the double-handed shot put. She also held records for the double-handed javelin throw, as well as being a leading sprinter and hurdler.

p. 106: **perhaps for the sole purpose of pleasing Lata**
The race was called the Cena Řídké – the Řídká prize – which to English eyes appears as near as makes no difference to the name of Lata's village but to Czech eyes is quite different, unless there was another variant of the spelling of Řitka of which no other record survives. In the absence of any alternative explanation, I am inclined to assume that there was.

p. 107: **'She began to respond to me particularly well'**
Lata interviewed by František Šírl in *Řitka v minulosti*.

p. 110: **'every inch a gentleman'**
Rudolf Deyl, quoted in *Taxis a ti druzí*.

p. 110: **Irma Formánková**
I am grateful to Martin Cáp for drawing my attention to this connection.
For more on Formánková, see 'Irma Formánková', *Veterán*, winter 2016,
pp. 25ff.

p. 111: **Hynek Býček . . . would be a hero of the anti-Nazi resistance**
See: 'Hynek Býček (1898–1992)' by Martin Cáp, at www.dostihy.cz.

p. 111: **Josef Charous**
See www.sports-reference.com/olympics/athletes/ch/josef-charous-1.html.

p. 111: **the all-male world of Pardubice's cavalry barracks and military
riding school**
The 8th St Wenceslas Cavalry Regiment had its equestrian barracks and
riding school on a site now occupied by the Pardubice branch of Tesco. For
more on the school, see *Taxis a ti druzí*, pp. 99–100; and 'Mjr Franjo
Aubrecht (1896–1985) a jeho boj proti totalitám', pp. 7–8.

p. 113: **he referred the matter up to . . . the English Jockey Club**
No direct documentary evidence of this correspondence survives. The
English Jockey Club destroyed its correspondence from this period
long ago; that of the Prague Jockey Club is also lost; and any letters that
remained in Ra's hands can be assumed to have perished in the Karlova
Koruna fire of 1943. But the gist of the exchange was repeatedly
attested to at the time by, among others, by Ra and Lata, and was not
disputed, and I see no reason to doubt it – partly because, had Ra not
found a way of resolving the dispute that more or less satisfied all
parties, Lata would probably not have raced.

p. 113: **she must be provided with a separate changing room**
These details appear in Lata's own account of the correspondence, in
František Šírl's interview in *Řitka v minulosti*. I am grateful to Martina
Růžičková-Jelínková for confirming that female riders in the Velká
Pardubická are still provided with a separate changing room.

p. 114: **a paper on 'Women's Participation in Athletics' presented to the
International Olympic Committee**
Quoted in 'Olympic Women: A Struggle for Recognition'.

p. 114: **There was even a life-size version of Taxis**
Some say that it was a few inches larger than life-size, so that the real thing
would be easier by comparison. The ditch is still there (I am grateful to
Count Francesco Kinský dal Borgo for guiding me to it and allowing me

to stand in it), but it is too over-grown by trees for fine measurement to be possible.

p. 116: **Countess Brandisová was not seriously hurt**
*Národní listy*, 7 October 1927, p. 6.

p. 117: **a medallion with an image of the Virgin Mary; another, depicting St Anthony**
I was told about the Virgin Mary medallion by Countess Génilde Kinský (whose special interest in the subject is explained in chapter 26). Jiří Kocman, who inherited Lata's helmet as well as her racing silks when he began to work at Chlumec, told me about St Anthony.

p. 117: **on Sunday the trains were overflowing**
*Venkov*, 11 October 1927, p. 6.

p. 117: **The weather was pleasant**
Rudolf Deyl's account, quoted in *Taxis a ti druzí*.

p. 117: **There were 650 cars packed into the car park**
My accounts of this and subsequent Velká Pardubickás are, as previously mentioned, heavily indebted to *Od Fantoma po Peruána*; as well as to Miloslav Nehyba's private archive. Passing details that are not attributed to other sources may be assumed to come from either the book or the archive; although whenever possible I have also confirmed them from other sources, such as contemporary news reports, or the collection of reminiscences in *Taxis a ti druzí*.

p. 118: **A well-dressed couple ... smile back**
The photograph appears in *Pestrý týden*, 12 November 1927, p. 8.

p. 118: **'If you sit on a horse, you must have your nerves properly together.'**
Lata in an interview in *Express Praha*, 20 October 1937.

p. 118: **get your approach to it wrong, and your race can be over before you've settled into it.**
My comments, here and elsewhere, on the ins and outs of riding in the Velká Pardubická are based mainly on interviews with jockeys with experience of the race (see Acknowledgements, page 402). However, I have also used the extensive jump-by-jump comments of the late Miloš Svoboda and the late Eva Palyzová, quoted in *Taxis a ti druzí*. This particular insight was emphasised by Palyzová.

p. 119: **'even with a woman in the saddle'**
*Národní listy*, 9 October 1927, p. 5.

p. 120: **'the time to give up is when you are in the ambulance'**
'For neck and honour', by John Oaksey, *Sunday Telegraph*, 14 October 1973, p. 37. I have not been able to trace the first use of his much-quoted remark about 'fools, bloody fools and those who remount in steeplechases'.

p. 123: **standing on benches**
Race-goers can be seen doing so in a picture in *Pestrý týden*, 12 November 1927, p. 8.

p. 124: **Charous … had the grace to say … that Lata's performance had been 'really impressive'**
*Pestrý týden*, 24 December 1927, p. 4.

p. 125: **'She was considered very grand and arrogant'**
This is true in the sense that it clearly became the received wisdom in some racing circles (not least in the Communist era); but it is not supported by anyone I have encountered who actually had contact with Lata. I should add that the expert in question, the Prague-based British academic Robin Healey, is spectacularly well-informed about Czech racing history (and much else) and has given me wise and generous support in my research. He admitted, however, that he had no special knowledge of Lata's story.

p. 126: **Avery Brundage … once complained rather pathetically**
The complaint was in a 1973 interview with Mary H. Leigh, quoted in 'The Pioneering Role Of Madame Alice Milliat and the FSFI in Establishing International Trade and Field Competition for Women', by Mary H. Leigh and Thérèse M. Bonin, *Journal of Sport History*, Vol. 4, No. 1 (spring, 1977), pp. 72–83.

p. 127: **the need to (as their mother put it) 'honour' the man of the house**
Johanna uses the word in her 1918 will.

p. 128: **Alžběta Jarocká**
I am grateful to Pavel Satorie, her step-grandson, for helping me to make sense of Gikina's otherwise mysterious role in Lata's story.

p. 129: **The village girls who watched them**
Jana Sléhová and Františka Mašková each independently mentioned this.

p. 133: **US stocks would be worth barely a tenth of their value**
See: 'Crash course: what the Great Depression reveals about our future', by Larry Elliott, *Guardian*, 4 March 2017; and *The Great Crash 1929*, by J. K. Galbraith (Hamish Hamilton, 1955).

p. 134: **'We used to play football with the boys from the German school ...'**
The speaker was Jaromír Konůpka, who grew up in Kopřivnice with the future athlete Emil Zátopek, the subject of my biography, *'Today We Die A Little ...':
Emil Zátopek, Olympic Legend to Cold War Hero* (Yellow Jersey, 2016).

p. 135: **Lieutenant Mellenthin**
There is an extended account of the Mellenthin affair in *Od Fantoma po Peruána.*

p. 136: **a flawless round in a show jumping contest at Velká Chuchle**
The contest, for men and women, was part of a meeting from 16–18 May 1930 and was reported in *Dostihový a jezdecký sport,* No. 12, p. 5.

p. 137: **commentators who, for the first time, were reporting live on the proceedings to radio listeners**
See: 'Rudolf Popler, nezapomenutelný hrdina Velké pardubické', in *Dostihový svět speciál,* October 2004, pp. 36ff.

p. 138: **performing a complete somersault**
See: *Od Fantoma po Peruána.*

p. 139: **his broken heart was a factor in his greatness**
This seems to have been the belief of Josef Pávek, Popler's friend and author of the biographical *Tisíc a jeden skok.*

p. 140: **he wrote to Weatherbys ... to enquire about the possibility of entering Gyi Lovam! for the Grand National**
The best account I have read of Popler's English adventure is in *Velká pardubická a Velká Národní Liverpoolska,* pp. 161–78.

p. 141: **President Tomáš Masaryk ... watched ... the Czechoslovak Derby**
The 'Cena prezidenta republiky', in October, seems to have started in 1920; but Masaryk showed no sign of wanting to come and watch it. See: 'Navzdory válkám a pohromám chuchelské dostihy přežívají', by Jiří Kábrt, čtidoma.cz, 23 February 2016.

p. 141: **He ... made a conscious effort to associate himself with his countrymen's equestrian traditions**
See Masaryk's obituary in *The Times,* 15 September 1937. Masaryk even went so far as to learn to ride, at the age of sixty-eight.

p. 141: **Lata ... may well have been introduced to him**
Martin Cáp, the greatest living expert on the history of Velká Chuchle, believes that Lata may even have bought her own horse (see page 147) with the aim of securing such an introduction.

p. 141: **Lata is thought to have been among the 1.25 million visitors**
See: *Knihu o městě Pardubice*; and the town's sporting history at http://work.
xhtml-css.cz/pardubice/en/the-history-of-sport.html#clanek4. Jiří Kotyk,
Pardubice historian, considers it highly unlikely that Lata would not have
been there.

p. 144: **'Everyone was glad that the race was over'**
*Od Fantoma po Peruána*, p. 62.

p. 146: **'like a cat'**
The words are attributed to Popler, perhaps fancifully, in Josef Pávek's *Tisíc
a jeden skok*, p. 213.

p. 146: **'courageous Amazon'**
*Hamburgischer Correspondent und neue hamburgische Börsen-Halle*, 23
September 1931.

p. 147: **she seems to have registered her own colours in 1931**
No official records survive for 1931, but her colours were not registered
the previous year and were by 1932. Given that Dante ran in the 1931
Derby, we can assume that they were registered by then.

p. 148: **Řitka was quite heavily mortgaged**
The Pospíšil papers suggest that the mortgage covered roughly half the
estate's value.

p. 149: **'the death of a young athlete, and of a friend'**
Quoted in *Tisíc a jeden skok*, p. 305.

p. 151: **'no one here will shed any tears for the disappearance of German
democracy'**
'In Germany, the elections', *Daily Mail*, 1 March 1933. Lord Rothermere,
the newspaper's proprietor, was a vigorous supporter of British fascism.
His notorious 'Hurrah for the Blackshirts!' editorial appeared on 15 January
1934. Some *Mail* staff are said to have worn black shirts to work during
this period, to signify their support. See *Reporting on Hitler*, by Will
Wainewright (Biteback, 2017); *Mail Men*, by Adrian Addison (Atlantic
Books, 2017).

p. 152: **support for fascist parties**
For example: Vlajka and Akce národní obrody.

p. 153: **frequent visits from the far-right leader General Radola Gajda**
See *A History of the Czechoslovak Republic 1918–1948*, pp. 302–3.

p. 153: **Leopold von Fugger**
The fullest and most balanced account that I have seen of Fugger's time in Pardubice is the chapter devoted to him in *Pardubický Zámeček a jeho osudy*, pp. 16–24.

p. 154: **Fugger's record as a much-decorated reconnaissance pilot**
According to his mother, Poldi flew nearly 200 missions over enemy positions, and his plane was hit at least thirty times. He was rewarded with eight decorations. See: *The Glory of the Habsburgs*, pp. 310–11.

p. 155: **almost certainly including ... Lata**
I base this assertion on the opinions of Dr Jiří Kotyk; František Bobek, who very kindly showed me round the Zámeček; and Génilde Kinský, who as a child often saw Ra, Lata and Poldi in the same place. Each thought it likely that Lata would have visited, but none was certain.

p. 155: **won at least one showjumping contest**
See: *Venkov*, 26 April 1933, p. 8. His horse was called Duruito.

p. 156: **her own relationship with Hanuš Kasalický – whose increasing closeness must ... have been creating confusion in her heart**
My evidence for this is simultaneously strong and vague. In addition to the gossip of young Řitka-dwellers, the relationship attracted attention in Všenory, and was eventually mentioned as a factor in Kasalický's post-war divorce. It was also mentioned in evidence, apparently originating from a Dr Forster from Všenory, that was cited in a letter from the Místní národní výbor ve Všenorech to the Okresní národní výbor, 17 November 1945, in relation to legal proceedings over Kasalický's collaboration. (The relevant documents are in Všenory Library.) Kasalický's grandson, Jan Doležal, who lives in Switzerland and as far as I can tell is Kasalický's closest surviving relative, confirmed that Kasalický's 'affair' with Lata was discussed in his family when he was growing up, although he knew nothing of the details. So we can be confident that something significant happened between them. What we don't know is what, or when – hence my speculative tone.

p. 156: **the press was reporting that Neklan would be Lata's mount**
*Národní listy*, 30 September 1933.

p. 157: **She was small – about fifteen and a half hands**
Norma's height was estimated at 165–167cm at the shoulder. As with other measurements, I have converted this into the imperial and pre-imperial measurements of the British racing world. Much of my information about

Norma, including this detail, comes from two articles published in *Dostihový zpravodaj* in 1980 ('Sága rodu Normy', Vol. 7, pp. 6–9) and 1981 ('Po stopách Normy', Vol. 5, pp. 12–14). The first of these was written by Dr Karel Trojan, a dragoons officer and friend of Ra's who rode Norma over the Kinskýs' replica Velká Pardubická course a few weeks after Lata's 1937 triumph. The second was written by the magazine's editors, correcting various alleged inaccuracies in Dr Trojan's account. Between them, the two articles paint a remarkably full picture. I have supplemented this with the memories of others who knew and rode Norma (e.g., Génilde Kinský, Jiří Kocman and – via their children – Eduard Zágler and František Schwarzenberg), along with evidence from the Kinský studbook and from contemporary reports. I am very grateful to Lenka Gotthardová and Miloslav Nehyba for their tireless efforts to trace further biographical details about the half-forgotten co-heroine of this book.

p. 157: **'they made a harmonious, attractive unit'**
Dr Karel Trojan, in 'Sága rodu Normy'.

p. 157: **'That's a beautiful lady ...'**
I was told this by Pavel Liebich – who may or may not have been the visiting jockey himself.

p. 158: **'She couldn't bear having a horse in front of her'**
Jiří Kocman.

p. 158: **'tough, brave and faithful horse ...'**
Lata in 'Vítěz Velké pardubické, slečna Brandisová, vypravuje', an interview in *Svoboda-Brno*, 22 October 1937.

p. 158: **'the cleverest horse I ever knew'**
František Horák, quoted in 'Sága rodu Normy', which also includes details of Nedejse's mathematical gifts.

p.159: **František Schwarzenberg ... described her as 'a love'**
Schwarzenberg used the expression when enthusing about Norma to his daughter, Ludmila. The family had moved to the US by then, and František, who was raised by English nannies, was speaking in English. According to Ludmila (now Ludmila S. Bidwell), he admired both Norma and Lata 'exceedingly'.

p. 159: **'Pan kůň'**
The phrase literally means 'Mr Horse'. Quoted by Dr Karel Trojan, in 'Sága rodu Normy', along with the observation about Norma's 'chiselled, lean legs', etc.

p. 159: **scorning treats such as sugar lumps**
Lata made this point in an interview for 'Žena a její svět', *Express-Praha*, 20 October 1937.

p. 160: **Henlein insisted on being greeted with the words: 'Heil, mein Führer'**
Reported in 'German and Czech', *The Times*, 3 December 1937.

p. 161: **'the best in history'**
Miloslav Nehyba and Jaroslav Hubálek in *Od Fantoma po Peruána*.

p. 162: **'she rode very beautifully'**
*Le sport universel illustré*, 28 October 1933, p. 854.

p. 163: **'the fearless Countess Brandisová'**
*Národní listy*, 16 October 1933, p. 5.

p. 165: **sixty-five-mile journey took them two days**
'Bůh, čest, vlast a koně', by Lenka Gotthardová (Klubu Equus Kinsky, 1998).

p. 166: **Kasalický sometimes gave them lifts in his**
In August 1930, Alžběta was in Kasalický's car when he was involved in a minor collision with a bus in Prague.

p. 167: **Norma ... certainly pulled a carriage ... Brutus ... sometimes pulled a plough**
The detail about Norma comes from Dr Karel Trojan, in 'Sága rodu Normy'. Martin Cáp has a photograph of Brutus pulling a plough.

p. 168: **the Nazis had weaponised sport**
A compelling account of this process can be found in *High Society in the Third Reich*, which also describes how the Grosser Preis der Reichshaupstadt ended up with a 100,000 mark prize.

p. 168: **'a young German must be ... as hard as Krupp steel'**
Quoted at Mémorial de la Shoah (http://sport.memorialdelashoah.org/en-nazi-germany-olympic-games.htm).

p. 169: **the Reich Ministry ... had decreed that all German riding associations must join one of the party's two paramilitary wings**
See *Himmler's Cavalry: the Equestrian SS, 1930–1945*, to which this and the two following paragraphs are heavily indebted.

p. 170: **whose bêtes noires included ... 'Amazons'**
See: *The Nazi Conscience*, p. 242.

p. 171: **Heinrich Wiese**
Wiese's SA records are partially preserved in the Bundesarchiv in Freiburg. See also *Der Grossdeutsche Reichstag 1938* (R.v. Decker's Verlag, G Schenk) p. 554.

p. 172: **eleven dissenting equestrians in Dachau**
The eleven men had been incarcerated in 1933 for refusing to take the SS oath. See: *Fegelein's Horsemen and Genocidal Warfare*, p. 17; and the previously mentioned *Himmler's Cavalry*, pp. 17–18. Both books have been invaluable sources for me for this and the following chapters; as, very generously, have both authors.

p. 172: **shot on Himmler's orders**
See *CIA Who's Who In Nazi Germany*, p. 67. Anton von Hohberg und Buchwald, described by the CIA as 'the leading horseman in East Prussia', was shot on 2 July 1934 for making disrespectful remarks about the SS.

p. 172: **SA-Sturmführer Helmuth von der Gröben**
For anyone interested in von der Gröben, a good starting-point would be *150 Jahre Amateur-Rennsport*.

p. 176: **she took part in a dressage display**
There is a picture of the event in *Wiener Salonblatt*, 18 November 1934, pp. 11–12.

p. 177: **a well-behaved eagle owl**
I am grateful to Jana Sléhová, Běhal's daughter, for showing me a picture of the owl, which certainly looks well-behaved. Apparently the owl's role was to act as a decoy, provoking unwanted birds of prey into showing themselves.

p. 177: **carved wooden chest ... etc.**
Most of these details come from the memory and the photo-album of Petr Jaroševský. The caricature is mentioned in 'V sídle amazonky'; the well-stocked gun-rack can be seen in 'U vítězky pardubické steeple-chase', *Pestrý týden*, 1 January 1938, p. 24.

p. 178: **'the older they get, the nicer they are'**
'Žena a její svět'.

p. 178: **hunting dogs of the pointer variety**
Lata's favourite breed was the Český fousek – which is like a more athletic, bearded version of the German wire-haired pointer.

p. 180: **support for far-right factions**
This manifested itself both in support for far-right parties and in increased far-right influence in centre parties, the biggest of which – the National Democrats, the Agrarians and the Catholic Populists – were increasingly linked with authoritarian and even fascist policies. See: *Noble Nationalists. The Transformation of the Bohemian Aristocracy*, pp. 131–2.

p. 180: **the biggest advances were made by Henlein's increasingly strident Sudeten German Party**
The SdP's 15.2 per cent vote share made it the biggest single party.

p. 180: **Sudeten German Nazi Party**
The German National Socialist Workers' Party (Deutsche National-sozialistische Arbeiterpartei, or DNSAP) was founded in 1919 and by the time it was banned in 1933 had more than 60,000 members. It was sufficiently close to the Nazi party (the National Socialist German Workers' Party – Nationalsozialistische Deutsche Arbeiterpartei – or NSDAP), for the jockey Hans Schmidt, who joined the DNSAP in 1925 and the NSDAP in 1931, to have attempted to get his membership of the latter backdated to his joining of the former.

p. 180: **Willibald Schlagbaum**
Existing Czech tellings of Lata's story, in which Schlagbaum is invariably the villain, are pretty cavalier with the details of his life, apparently relying mainly on Lata's views, which were not necessarily very well-informed. I am very grateful to Schlagbaum's family – and particularly to his great-grand-daughter, Mandy van Häigeling – for supplying a fuller biographical picture of his life (including a detailed German-language obituary published in 1971). It seems reasonable to suppose that, from Schlagbaum's point of view, Lata was the villain: over-privileged and grand, with the best horses provided to her as a family favour, whereas he had had to fight for everything he had achieved. On the other hand, it is hard to dispute his ideological leanings. As Mandy van Häigeling dryly observed: 'I'm pretty sure he was no anti-Nazi ...'

p. 181: **'It is always worse when a woman is racing'**
Lata, interviewed in 'V sídle amazonky'.

p. 182: **'take hold of the frying pan, dustpan and broom, and marry a man'**
This was one of Göring's 'Nine Commandments for the Workers' Struggle' (published in May 1934 as *Für den Berliner Arbeitskampf: Neun Gebote*).

p. 184: **Trakehner horses were a living symbol of East Prussian uniqueness**
East Prussia's subsequent disastrous history meant that the remarkable heritage of Trakehnen has been largely forgotten in the west, although pockets of Trakehner enthusiasts can be found in Germany and North America. Patricia Clough's heartbreaking *The Flight Across the Ice* offers the best English-language introduction, but focuses mainly on the final tragic chapters of the story. Martin Heling's *Trakehnen* gives a good overview in German.

p. 184: **these had been celebrated as East Prussian successes**
See: 'Kameradschaftsgeist und Gemeinsinn', by Karl August Knorr, *Das Ostpreussenblatt*, 23 June 1973, p. 10; and 'Die Abstammung des Pardubitz-Siegers Herold', *Sankt Georg*, Vol. 38, 1937.

p. 185: **murky water jump ... called Jew's Creek**
My thanks to Martin Cáp for pointing this out to me on a map in *Führer durch das Hauptgestüt Trakehnen*, by J. von Henninges (H. Klutke, 1939).

p. 185: **Martin Münzesheimer**
I know nothing about Münzesheimer beyond the fact that he rode for Stáj Jirka.

p. 186: **in 'sinewy form'**
Dr Karel Trojan, in 'Sága rodu Normy'.

p. 188: **Racegoers greeted the German triumph 'coldly'**
Miloslav Nehyba and Jaroslav Hubálek in *Od Fantoma po Peruána*.

p. 188: **'SS riders' triumph in Czechoslovakia'**
'SS-Reitersieg in der Tschechei', *Das Schwarze Korps*, 31 October 1935, p. 4.

p. 188: **Poldi von Fugger disappeared**
For a full and balanced account of what is and isn't known about Fugger's disappearance, see *Pardubický Zámeček a jeho osudy*. Full documentation of the 'Fugger case' was deposited in the Pardubice State district archive in folder number 37 from 1937.

p. 188: **by one account he was still in Czechoslovakia**
In *Zu Pferd und zu Fuss* (p. 123), Ra claims to have seen Fugger at a drag hunt. I have no idea how to account for the inconsistency with all the other evidence. Perhaps Ra misremembered something; or perhaps Fugger wanted to hide in plain sight for a while before completing his escape.

p. 189: **an instructor in aerial photography**
See also: *Staré domy vyprávějí*, by Jiří Kotyk (KPP, 2014).

p. 192: **Stable lads were occasionally dispatched to the rafters to retrieve stuck balls.**
This would have been a perilous pursuit: the rafters were about 20 feet off the ground.

p. 194: **'So no one was afraid they might get hurt'**
'Můj život s koňmi', by Radslav Kinský, *Chlumecké listy: časopis chlumeckého regionu*, 2001 (3), pp. 18–19.

p. 195: **noble families would soon supply getting on for a fifth of senior SS officers**
See: *High Society in the Third Reich*.

p. 195: **roughly two-thirds of Czechoslovakia's former nobility ... would identify themselves as pro-German**
I base this crude estimate on a long discussion with Dr Zdeněk Hazdra (author of *Šlechta střední Evropy v konfrontaci s totalitními režimy 20. století* and *Ve znamení tří deklarací: Šlechta v letech nacistického ohrožení československého státu*) and on the more nuanced figures in Eagle Glassheim's *Noble Nationalists: the Transformation of the Bohemian Aristocracy*. The proportion varies depending on when you take the snapshot. (Czechoslovaks regularly stated their preferred nationality in censuses.) The moments of choice that mattered came from September 1938 onwards.

p. 196: **considered himself bound by his oath**
*Situace české šlechty po roce 1918 na příkladu rodu Kinských (do roku 1939)*, by Veronika Kinclová (Brno, 2007), p. 20.

p. 198: **well-advanced plans for an alternative, non-Nazi Games**
See: *Thinking Barcelona*, by Edgar Illas (Liverpool University Press, 2012).

p. 198: **minus its Jewish athletes, who refused to participate**
See: *Zionists in Interwar Czechoslovakia*, by Tatjana Lichtenstein (Indiana University Press, 2016), p. 227.

p. 199: **Germans all seemed suspiciously well prepared**
Their remarkable confidence at the obstacle is evident even in Leni Riefenstahl's notorious propaganda film of the Games, *Olympia*.

p. 200: **conservatives who disapproved of any kind of female participation in 'male' events**
For example, Avery Brundage: see *Time* magazine, 10 and 24 August 1936.

p. 200: **Zdeněk Koubek**
The Czech sportswriter Pavel Kovář, author of a much quoted article on Lata, published a fascinating book about Koubek, *Příběh české rekordwoman*, in 2017. Its subtitle describes Koubek's gender-change as 'the greatest sporting scandal of the First Republic'.

p. 200: **gave an interview to *Time* magazine**
'Medicine: Change of Sex', *Time*, 24 August 1936.

p. 202: **Hermann Fegelein**
Fegelein's bizarre story is well-told both in *Himmler's Cavalry* and in *Fegelein's Horsemen*. I have relied slightly more on the former for the early

part of Fegelein's career and more on the latter for the later stages. But the books complement one another. I recommend both.

p. 203: **'pretty as a picture'**
'Rennreiter in Ostpreussen', by Walter Stöckel, *Ostpreussische Erinnerungen und Gegenwartsgedanken von einem Amateur-Hippologen oder 'Zusammenengeschrappte Pferdeäppel'.*

p. 203: **Herold ... pined disastrously**
In 1931, the German Olympic Committee for Equestrian Sports persuaded Lengnik, with difficulty, to sell Herold, hoping to take advantage of the six-year-old's remarkable jumping abilities for the Olympics. Herold was moved to the military stables in Hanover, but quickly became a sullen underachiever. Returned to Lengnik a couple of years later, he once again thrived – and became the most successful Trakehner steeplechaser of all time. See: 'Die Abstammung des Pardubitz-Siegers Herold', *Sankt Georg*, Vol. 38, 1937.

p. 203: **a participant in Himmler's ... Lebensborn programme ... possessor of a Julleuchter**
Lengnik's SS records give no clue as to when the participation (or possession) began. Most of his records, in the Bundesarchiv in Freiburg, are too damaged by fire to be legible.

p. 204: **Lemke ... was in the process of being thrown out for being too 'unpleasant'**
This is a slight oversimplification. Lemke's membership was revoked for several reasons, including non-payment of financial dues. But 'unpleasant' police reports on his character were among the factors cited; as was his expulsion from a Reich Sports School for 'improper behaviour'. The revocation of his membership was finally confirmed in May 1937. The SA, on the other hand, seems to have been happy to continue to have him as an officer.

p. 204: **howls of public disapproval**
See: 'Der Doktor und Seine Rösser', by Gerhard Merzdoff, *Das Ostpreussenblatt*, 15 September 1990, p. 8.

p. 205: **greeted 'by louder cheers than the winner'**
Miloslav Nehyba and Jaroslav Hubálek in *Od Fantoma po Peruána.*

p. 205: **'Damn these Germans!'**
Quoted in a profile of Lengnik by O. Christ in *Sankt Georg*, 1936. The words were spoken in Czech but reported in German as 'Die Deutschen sind doch verfluchte Kerle' – literally, 'These Germans are damn fellows'. I assume

the heckler meant something along the lines of 'Damn these Germans, they're good'.

p. 205: **promptly won the next race**
Lengnik rode Solo, another of his own horses.

p. 205: **adapting a traditional song to praise the great Oskar Lengnik**
Profile of Lengnik by O. Christ in *Sankt Georg*, 1936.

p. 209: **'the thing is: I'm not all that attached to life'**
This exchange was relayed to me, very confidently, by Zagler's son, Jan.

p. 211: **Traffic came to a virtual standstill**
The events following Masaryk's death were reported extensively in *The Times*. I have quoted details from: 'Crowds pouring into Prague', 18 September 1937, p. 9; 'Last homage to Dr Masaryk', 21 September 1937, p. 14; and 'Prague farewell to Dr Masaryk', 22 September 1937, p. 12.

p. 211: **more than four miles of silent, crowd-lined streets**
See: 'Po stopách posledni cesty TGM', TV Vona, 27 April 2009 (https://tvvona.wordpress.com/2009/04/27/783491-po-stopach-posledni-cesty-tgm/). It is also worth looking at the Pathé News footage, if you can find it.

p. 211: **an open train ... took the coffin back to Lány**
For this part of the account I am grateful for the memories of the former Olympic javelin champion Dana Zátopková, whose father was part of the guard of honour; and of the former Olympic wrestler Karel Engel, whose grandfather drove the train.

p. 211: **'a single desire: to be worthy of this rare and exceptional figure'**
'Po pohřbu', by Eduard Bass, *Lidové noviny* 23 September 1937, quoted in 'Mourning becomes a nation', by John Bolton, *Bohemia Band* 45 (2004).

p. 211: **'That was not a crowd. That was a nation'**
'Zástupové' by Ferdinand Peroutka, *Přítomnost*, 22 September 1937, p. 1.

p. 212: **'Pravda vítězí'**
*The Times* ('Last homage to Dr Masaryk') quotes a Slovak version of the words, '*Pravda víťazí*', but Czechs remember it in Czech. I cannot explain the inconsistency. The motto echoes the famous words of the fifteenth-century Czech martyr Jan Hus: 'Seek the truth, hear the truth, love the truth, speak the truth, hold the truth and defend the truth until death' – and foreshadows the declaration of Czechoslovakia's last president, Vacláv Havel: 'Truth and love must prevail over lies and hatred'.

p. 212: **killed hundreds of civilians in Guernica**
There is no agreed figure. Estimates range from 200 victims to 1,654.

p. 213: **at the Pardubice Zámeček ... the Czechoslovak army was training its cavalry**
The town of Pardubice bought the Zámeček for that purpose on 22 May – see: *Kniha o městě Pardubice*, p. 178.

p. 215: **In some Czechoslovak minds, it had begun to seem like a law of nature**
The *Star* newspaper spoke for many when it reflected that autumn: 'Every year we admire the abilities of the German steeplechasers, and we consider it a success if a Czech horse gets a place.'

p. 215: **German footballers always win penalty shoot-outs**
In deference to Czech patriots and pedants, I concede that this law did not work at the European Championships in Belgrade in 1976.

p. 217: **the mare's appetite for food gradually declined**
See: Lata's comments in 'V sídle amazonky' and also Dr Karel Trojan's observations in 'Po stopách Normy'.

p. 217: **a few weeks before the 1 September entry deadline**
See: the 'Norma' chapter in *Slavní koně*. Frantisek Šírl in *Řitka v minulosti* claims that Lata was still contemplating riding Čibuk the day before the race. This seems implausible, given Lata's commitment to Norma.

p. 218: **Rumours that Duke and Duchess of Windsor would also be in attendance**
This and other titbits were reported in the official race-day programme. I am grateful to Miloslav Nehyba for showing me his copy.

p. 218: **The Women's Club of Pardubice staged a special event at the Veselka**
See: 'Činnnost Klubu Ženské Národní Rady v Pardubicích v letech 1936–42', by Dr Jiří Kotyk, *KPP*, 24 June 2010.

p. 219: **some claimed to have seen German riders drinking**
A report in *Štít* magazine suggested that some of them had over-indulged in beer and brandy. The *Východočeský republikán* newspaper repeated the story but later apologised after being accused of making light of Lata's success.

p. 219: **Schmidt and Scharfetter were known to enjoy a post-race party**
According to Trakehnen veteran Fritz Alshuth, the two men often joined celebrations at the Hotel Elch. See: 'Erinnerungen an die Kindheit und

die Jugendjahre in Trakehnen: Ein Zeitzeuge berichtet', published post-humously in September 2017 at trakehnenverein.de.

**p. 219: Guests included the Count and Countess of Paris ...**
Details of the diversions can be found in *Zu Pferd und zu Fuss*, pp. 136–8; and in *Wiener Salonblatt*, 31 October 1937, pp. 7–9. Génilde's involvement (on Neva) in Lata's final preparations is also mentioned in the official Velká Pardubická race-day programme.

**p. 221: they confuse the Velká Pardubická with a fight in a cloakroom of a Prague movie theatre**
For a detailed contemporary 'colour' piece on the great race-day, see: 'Dame gewinnt "Grosse Pardubitzer"', *Prager Tagblatt*, 19 October 1937, p. 8 – which also mentions that Norma was 'trembling' before the race.

**p. 221: a 'foal coat'**
It's pretty clear from the context that this isn't a mistranslation. According to *Prager Tagblatt* ('Dame gewinnt "Grosse Pardubitzer"'), the garment fascinated the public and caused grief among the horses: 'Ein Fohlenmantel erregt Neugier im Publikum und Trauer unter den Pferden ...'. If it is any comfort, it is also evident that such garb was not considered normal.

**p. 223: 'Once you're on horseback ... you know that the battle is coming'**
Lata in an interview in *Express Praha*, 20 October 1937.

**p. 224: several ditches had been widened**
Between 1932 and 1935, at least five obstacles were enlarged. The ditches were broadened at the eighth, the eleventh (the English jump), the thirteenth (railed fence) and the twenty-first (water-jump); in addition, the hedge at Taxis was raised at some point, to 140 cm. See *Od Fantoma po Peruána*'s '1936' section.

**p. 224: 'You have to, when you want to achieve something'**
Lata, in an interview with *Svoboda-Brno*, 'Vítěz Velké pardubické, slečna Brandisová, vypravuje' (22 October 1937). This was one of her most detailed blow-by-blow accounts of the race, and this chapter uses several other details from it.

**p. 224: a horse-drawn ambulance coach ... waited ominously**
'Dame gewinnt "Grosse Pardubitzer"'.

p. 225: **prompting Konrad Heinlein to call for 'the Sudeten German issue to be decided with the help of the German Empire'**
See: 'Československo a Evropa v čase skonu T. G. Masaryka', by Robert Kvaček, in *Už vícekrát nezazní tak těžce requiem ...*, p. 3.

p. 226: *'Gehen! Jděte!'*
In other words, 'Go!' See: *Taxis a ti druzí*, p. 59. I am assuming, however, that in 1937 German rather than English would have been used.

p. 226: **'You need to ... focus on maintaining a straight approach ...'**
The advice in this paragraph, from Eva Palyzová, is quoted in *Taxis a ti druzí*; as is Václav Chaloupka's advice about the Irish Bank four paragraphs later and, later still, Lata's remarks – relayed by Palyzová – about the ploughed land.

p. 228: **Lata was always superstitiously relieved to get the thirteenth behind her**
Lata mentioned this in 'Vitěz Velké pardubické, slečna Brandisová, vypravuje'.

p. 228: **'Without the November mud the track is a billiard table'**
Bizarrely, this piece appeared in the official race-day programme.

p. 230: **'it would be easier if it was twenty centimetres higher'**
Liebich is quoted in *Taxis a ti druzí*.

p. 230: **'The race is mine!'**
Lata, quoted in 'Vitěz Velké pardubické, slečna Brandisová, vypravuje'.

p. 230: **'Several times he tried to push us aside'**
This quote comes from Šírl's interview in *Řitka v minulosti*. Lata gave similar accounts elsewhere.

p. 232: **'At last, it is done'**
The quote from Wiese is reported in 'Vítězství sl. Brandisové a zahranicní tisk' – unidentified Czech newspaper cutting from 1937 in the Kinský archive in Zármsk.

p. 232: **V-for-*vítězství***
Soukup's son – also Josef Soukup – was certain that his father pre-prepared this sash with no other purpose than to symbolise this provocative word.

p. 233: **'it seemed to me that never before were people so truly and amicably united'**
Lata's remarks here and in the final two paragraphs of the chapter can mostly be traced to Lata's radio interview for Český rozhlas on 10 November 1937. However, the 'I walked with my beloved Norma ...' quote seems to have

appeared first in *Express Praha* on 20 October. The 'Never have I known such happiness ...' remarks, quoted in *Příběhy předmětů* and also in *Slavní koně*, are attributed to a Český rozhlas interview but do not appear in the only transcript I have been able to trace.

p. 235: **A photograph shows Lata sitting on a gilded chair**
The picture appears in *Wiener Salonblatt*, 31 October 1937, pp. 7–9. It is possible that the photograph was taken in a studio rather than at the ball, but it must have been taken very close to the same time.

p. 235: **Jan Masaryk was among those who sent telegrams**
Interview with Lata by 'Hilda' in 'U vítězky pardubické steeple-chase', *Pestrý týden*, 1 January 1938, p. 24.

p. 236: **'I won it for you'**
Obviously Petr Jaroševský, who told me this, could have no direct memory of it; but he was reminded of it many times when he was growing up.

p. 236: **'victory for our breed' ... etc.**
From an unidentified newspaper clipping, under the headline 'Sensační vítězství Normy se sl. Brandisovou', in the Pospíšil papers. The other quotes in this paragraph are from, respectively, another unidentified clipping in the Pospíšil papers; 'Lata Brandisová, vítěz Velké Pardubické', *Republikán*, October 1937; unidentified newspaper clipping ('Velká Pardubická steeplechase 1937') in the Pospíšil papers; 'Žena vítězí v nejtěžším překážkovém dostihu kontinentu', *Národní listy*, 18 October 1937, p. 5; 'Kazí sport ženy?' *Pražanka, Praha*, 10 November 1937; 'Žena a její svět', *Express-Pruhu*, 20 October 1937.

p. 237: **Konstantin von Neurath ... was summoned to a meeting with Hitler**
See *Prague in Black*, p. 24, for an account of the meeting.

p. 237: **Hitler ... would create a lucrative new race**
*High Society in the Third Reich*, p. 126.

p. 237: **'the most violent used by Germany against another country since 1918'**
Report in the Danish periodical *Nationaltidente*, quoted in 'Československo a Evropa v čase skonu T. G. Masaryka', by Robert Kvaček, in *Už vícekrát nezazní tak těžce requiem ...*, p. 3.

p. 238: **'We must always demand so much of them that we can never be satisfied'**
Quoted in *Prague in Black*, p. 24.

p. 238: **Perhaps, even now, he and she were still seeing one another**
Kasalický seems to have helped put *Pestrý týden*'s journalist in touch with
Lata for the interview published in January 1938 ('U vitěsky pardubické
steeple-chase'); Lata, in turn, made a point of acknowledging Kasalický's
contribution to her career in her Český rozhlas interview in November 1937.

p. 239: **a springtime adventure on horseback involving Ra and ... Sylvie
Münster-Fuggerová**
See: *Zu Pferd und zu Fuss*, p. 140; Aleš Valenta's *Dějiny rodu Kinských*,
p. 200. Valenta raises the possibility that Lata may have been present when
Lord Runciman visited Žďár nad Sázavou.

p. 240: **'Czechoslovakia is a Bolshevik monster and must be destroyed'**
The account of Kinský's words was Jan Masaryk's, quoted by Eagle Glassheim
in *Noble Nationalists*, p. 175.

p. 240: **Runciman reported that ... their desire to join the Reich was 'a
natural development ...'**
*Documents on British Foreign Policy 1919–1939*, Vol. 2 (London, 1949),
appendix II, p. 677.

p. 243: **More than 20,000 Jews were driven out of public life**
See: *Prague in Black*, pp. 24–5.

p. 244: **The nobility ... were mostly enthusiastic about their nation's new
German rulers**
The examples in this paragraph are cited by Eagle Glassheim in *Noble
Nationalists*.

p. 245: **another declaration from a group of Czech nobles**
Eagle Glassheim and Zdeněk Hazdra have both written authoritatively
about the nobility's declarations of 1938 and 1939. Readers puzzled by
the strange mathematics (eighty-five signatories, sixty-nine signatures,
thirty-three families) may also want to consult Czech Tourism's report,
compiled to accompany an exhibition at Prague Castle marking the 75th
anniversary of the 1939 declaration: http://www.czechtourism.com/e/
prague-aristocratic-tidings/.

p. 247: **Lata was responsible for three horses**
See: 'Můj život s koňmi', by Radslav Kinský, in *Chlumecké listy: časopis chlumeckého regionu*, 2001 (3), pp. 18–19; also *Ročníková práce: Lata Brandisová*,
by Ester Pospíšilová (Gymnázium, 2016–17; an account prepared with input
from the Pospíšil family). The other two horses were Horymír and Hostivít,
although it is possible that Hostivít was kept somewhere other than Řitka.

p. 248: **the new Reich-approved authorities melted down the town's commemorative statue**
I am grateful to Dr Jiří Kotyk and his colleagues in the Klub přátel Pardubicka (KPP) for this and countless other details about life in Pardubice under Nazi rule. For more on this particular episode, see: 'Pravda o zničení pomníku T.G.Masaryka v Pardubicích', by the KPP editors, 3 June 2009.

p. 248: **helping to distribute an illegal magazine**
See: 'Mjr Franjo Aubrecht (1896–1985) a jeho boj proti totalitám', pp. 7–8.

p. 248: **eventually judged sufficiently 'German' in outlook**
Mauve's suitability is discussed in a long internal Böhm-Mähr Jockey-Club memo, dated 8 April 1943.

p. 249: **the SS Cavalry Brigade slaughtered at least 15,878 men, women and children in the Pripet Marshes**
See: *Himmler's Cavalry*, pp. 152–5.

p. 249: **a holding camp for the Protectorate's Jews in the Bohemian town of Terezín**
The actual camp was more usually referred to by its German name of Theresienstadt.

p. 249: **'Germanise the Czech vermin'**
Quoted in *Encyclopedia of War Crimes and Genocide*.

p. 249: **abruptly taken into administration**
Řitka was taken into administration on 16 July 1941.

p. 250: **dismissed ... a cook, a maid and a coachman**
*Ročníková práce: Lata Brandisová*, by Ester Pospíšilová.

p. 251: **'It does not cross my mind at all to complain ...'**
Letter to Lori Kinský, 22 July 1941 (in Kinský archive at Zármsk).

p. 251: **Košťál ... gave ... Valčík, a job in his wine cellar ... and persuaded him to drop ... a large pile of plates**
I was told this both by Dr Jiří Kotyk and by František Bobek. See also: 'Hotel Veselka byl zbořen před 40 lety' – pardubice.cz/zpravy.

p. 252: **Most were kept beforehand in what had once been Poldi's well-stocked wine cellar**
I will not easily forget the experience of standing in the cellar with František Bobek of the Československá obec legionářské before being walked, as the victims were, to the place of execution on the Zámeček grounds. Mr Bobek

is overseeing an ambitious project to restore the currently derelict Zámeček to be a permanent memorial to the Nazis' Pardubice victims.

p. 252: 'do not look for it on the map; it has been swept away ...'
*The World of Yesterday*, Preface.

p. 253: 'fighting the Bolsheviks'
Lengnik's death was reported in, among other publications, the Dutch SS journal, *De Zwarte Soldaat*.

p. 253: **Similar fates would in due course befall Curt Scharfetter, Hans Schmidt and Heinz Lemke**
So many records were lost in the war that it is not always possible to state precisely what happened to each jockey. *150 Jahre Amateur-Rennsport* records that Scharfetter and Schmidt, like Lengnik, 'fell' in the war. Lemke went missing at Wolossowo, near Leningrad, in January 1944, but his family appear to have held out hope that he survived until at least 1950: they placed an advertisement in *Das Ostpreussenblatt* (20 August 1950) appealing for information.

p. 254: **their credibility as potential members of an elite killing force had been undermined by their humiliating defeat by a woman**
This speculation may sound far-fetched. We must not forget that everything about Himmler and Fegelein's weird, grotesque vision for an elite cavalry of SS enforcers was far-fetched. When I put this specific idea to the historian Henning Pieper – author of *Fegelein's Horsemen and Genocidal Warfare* – he said he considered it 'possible' that their defeat by Lata would have discredited individual SS men in the eyes of an 'arrogant, bossy parvenu like Hermann Fegelein'. Paul J. Wilson – author of *Himmler's Cavalry: the Equestrian SS, 1930–1945* – felt that the defeat was more likely to have been a one-off embarrassment, but agreed that closeness to Fegelein played a significant part in determining who would be honoured with selection for his wartime cavalry. Defeat by Lata would not have endeared any of the Velká Pardubická jockeys to Fegelein and thus can hardly have helped their prospects.

p. 254: **Schlagbaum ... returned to Germany and became a successful ... innkeeper**
According to his family, Schlagbaum left Prague in 1946, with his possessions in a cart. He ran a restaurant in Geiselhöring (Bayern) for a while, then – around the time that Lata was being packed off to her cottage in the woods – he set up an inn in Pfatter, near Regensburg. It was reported in 2015 that this inn, still owned by his descendants, was being used largely

to provide accommodation for some of the refugees that a more generous German leader, Angela Merkel, had invited into Europe. See: 'Pfatterer bietet Plätze für Flüchtlinge', by Walter Schiessl, *Mittelbaterische*, 12 March 2015. According to his grand-daughter, Josephine Huber, Schlagbaum would become very emotional whenever the 1937 Velká Pardubická was discussed.

p. 254: **Helmut Böttcher ... mourned for his 'gentle, modest' nature**
Obituary, *Sankt Georg*, Vol. 385 No. 7, p. 25.

p. 254-5: **Wiese ... was awarded the War Merit Cross**
Wiese's decoration was 'without swords', indicating that his meritorious service was performed as a civilian.

p. 255: **Wiese ... raced again**
Hans-Heinrich von Loeper, long-time secretary-general of Germany's Board of Thoroughbred Breeding and Racing, rode against Wiese (and beat him) in the first German Cross Country Steeplechase after the war.

p. 255: **one among fifty former Olympic competitors to die in Nazi concentration camps**
Their names (and camps) are recorded in 'Olympians Who Died in Nazi Concentration Camps' at sportsreference.com.

p. 255: **Kasalický applied for German citizenship and membership of the Nazi Party**
See note to page 83. His application for party membership was eventually turned down.

p. 256: **Soukup was the main operator of Ra's high-risk scheme to spare his horses conscription**
The scheme was explained to me by Soukup's son. See also: *Sága rodu Kinských*, by Karel Richter.

p. 256: **Norma ... gave birth to five foals**
Their names and dates of birth were Napoleon (2 February 1939), Nora (19 February 1941), Nurmi (21 January 1942), Natura (11 January 1943) and Naďa (15 April 1944). I have made extensive enquiries – with particularly generous help from Lenka Gotthardová and Miloslav Nehyba – but it appears that no trace survives of what happened to Norma after Naďa's birth.

p. 257: **Ra was unable ... to save ... Norbert from forced labour**
See: 'History of Kinský family' at hrad-kost.cz. Norbert is reported to have escaped from Germany, eventually, by bicycle – hence his subsequent involvement in events in Czechoslovakia in May 1945.

p. 257: **'a gentleman does not behave like this'**
I can find no record of this event beyond family memories, but Jan Pospíšil is very confident that something along these lines took place.

p. 258: **Kasalický appears to have used his influence to make the case go away**
Kasalický cited this in his defence when accused of collaboration. Statement of evidence from Hanuš Kasalický to the Místní národní výbor ve Všenorech, dated (presumably in error) 5 May 1945; document in Všenory Library.

p. 258: **a close relationship with Lata's resident cousin, Gikina**
Pavel Satorie – Josef's grandson and Gikina's step-grandson – believes that Josef and Gikina were lovers by now.

p. 260: **'when my heart becomes very heavy …'**
Letter from Lata to Lori Kinský, 6 December 1944; the 'In these hard times …' quote comes from a subsequent letter, dated 22 December 1944. Both letters are in the Kinský archive in Zármsk.

p. 261: **Horses still raced, but only in Saturday 'breeding tests'**
A series of fascinating articles by Petr Feldstein about Velká Chuchle during the war can be found at http://www.dostihovy-svet.cz. See also the 'Velká Chuchle válečná' chapter in *Velká Chuchle dostihová*.

p. 261: **Lata came across a wounded man**
I first encountered this family memory in Ester Pospíšilová's *Ročníková práce: Lata Brandisová*.

p. 262: **Czech partisans … moved closer to Řitka**
Several villagers confirmed the presence of partisans and Lata's dealings with them. However, it is sometimes hard to disentangle memories of Czech partisans from those of Soviet soldiers, who also made use of the woods in 1945. From the Gestapo's point of view, of course, it came to much the same thing.

p. 263: **fighting in and around the radio building**
The names of the seventy-nine civilians who died in the fighting can still be seen on a plaque at the radio building. For more on the role of Czech radio in the uprising, see 'Calling all Czechs', by Rob Cameron, 'Current Affairs – Czech Radio History Part III', Radio Prague, 23 May 2003 (http://www.radio.cz/en/article/41012).

p. 263: **Poldi von Fugger … was among those who did so**
There is a rather touching description of Fugger's last moments in German uniform in Celia Sternberg's *The Journey* (pp. 180–3). Urged by friends to

make himself scarce, he insisted on keeping his uniform on and doing what he saw as his duty. Days later, he was captured by the Soviets, who kept him prisoner for the next decade.

**p. 264: Šmejda walked to the stables to feed, water and reassure them**
This is a simplified version of a long and moving hand-written account shared with me by his grand-daughter, Božena Osvaldová.

**p. 265: SS-Gruppenführer Count Pückler-Berghaus ... killed first his family and then himself**
There is a fascinating account of the Count 's last hours, based on the memories of a child eyewitness, by Zdeněk Oškera at pribehy2ostoleti.cz, under the heading: 'Sebevražda generála hraběte von Pücklera – autentické svědectví mé maminky'.

**p. 265: 'the last shot fired in the war in Europe'**
I came across this description ('Zastřelil se a byl to symbolický poslední výstřel druhé světové války v Evropě') in an article on the website of the old Czech Communist party (KSČM). See: 'Válka skončila u Čimelic', 17 December 2010, http://old.pisek.kscm.cz/article.asp?thema=5147&item=52526.

**p. 265: Thousands camped there until June**
Local historian and chronicler Antonín Dvořák estimates the number at 6,000. Mr Dvořák's private archive includes photographs of Soviet soldiers being presented with flowers, and local young men kitted out with light weaponry.

**p. 266: leading ... separate lives**
A summary of the divorce proceedings on 4 January 1947 (in the national archive) reveals that, among other things, they espoused separate nationalities: him German, her Czech.

**p. 267: most confiscated land was ... allocated to small local landowners**
Roughly two-thirds of 1.8 million hectares of agricultural land confiscated in 1945 was redistributed in small lots. See: *A History of the Czechoslovak Republic, 1918–1948.*

**p. 267: placed almost immediately into provisional administration**
Hand-written case-note dated 6 November 1945. My phrasing is vague because it is impossible to tell who wrote the note or why. Like all the surviving documents that I am aware of relating to the successive stages of Řitka's confiscation, this can be found among the Pospíšil papers – which were still in the process of being sorted in the state archive at Dobřichovice when this book went to press. I will not attempt to identify individual documents relating to this strand of the story.

p. 267: **no proof that Norma survived the war**
Records preserved at Kladruby show that Norma was alive in 1943; the April 1944 comes from 'Po stopách Normy', *Dostihový zpravodaj*, Vol. 5, pp. 12–14.

p. 270: **a westward journey so cruel that, even now, it hardly bears thinking about**
If you can bear to think about it, you will not find a better account than *The Flight Across the Ice*. It is possible that Herold, who was still alive and in Insterburg as late as 1942, was involved in the forced migration.

p. 271: **a legislative attempt . . . to complete the unfinished business of land reform**
For a less over-simplified account, see: 'Collectivization in Czechoslovakia in comparative perspective, 1948–1960', by Jan Rychlík, in *The Collectivization of Agriculture in Communist Eastern Europe: Comparison and Entanglements*, ed. Constantin Iordachi and Arnd Bauerkamper (Central European University Press, 2013), pp. 181–210; or the Univerzita Karlova informační systém briefing: 'Development of the ownership right to the land in the Czech Republic'.

p. 272: **Most woodland ended up with the State Forest Administration**
*A History of the Czechoslovak Republic, 1918–1948*, p. 442.

p. 272: **'a bit of a family affair'**
Quoted in *Sága rodu Kinských*, by Karel Richter, p. 129.

p. 273: **after killing his groom with a bite to the neck**
I am grateful to Martin Cáp for sharing with me the note about this incident written by Dr František Lerche, long-time director of the Kladruby and Napajedla studs. According to Dr Lerche, Othello killed his groom with a bite to the neck, and was put down despite energetic protests by Ra.

p. 276: **accepting a lift from a drunken motorcycle rider**
According to the current Karel Schwarzenberg (the seventh prince), the motorcyclist was one of the Schwarzenbergs' many tenants.

p. 276: **according to Karel's son (then aged ten)**
Just to be clear, the son in question was Prince Karel 7th of Schwarzenberg, born in 1937, and in later life a senator, foreign minister and candidate in the 2013 presidential election. It is difficult to avoid confusion when writing about eldest sons in the Schwarzenberg family as they are all called Karel. I understand that the full title (in English) of the seventh prince is: His Serene Highness Karel Jan Nepomuk Josef Norbert Bedřich Antonín Vratislav

Menas The 12th Prince of Schwarzenberg (First Majorat) and 7th Prince of Schwarzenberg (Second Majorat), Count of Sulz, Princely Landgrave in Klettgau, Duke of Krumlov.

p. 277: **then close to their fifth and second birthdays**
Václav, Génilde's eldest son, was born on 9 October 1943; Hendrik was born on 11 November 1946. The 1948 Velká Pardubická took place on 10 October.

p. 281: **300,000 horses were sent to the slaughterhouse**
This figure comes from Cyril Neumann, founder of Prague's Equestrian Club Ctěnice and energetic campaigner to revive the Czech nation's equestrian heritage. The figure should be considered a back-of-an-envelope estimate, but a well-informed one.

p. 283: **'afraid to ride without it'**
Eyewitness account by Dr Radovan Brož, in 'Mých sedmdesát návštěv Velké pardubické', KPP, 2017; also mentioned in Střecha and Žmolík's 'O Latě Brandisové' and in Kovář (*Reflex* and *Šampaňské s příchutí pelyňku*).

p. 285: **added the insinuation that ... the former countess had deliberately tried to kill herself ...**
Alleged in *Příběhy předmětů*. Miloslav Nehyba also assured me that this was the case.

p. 285: **a fractured skull, a broken collar bone, a complex fracture of her left leg ... etc.**
All medical details are taken from the medical report issued by Masaryk state regional hospital in Pardubice, surgical and urological ward (head doctor: Jaroslav Snopek), 17 February 1950.

p. 285: **She wanted someone to summon a vet**
This detail comes from Génilde Kinský.

p. 286: **'There were two horses lying in the Snake Ditch. When I saw them, it was too late ...'**
Quoted in Kovář.

p. 286: **'Oh yes I will ... Like the devil!'**
This also comes from Génilde Kinský.

p. 287: **In Řitka, the Action Committee ... approved a statement calling for the 'severest possible penalty'**
The original letter is supposedly in the national archive (A, f. Státní prokuratura Praha, PSt I 774, 1950, nezprac.; Místní akční výbor NF v Řitce – Rezoluce odhlasovaná na veřejné schůzi 7. 6. 1950 v obci Řitka, okres

Praha-jih a zaslaná ministerstvu spravedlnosti) but was temporarily irretrievable for inspection during my research. It seems inconceivable, however, that – if Lata had signed the letter – the regime would not have drawn public attention to the fact.

**p. 288: A secret police report a few months earlier**
The report, dated 27 October 1949, focuses on the misdeeds of one of the Brandis sisters' unsuitable friends: a former Buchenwald inmate called Karel Blumentritt. It can be found in the archive of the Ústředna Státní bezpečnosti Praha, Signature 305–332-6, pp. 129–30.

**p. 289: she was still troubled by memory disorders, mood swings … etc.**
Statement from Dr Karel Mathon, university neurologist, Prague, 18 November 1950.

**p. 290: Lata … did make friends with several of the new farmworkers**
At least one of these workers, Ruth Kopecká, would continue to visit the sisters even in the next phase of their life. See: 'Příběh dětství mé babičky', by Katerina Kopecká, at pribehy2ostoleti.cz.

**p. 290: Hejmovský … fell – or "jumped" – from a window**
There are still some who believe that Hejmovský's death was either accident or suicide. Those who insist that he was murdered include Mirek Petráň, former managing director of Pardubice racecourse.

**p. 291: Řitka showed less enthusiasm for the cause than most villages**
Analysis in *Řitka v minulosti* suggests that even in the 1946 elections – their high point – the Communists received less than a third of the local vote.

**p. 291: 1 per cent of the population … were sent to prisons, camps and mines**
*A History of Eastern Europe: Crisis and change*, p. 531.

**p. 291: Arnošt Schwarzenberg … spent four years in custody**
See: *Noble Nationalists*, p. 222.

**p. 292: a radical reform of the currency**
Perhaps the most shocking thing about this crudely transformational policy was the fact that, the night before it was introduced, President Antonín Zápotocký addressed the nation on radio to insist that 'monetary reform will not take place'. See: *The Czech Crown – A Brief History of a Currency*, by Mojmír Hampl, Czech National Bank, Liberec Economic Forums, 16 September 2015.

**p. 297: the sisters would talk briefly to the priest, Father Josef Javůrek**
One local told me that Lata got on better with Father Javůrek's predecessor, Karel Kroupa; but she clearly developed a close relationship with Javůrek, who took over in 1956, as well.

p. 298: **a Czech-language broadcast ... transmitted from the West**
The great-nephew who told me this insisted that this was 'Radio Washington' rather than Radio Free Europe, but I can find no record of such a channel having existed. The Voice of America seems the only plausible alternative.

p. 299: **she had won most major steeplechases in Czechoslovakia**
For example: the Velká Olomoucká, the Velká Pražská, the Velká Karlovarská, the Velká Poděbradská, the Velká benešovská (five times), the Captain Popler Memorial Race (as Pardubice's Kinský Memorial Race was by then called).

p. 300: **who had ridden in the Velká Pardubická himself**
Kocman rode Lotos-1 in 1963 but failed to finish.

p. 301: **'There was no way that an article about the life of the woman who won the Velká Pardubická could be published'**
Kovář (*Reflex* and *Šampaňské s příchutí pelyňku*).

p. 302: **'Hanuš Kasalický ... disgraced, dispossessed and bitterly resentful'**
According to his grandson, Jan Doležal, Kasalický was 'not at all happy' in the last years of his life. His dreams of upward mobility lay in ruins, along with his marriage and his romance with Lata; and Czechoslovakia had become what his family considered a 'Stalinist hell'. The Doležals fled to Switzerland in 1968.

p. 303: **'We closed the book ... and we never opened it again'**
Quoted in *Příběh předmětů*.

p. 304: **According to one account of their conversation**
The conversation appears in a short dramatised account of Lata's life broad-cast as part of the *Jak to bylo dopravdy* series by Český rozhlas: Plus, 20 February 2017. But Lata's remarks about Communism are also quoted in *Příběh předmětů*.

p. 306: **She didn't contribute much, beyond saying how saddened she had been by Popler's death**
There is a detailed account of the meeting in Josef Pávek's *Tisíc a jeden skok*.

p. 306: **the British ambassador to Prague ... had written an article for** *Country Life*
'An Aintree in Bohemia', by Ronald Scrivener, *Country Life*, 29 March 1973.

p. 308: **the director ... 'looked as though he spent most of his life interrogating people in a basement'**
This would have been Vojtěch Babánek, head of the Státní závodiště for most of the 1970s. As far as I am aware, he never interrogated anybody.

p. 309: **rugged and inscrutable as an Easter Island statue**
The photograph appears in *Taxis a ti druzí*, p. 180.

p. 310: **The savagery of the collective response**
Charlotte Budd has been very kind in sharing her memories of her remarkable racing experiences at Aintree and Pardubice. For the build-up to the 1977 Grand National, however, I have also drawn on Anne Alcock's detailed and shocking near-contemporary account in *They're Off! The story of the first girl jump jockeys*, pp. 114–24.

p. 316: **the tomb had ... been damaged (some said vandalised)**
See: *Řitka v minulosti*; and the article about the tomb at http://www.prostor-ad.cz/pruvodce/okolobrd/ritka/hrobka.htm. The tomb of the Nolč family (Kasalický's in-laws) in the woods above Všenory met a similar fate around the same time.

p. 317: **a 'horse paradise'**
Lenka Gotthardová in 'Perličky vzpomínek na Latu Brandisovou'.

p. 318: **'I have loved justice and hated iniquity ...'**
The Latin words, 'Dilexi iustitiam et odivi iniquitatem propterea morior in exilio', are carved on Pope Gregory's tomb in Salerno. They are a play on a less negative sentiment to be found in Psalm 44, verse 8.

p. 318: **the last surviving snapshots of Lata's life**
Both pictures are in the private collection of Petr Breyer.

p. 320: **a 416-page compilation of mini biographies**
*Naši slavní sportovci*, by Ivan Hanousek and Jiří Lacina (Albatros, 1987).

p. 323: **'I have a theory ... that Ken is locked up somewhere ...'**
'Sweet Sixteen as legend Vana proves king of Pardubice again', by Alastair Down, *Racing Post*, 15 October 2007.

p. 323: **he had seen the light – 'actually, the flashing blue light'**
'Czech Grand National makes its European cousins look like a stroll in the park – as I learnt to my cost', by Marcus Armytage, *Daily Telegraph*, 5 October 2016.

p. 325: **Gavin Wragg's exuberant encounter with an equestrian statue**
It is hard to explain this sensibly beyond saying that the statue is on a tall pedestal; and that alcohol may have been involved; and that, as Martin Šabata put it, 'No one could work out how he got up there.'

p. 330: **a recent set of UK figures**
The fourteen-year study, led by Vanessa Cashmore of the Northern Racing College and carried out through the University of Liverpool Management

School's Thoroughbred Horseracing Industries MBA, analysed 1.25 million available rides during that period. See: news.liverpool.ac.uk/2018/01/30/female-jockeys-good-males-suggests-thoroughbred-horseracing-industries-mba-study/, 30 January 2018; and 'Trainers "do not use female jockeys" despite findings of new study', BBC Sport, 30 January 2018.

p. 335: **in many countries it is nearer 80 per cent**
For example: 78 per cent of riders in France are female and 80 per cent of riders in the US are female. In the UK, according to the British Equestrian Trade Association's National Equestrian Survey 2015, 74 per cent of riders are female.

p. 336: **champions of natural training methods, such as Monty Roberts and Pat Parelli**
My thanks to Martin Cáp for pointing out the similarities between Lata's approach and theirs. Roberts even echoes Lata's words with a (trademarked) training programme for producing well-adjusted horses called the 'Willing Partners' programme.

p. 338: **'a complete trust, one to another ...'**
Lata was writing to Petr Breyer to congratulate him on his impending marriage.

p. 339: **'a lover of honour and modesty and temperance, and a follower of true glory'**
*Phaedrus*, Plato (246a ff), translated by Benjamin Jowett.

p. 340: **'beareth all things, believeth all things, hopeth all things, endureth all things'**
1 Corinthians 13: 7 (King James Bible).

p. 341: **good and faithful servant**
The biblical 'parable of the talents' appears in Matthew 25: 14–30 and in Luke 19: 12–27.

# Acknowledgements

Lata Brandisová was largely forgotten when I first set out to write this book. It turned out that there were many people, in at least seven countries, who felt strongly that she deserved to be remembered. Without their help this book could never have been written.

My greatest debt is to Lata's family: particularly to Jan Pospíšil and Gabriela Křístková, current owners of Řitka, whose inexhaustible encouragement, hospitality and often-inspired g uidance s ince I fi rst approached them out of the blue in early 2017 have been both breathtaking and humbling – and wonderfully enjoyable.

I am also more grateful than I can say to Petr Jaroševský, Alexandr Jaroševský, Countess Radslav (Thamar) Kinský, Countess Génilde Kinský, Count Konstantin Kinský, Count Francesco Kinský dal Borgo, Prince Karel VII Schwarzenberg, Dietmar Haan and Ludmila S. Bidwell – each of whom has a family connection to Lata's story and each of whom has helped me in important ways.

I wish there was space to thank everyone else who has helped me as effusively as they deserve. Instead, a mere name-check will have to suffice. I hope those listed will believe me when I say that my gratitude is out of all proportion to this brevity. If by some terrible oversight I have omitted someone's name, I hope they will forgive me.

In the village of Řitka, I am particularly grateful to Pavla Novotná, Jiří Mudr, Radek Brabenec and Alena Brabencová, Jana Sléhová, Jaroslava Orolová, Irene and Petr Kotálová, Františka Mašková, Vlasta Klabíková, Antonín Dvořák and Josef Mudr – who were extraordinarily patient and helpful in the face of seemingly insatiable questioning; and, indeed, to most of the rest of the village. I am no less grateful (radiating vaguely outwards across the Czech Republic) to Petr Breyer, Marie Obermajerová, Vilibald Hořenek, Vlastimil Kaščák and Pavel Liška (in Líšnice); to Jan Dlouhý (in Mníšek pod Brdy); to Alena Sahánková (in Všenory); to Jan Zágler, Eva Chaloupková, Jiří Zlámaný, Petr Drahoš and Božena Osvaldová (in and around Velká Chuchle); to Pavel Satorie and Alena Šípová (in Prague); to Petr Dubják (and his colleagues at Metalcom, current owners of Úmonín); Dobroslav Vepřek and his family (in Kutná Hora); František Bobek, Martin Korba, Kateřina Nohavová and Miroslav Petráň (all in Pardubice); Pavel Fiala, Josef Soukup, Jiří Kocman and Marcela Zahálková (in and around Chlumec nad Cidlinou); Petr and Libuše Půlpán (in Hradištko u Sadské); and Sandra Resselová (in Ostrov).

Martina Růžičková-Jelínková, Lucie Baluchová, Pavel Liebich, František Vítek, Charlie Mann, Christopher Collins and Charlotte Budd all very kindly shared their experiences of riding in the Velka Pardubická. The great John Francome also gave me helpful advice.

I have received tireless and spectacularly well-informed support from Miloslav Nehyba (author and self-confessed Velká Pardubická obsessive) and Lenka Gotthardová (author, publisher and president of the Czech association for breeders of Kinský horses), while other wise and distinguished figures in the Czech racing world have also been generous with their advice, notably Petr Feldstein, Martin Šabata, Cyril Neumann, Zdeněk Mahler, Michal Horáček, Petr Guth and Vlastimil Weiner. In the British racing world, John Pinfold, Tim Cox and Diane Hill were very kind and encouraging.

Historians who have helped me include Henning Pieper, Paul J. Wilson, Aleš Valenta, Zdeněk Hazdra (director of the Institute for the Study of Totalitarian Regimes), Jiří Kotyk, Radovan Brož. I am also very grateful to the tireless and well-informed members of Axis History Forum (forum.axishistory.com).

Patricia Clough, David Conolly-Smith, Gerd von Ende, Hans-Heinrich von Loeper, Dr Horst Willer, Christoph Neddens, Daniela Wiemer, Harald Siemen, James Fry, Veronika Siska, Renate Rüb, Benjamin Haas, Thomas Poehlmann and Lütz Möser all played valuable parts in helping me to trace the background of Lata's German rivals. Mandy van Häigeling and Josephine Huber, in the US, generously shared what they knew about their forebear, Willibald Schlagbaum, as did Jan Doležal, in Switzerland, about his, Hanuš Kasalický. Additional thanks are due to Igor Kasalický, Libuše Křístková, Jaroslav Křístek, Jan Pipek, David Vaughan, Dana Zátopková, Karel Engel, Kateřina Mikulcová, Ivo Strauss, Jaroslav Bušta, Lucie Weitzová, Rachel Jeffries, Jon Shack, Ruzena Holub, Jana Slavíková, Jiří Šebek and Libor Sečka.

ACKNOWLEDGEMENTS

I owe a huge debt to Eva Krákorová-Jindrová and her colleagues at the state archive in Dobřichovice, who have tolerated my repeated interruptions of their cataloguing of the Pospíšil papers and patiently shared their findings with me. Zuzana Ouhrabková guided me through many otherwise forbidding archives and made valuable discoveries. I am also grateful to Stanislav Mikule at the regional museum in Žďár nad Sázavou; Michael Skopal at the state regional archive in Zámrsk; Jitka Bílková and Petr Zeman at the security services archive in Prague; and to the staff at the National Library of the Czech Republic, the British Library, the state archive in Prague and the regional archive in Pardubice. Renáta Tetřevová, at Pardubice's Východočeské museum, was enormously helpful when it came to tracking down photographs, as was Vlastimil Šimůnek, director of Česká televize's *Podkova Laty Brandisové*.

My particular thanks are due to Martin Cáp, Kamila Pecherová, Robin Healey, Jiří Pšenička and Dr Jon Hughes (of Royal Holloway, University of London) – all experts in their different fields – who not only gave me generous quantities of wise and expert advice but also very kindly read my manuscript (in some cases several versions of it) and pointed out numerous errors. Needless to say, mistakes that remain are mine alone.

From beginning to end, an essential role in my research has been played by three gifted and loyal interpreters, who have supported me in ways that went far beyond mere translation. Anna Kudrnová, Petr Bráník and Radka Brahová all have cause to think of this as 'their' book. I hope that they are not disappointed. I am also grateful to Tim Broughton, editorial director of Yellow

Jersey, Frances Jessop, my brilliant editor, and Victoria Hobbs, my agent, for their guidance and support. Above all, I thank my family – Clare, Isobel, Edward, Anne – for their love, encouragement and, not least, patience. My previous book had a Czechoslovak subject (the athlete Emil Zátopek). When I finished that, in 2016, I promised that my next project would not involve endless research in a faraway country where everyone spoke Czech. Then I came across Lata's story. This time, I really do promise – with the proviso that, when I look at the list above and think about the kindness so many Czech people have shown me, I already feel tempted to break my word again.

# List of Illustrations

End papers: profiles of the Velká Pardubická jumps in 1937, based on the official race-day programme (with additional acknowledgements to Jaroslav Hubálek, Miloslav Nehyba and the late Miloš Svoboda). Taxis is obstacle No. 4

Every effort has been made to trace copyright holders. The publishers would be pleased to correct any inadvertent omissions or errors at the earliest possible opportunity.

# Index

LB indicates Lata Brandisová.